The City

THE CITY
An Urban Cosmology

Joseph Grange

STATE UNIVERSITY OF NEW YORK PRESS

Published by
State University of New York Press, Albany

Printed in the United States of America

For information, address State University of New York Press,
State University Plaza, Albany, N.Y., 12246

Production by Dale Cotton
Marketing by Fran Keneston

Library of Congress Cataloging-in-Publication Data
Grange, Joseph, 1940–
    The city : an urban cosmology / Joseph Grange.
        p.   cm.
    Includes bibliographical references and index.
    ISBN 0-7914-4203-9 (hc : alk. paper).—ISBN 0-7914-4204-7 (pbk.
: alk. paper)
    1. Urban ecology.   2. Sociology, Urban.   3. City and town life.
I. Title.
HT241.G73   1999
307.76—dc21   98-30459
                                                               CIP

10 9 8 7 6 5 4 3 2 1

For John Grange
and
The Members of the Saint Jerome Community

Contents

PART ONE
CITYSCAPE

PART TWO

URBAN SEMIOTICS

PART THREE

URBAN PRAXIS

Preface

This work goes as far back as my childhood. As a youngster born and raised in the South Bronx, I was a child of the city. My earliest memories involve such urban structures as the Third Avenue "El," the Museum of Natural History, the 136th Street Playground, St. Jerome Church and School, Beck's Bakery, Macomb's Dam Park, Yankee Stadium, the Polo Grounds, the Harlem and East Rivers, 455 East 136th Street, 447 East 136th Street, the Kilpatrick P.A.L. Center, Randall's Island, the Freight Yards, the Subway, the Empire State Building, the Chrysler Building, the Staten Island Ferry, Wall Street, 42nd Street, Macy's, Gimbel's, Madison Square Garden (the old one). I stop here even though I could seemingly go on forever.

My earlier work, *Nature: An Environmental Cosmology*, developed a schema of speculative categories designed to provide a generic understanding of any environment whatsoever. Thus, the schema could be applied indifferently to a river valley, a mountain range, or a barren desert. It also should be able to help us understand the processes of city life. The aim of this work, *The City: An Urban Cosmology*, is to examine urban experience with the aid of the environmental categories developed in the first book. Their use should provide the same sense of depth and connection with experience that was achieved in the study of natural environments. Most especially, this study of the city should demonstrate the adequacy of the categoreal scheme for understanding the continuum of values that spans natural and urban domains. While the modalities of these values shift and alter in terms of their contexts, it is the thesis of this study that a fundamental unity underlies all environmental processes, both natural and urban. At the end of this work there should be solid evidence that these categories have produced important knowledge about the urban environment in which humans dwell.

To return to the autobiographical, some twenty-five years ago I left New York City to live in southern Maine. For a "Bronx Boy" that was quite a change. A change, however, that grew on me as I explored regions vastly different from what I had left. In place of concrete and traffic, I encountered seemingly endless empty roads that stretched through enormously thick forests. In place of downtown and uptown, west side and east side, I was told about north by northeast and "past Booty's Corner by the old Beech tree." Then there was the sense of quiet that in the beginning was far more unnerving than the screeching noises of a South Bronx street corner. All in all, the differences were overwhelming and yet I also felt "at home" in nature. What were the lines of continuity that enabled me to span these starkly different environments? Fundamental to finding an answer to this question was the philosophy of Alfred North Whitehead. His *Process and Reality* provided an example of what could be done if one allied speculative daring, logical rigor, concrete human experience, and imagination.

As was true of *Nature*, this work owes its inspiration to many people. In the first place I must thank my parents for giving me such a rich childhood. My father, Joseph Grange, took us Grange kids all over the Bronx and Manhattan. He showed us urban experience firsthand. My mother, Margaret Grange, taught us to be open and generous in our dealings with others and thereby gave us a sense of confidence in dealing with what is different. My twin brother John, who to this day works as a priest in the South Bronx, was my companion on many of these adventures. Even to this day he shares my sense of enthusiasm for the riches of city life. In contrast, my youngest brother Malachy in his mountain haunts in the Pacific northwest has taught me how to appreciate the wild side of nature.

My understanding of the importance of Whitehead's thought for contemporary culture has grown under the tutelage and example of Robert Neville, David Hall, and George Allan. Each in his own way has shaped my sense of the purpose and value of process thought. Though I doubt they would agree with all my conclusions. A similar compliment is owed to my colleagues in the Society for the Study of

Process Philosophies. Over the last decade they have provided me
with invaluable advice.

A final word about the relation of this work to the earlier study
of nature. It is not necessary to read that study to comprehend the
argument worked out in this analysis of the city. The two works,
however, do complement each other. The introduction to this volume
presents a compressed version of the systematic cosmological specu-
lations of the first book. In dealing with the city, the ground level of
the analysis—that environmental reality is best understood through
categoreal analyses and application—remains the same. There is,
however, an inevitable change in emphases. The city requires con-
centration on the cultural level of normative participation. As such,
major concerns involve propositional contrasts and types of higher
consciousness. In a city, how things appear to us is almost as important as what they are in reality. In fact, urban experience ties appearance and reality so tightly together that often it is impossible
and unwise to separate them in any final way. The city is a magnifi-
cent organism whose interrelations from the physical through the
living to the cultural levels demand exacting analysis.

There is a natural transition from the cosmological categories of
space, time, and place to an urban semiotics that features icons, indices, and symbols as the heart of cultural participation experienced
within the urban environment. As I argue throughout this work, the
physical level converts to the biological level, which in turn continuously transforms itself into modes of cultural participation. Likewise, what requires this transition from cosmology to semiotics is
the very size of the contemporary city. Furthermore, what gains critical mass in any authentic urban environment is the communicative
level of cultural participation. Consequently, what distinguishes the
city from other forms of social dwelling is the way in which the experience of meaning transmitted through different kinds of signs reor-
ganizes the conditions of the human habitat. To be human in an
urban environment requires modes of intelligence-in-action unnec-
essary in village life. Thus, the last part of this work concentrates on
the theme of urban praxis.

It is for these reasons that I have expanded the resources for this
book. By engaging the metaphysics and semiotics of C. S. Peirce, the
social thought of G. H. Mead, and John Dewey's understanding of
community, intelligence, and justice, I have attempted to deepen and
extend the scope and applicability of this cosmology.

My hope is that this study helps our culture understand just
how extraordinary an expression of process the city really is.

* * *

Finally, there are other people in my life whose support, encouragement, wisdom, and advice made this book possible. I wrote the better part of this work while Exchange Professor of Philosophy at the University of Hawaii. The kindness and generosity of the Philosophy Department was extraordinary. I wish especially to thank Roger Ames, Chung-ying Cheng, Elliot Deutsch, Linyu Gu, Steve Odin, James Tiles, and Mary Tiles. James Behuniak, a Doctoral Fellow of the same institution, prepared the index and offered valuable advice while reading the entire manuscript. I also thank George Caffentzis, Joseph Conforti, Jim Drake, Jeannette Haas, Bess Harrod, John Kinsella, Brian Martine, The Olivas (Sheri, Frank, Leo, Henry, and Joseph), Jessica Roberts, Linda Sanborn, Lee Stuart, Maria Truman, and Yuri Van Mierlo. Most especially, I want to thank Claudine, Anya, and Robin Wilhelmi.

Introduction: Cosmology and Urban Culture

The city is the place where human beings express to the fullest degree the perspectives on importance that their culture has bequeathed them. It is the environmental region within which ideals become enacted, signifiers are elaborated, and categories establish themselves as culturally normative. It is, par excellence, the place where human values come to their most concrete expression. The city is the form of the good for human civilization. It is therefore an exceedingly complex, nuanced, and even delicate cultural instrument. To understand its process of becoming, as well as the values it upholds, requires both deftness and patience. This introduction lays out the argument employed to get to the heart of city values as well as the manner in which the study is organized.

Process and Urban Values

This work is an exercise in building a cosmology in the tradition of Alfred North Whitehead. Its basic assumptions, methodology, and aims should be clearly stated from the outset. My thinking runs along the lines of what I call Platonic naturalism. This manner of doing philosophy seeks to unite the insights of the Platonic tradition of normative thinking with the interests, aims, and methods of American naturalism. Philosophy is therefore always an attempt to rule well where this obligation is exercised through intellectual responsibility, social action, and personal conduct. The key to this way of understanding reality is through the normative analysis of the structures that create certain types of value instead of others.

An introduction to this work must include a few words about metaphysics, ontology, and cosmology.[1] The relation between ontology, metaphysics, and cosmology is one of dependent theoretical entailment. Thus, cosmology seeks the generic traits of this actual world. It results in a theoretical vision of this world as sets of systems upon systems of events whose interlocking quality is the outcome of the norms used to set up such value structures. Metaphysics, on the other hand, deals with the fact that all these events are determinate. It therefore asks about the grounds and conditions of determinateness as such. Finally, ontology asks about why there is this kind of determinate world and not another. Ontology grounds metaphysics and metaphysics provides cosmology with the grounds for the categories it employs to understand the basic traits of this particular world.[2]

My earlier work, *Nature: An Environmental Cosmology*, argued the following worldview. Reality is composed of events, each one of which is a value in itself, for others and for the whole. Therefore all modes of reality—natural, urban, or whatever—are distinguished by internal relations and interconnections. Furthermore, these events link up in discernible patterns that express different values, and when they do so, they express varying contrasts of actual and possible feelings. Thus, all reality is a process of weaving real events out of the warp and woof of the actual and the possible. The environment is what results from these interlocking events and the degree to which they shade the relation between the actual and the possible. The possible enters the reality of process as potential forms of definiteness. These are to be understood along the lines of Whitehead's eternal objects and Plato's forms. They function in the environment as structural norms that measure out the ways in which the actual and the possible are mixed in the concrete events that make up specific environmental regions.

Likewise, spacetime is the outcome of these events. Space spreads itself according to the dimensions of the events that make it up. Thus, it is perfectly logical to speak of natural space and human space. Also, time is given in these events, which are best understood as drops or epochs of experience. The contours of spacetime as well as their configurations are therefore concrete, specifiable, and entirely the outcome of the events that make them up. Bonded together they form the environmental structures that make up the world encountered by human beings. Following George Allan I call this world the "mesocosm."[3] This study is dedicated in part to finding out the ways in which such events brings about the spacetime values experienced in urban regions.

Central to this study is the term *value*. It signifies the actual worth of that which emerges from the process that makes up the reality. Each of these values is a unique, determinate moment of importance. Its being is its becoming and its becoming and perishing is the expression of its value. The common element in all forms of value is intensity, for all these events are "felt" in some way or other both by the events themselves as well as the events that environmentally surround them. So the world of process—be it natural or urban—is to be understood as sets of feelings of feelings. These sets make up the actual world we experience.

This world is called a process because it is characterized by the emergence of novelty. Each event is a newly unique expression of value that is superseded by its successors. The line of process is not a smooth linear one but rather a maelstrom of activities intervening to produce this present moment "right now," which in turn is surpassed by this present moment "right now." Whitehead calls this advance into novelty the "category of the ultimate" for it names the creativity that is the meaning of process itself. Process is reality in the sense that the many always become one and are always increased by one.

The contemporary philosophical movement known as postmodernism holds metaphysics, ontology, and cosmology in the greatest contempt. It charges all these forms of systematic and speculative thinking with arrogance and power mongering. In short, it calls what I am about to set out to do an exercise in intellectual arrogance. It indicts me and all others who follow such a path with the crime of intolerance. For, so they claim, what gets swallowed up by systematic speculative philosophy is the unique and the different. While I have responded to these charges in detail elsewhere,[4] it is important to provide at this time a set of general remarks.

In the first place, the charge of generalizing the specific out of existence misunderstands the role of the vague in creating a cosmology. The vague is not the fuzzy or the ambiguous, rather it means that which can function as an "any" in a generalized description of reality. Vague therefore means that which requires further specification in order for its full meaning to become apparent. Thus, this cosmology says that everything is either an event or a set of events. That is a vague hypothesis. It does not say that all events are the same. A racehorse is an event and so is a flea but each has its own specific uniqueness. When the cosmological scheme is applied to real experience these modes of difference emerge with startling clarity. If anything, vague cosmological categories preserve more of difference than any other form of thought. This is because both identity and difference are embraced by the vague. Like the variable in algebra, vague categories let the world hang together in ways that require further empirical investigation to fill out the uniqueness of the actual process of the world. Let x be the function of any category, then what x stands in for determines the specific meaning of that function. Vague cosmological categories are the opposite of scientific generalizations or laws. Science seeks to clothe its theory in universality and necessity. Cosmology seeks to provide a vaguely representative scheme that will make possible a rich understanding of the connections of sameness and difference spanning the actual world. Cosmology tries to assist human beings in their aim to rule well. Science tries apodictically to explain everything through causal inference and theory.

In a similar way, the charge of intellectual arrogance misreads cosmology's hypothetic character. The categoreal scheme is not a stipulative tablet of commandments laid over the intricacies of experience. It is, rather, something to be tried out and tested so that its worth is proved both theoretically and practically. The theoretical proof lies in the logical rigor, consistency, and noncontradictory character of the categories. Its practical worth is discovered gradually as the scheme is found to apply adequately and well to different dimensions of experience. In the end, use of the categoreal scheme should result in a richer appreciation of the values of the concrete world both in their unique dimensions and in their relations to other kinds of values.

The term *appreciation* lies at the heart of this cosmological effort. The purpose of this study is to allow us to prize, esteem, and assess the many different values that come to be in an urban environment. My earlier work, *Nature*, dealt with natural processes and their importances. I turn now to the urban dimension of human experience. Some regard the city as the very height of human growth and development. Others view it as anathema, the work of the devil and the symbol of all that is corrupt in Western civilization. Neither is wholly right nor wholly wrong. The answer lies somewhere in the middle. The great art of cosmology is to make a virtue of the middle ground. My aim in framing this cosmology is to establish a clearing, a middle ground within which the virtues and the vices of the city can be well appreciated and understood. Urban values are best discussed in the framework of a specific categoreal scheme. For without such a formal instrument the discussion quickly loses its way and becomes a mere tour of interesting urban sights. Such highlights might please the postmodernist who equates the interesting with the true. But I am after a bigger prize: the real urban values that are cosmologically present in any urban environment whatsoever.

The Categoreal Scheme

Inscape, contrast, pattern, and transmission are still the central categories of the categoreal scheme (see fig. 1). Just as they served well to articulate the dimensions of the natural world, so also here they bring out the basic components of the urban domain. In explaining each of these basic structures of urban existence, I ask the reader to be mindful of the fact that they were also employed to appreciate the values achieved in the natural environment. They therefore provide basic proof that the thesis of my earlier study is fundamentally correct. That argument was: There exists a continuum of value between the natural and the human, the organic and the artificial, and the city and nature such that there is no ultimate metaphysical distinction between these regions of experience.

Category One: Inscape. Every event has its own unique status in the universe. The value it expresses is singular, being tied to its own special location in space and date in time. Its specialness will never be repeated in exactly this way in the universe of process. In addition, how it forms itself out of its environmental conditions is its own special creative task. This radical pluralism is the outcome of the determinateness that is the mark of each event that emerges from the welter of process.

Determinateness means that something is this and not that. As such it entails certain other aspects of the category of inscape. The inscape of every urban event involves essential and conditional features and simple and complex components. The *haeccitas*[5] that is the primary characteristic of the category of inscape results from the unique way in which the essential features of each event compose their environmental conditions so as to become just this entity and no other. The conditional features are those environmental influences that literally condition the coming-to-be of the essential features. Every event must therefore have a component of simplicity in

Figure 1:
THE CATEGOREAL SCHEME

The Category of Inscape   *Haeccitas*

The Category of Contrast   The Unity of Actuality
                                   & Possibility

The Category of Pattern   Mesocosmic Forms
                                   of Process

The Category of Transmission   The Transfer of Values

i. Physical Feelings (The Material World)

ii. Conceptual Feelings (Possible Forms of Determinateness)

iii. Propositional Feelings (Contrasts of the Actual
& the Possible)

iv. Feelings of Stillness

its inscape as well as a component of complexity. To be simple is to be
this irreducible event. To be complex is to take account of the conditions of the environment within which the event comes to be.

Therefore, an environmental event is always a harmony that exhibits both oneness and manyness. It is this unique togetherness of
the oneness of the event and the manyness of the environment that
constitutes the creative advance of process. This advance into novelty is not necessarily good. It may, indeed, be quite evil. Still: the
point of the category of inscape is not to be lost. Novelty, uniqueness,
particularity—in a word, *haeccitas*—is the result of this basic trait of
the process of reality.

Category Two: Contrast. The metaphysical implications of the novelty
of the universe involve the recognition of two different dimensions of
reality: the actual and the possible. The actual is that which is ultimately real. It is the concrete world of happenings, undertakings, doings, and sufferings. It is active in the sense that it participates in its
own self-formation. The actual realm is composed of all those events
that really come to be and perish in the course of the ongoing rush of
process. To be actual is to be always this concrete specific event. There
is about the actual an inevitable atomic quality. This is due to the ir-

reducible plurality that marks the basic makeup of the process universe. On the other hand, the possible is that region of experience marked by what can be as opposed to what is. Furthermore, possibility is parcelled out, as it were, in forms of definiteness that exclude each other. Thus, incompatibility is as much a gift of possibility as compatibility. This aspect of possibility is what gives it the sense of normative measure that will grow in importance as this study develops its understanding of urban experience. But even though there is this exclusionary dimension to possibility whereby, for example, a square cannot at the same time be a circle, possibility, unlike actuality, displays the character of fundamental continuity. Thus, even though a square is not possibly a circle, both are shapes of space. They are connected by reason of the continuity of the concept of shape and the concept of space. It is for this reason that in this cosmology possibility is always spoken of as a "conceptual feeling." When possibility is felt, it is felt as a specific form of definiteness awaiting realization in the temporal world. What marks its possibility is the fact that in addition to its specificity, there clings to it a sense of further possible development whereby an enlargement of experience can be carried out.

Thus, the category of contrast describes a generic trait of all events in the process of reality. Each of them is a unity of what is and what can be. The fundamental meaning of contrast is therefore: To put into a unity with . . . . What is unified is the atomicity of actuality and the continuity of possibility. The result of all such contrasts is that a potential enlargement of experience always lurks in the heart of a process universe. For the most part this sense of enlargement is unconscious and recessive. As I argued in *Nature*, the emergence of novelty in the natural world is a slow process marked by the evolution of new forms of reality over long periods of time. But we are here talking about the city as the residence par excellence of human consciousness. Consciousness itself is a contrast. It is the "affirmation of a negation" for it unites in one experience the sense of what is with the sense of what can still yet be. This definition grows in importance as this essay in urban cosmology proceeds. As the affirmation of a negation, contrast as the ground of consciousness is the revolutionary drive underlying many forms of urban development. It is the structure whereby refusal and revolt enter urban experience. This is one of the reasons my study of the city moves from a cosmological perspective to a semiotic analysis. Because the urban environment is saturated with the experience of meaning, contrast inevitably takes on a semiotic character. Thus, continuity of meaning is established in city life by the transmission of contrasts felt as moments of symbolic breadth. Simply put, successful city experience turns contrast into what Peirce calls feelings of continuity.[6]

Furthermore, contrast is also the basic structure of the experience of beauty, which, as my earlier work demonstrated, is the supreme value of the natural world.[7] When something is beautiful, it has harmonized the relations between the actual and the possible in so novel a way as to bring forth new forms of truth into the process of reality. The category of contrast is therefore central to an understanding of the ways in which important values are achieved in urban experience. Finally, whenever contrast is present, a heightened level of intensity accompanies it. Thus, since value is understood as modes of intensity, contrast is the way in which value is increased, amplified, and spread throughout the universe of process. In terms of urban experience, contrast becomes singularly important for it is the way in which both consciousness and cultural ideals combine to express deeper levels of importance. It also has important connections with the theory of urban semiotics to be developed later. Similarly, contrast converted into symbolic breadth then requires another transformation. Urban semiotics must be actualized through an appropriate praxis. Contrast felt as beauty is the fundamental inscape of community. Without an urban praxis dedicated to such a goal, urban life withers and eventually dies.[8] In sum, a clear understanding of the category of contrast is indispensable for following the developing argument of this study.

Category Three: Pattern. When events interlock so as to form the large-scale objects of ordinary human experience we are in the effective presence of the category of pattern. Pattern implies order and it is the order of events that establishes the particular patterns we experience in urban environments. Human experience is woven out of the myriad events that make up the reality of process. Just as we notice the images on a television screen and not the individual dots that make them up, so also in the regions of human experience we notice the patterns formed by events and not the individual events that make them up. It is therefore the recognition of these patterns that is at the base of forms of human perception.

Now, there are two different ways to notice patterns: logical and aesthetic.[9] The logical recognition of patterns subsumes the particular under the general. Thus, in a logical mode of pattern recognition it would be "an" automobile that is noticed and not the particular make of automobile. In pattern recognition dominated by aesthetic interests, the opposite is the case. It is the particular that is of concern and not the general logical type. I notice the red Mazda convertible and not the automobile. Aesthetic attention is crucial for understanding the varieties of cosmological value active in urban areas. Without a feel for the particular in its concrete *haeccitas* it is impossible to distinguish the subtle differences that mark out the presence of real novelty. In fact, the term *to feel* is central to this cosmology for the structure of the universe of process is discoverable only through the recognition and expression of feelings and sets of feelings. It is this particular pattern arising from this particular set of events that grabs our attention. A form of pattern recognition that merely emphasizes the general is likely to eliminate precisely what we are supposed to look for: the *haeccitas* infecting this region of experience and no other. Again, this is yet one more reason an urban cosmology should develop into both an urban semiotics and an urban praxis. Pattern symbolically expressed is felt as semiotic continuity. A distinctive whole emerges out of the relations of the parts. Urban praxis then ought to continue this transmission of values by enacting important ways to actualize community. This is the salient responsibility of social institutions. What was a pattern becomes a symbol whose breadth then expresses feelings of community that can flood distinctive urban regions. A village is not a city, because its felt values establish different patterns of experience and meaning. Specifically, the size of the city transforms it into a unique entity whose environmental patterns demand experiences of meaning and action unique to such an immense number of human beings living together. To borrow from *Nature*, in the city the cultural continually overwhelms the physical and biological. This precise transmission of semiotic and practical energy does not happen in other forms of human dwelling.[10]

Once again, it is important to note the difference between the vague and the general. By insisting on vague categories that require further experiential specification, this cosmology safeguards the uniqueness of its constituent members. It would, therefore, not be an exaggeration to call this an essay in aesthetic cosmology. It is the particular feel of the particular urban environment that is the subject matter of concern. When these patterns become institutionalized, they then serve to structure important dimensions of urban experience. The traffic light, the highway sign, the public monument, the shopping mall, and the sports complex—all these are patterns whose recognition is specifically necessary for thriving in an urban culture. Furthermore, these patterns are continually transmitted throughout environments.

Category Four: Transmission. This category underlies the dynamism of urban environments. Where inscape, contrast, and pattern focused on the structures found in urban environments, the category of transmission speaks to the dynamics of such an environment. An urban region is active, alive, and always in motion. What is transferred through such a region is best understood as different types of feelings. As has been already noted, this term, *feeling*, designates the basic experience of the transfer of values in a process universe. Not all feelings are the same. There are four different types that can be singled out for categoreal notice and analysis: physical feelings, conceptual feelings, propositional feelings, and feelings of stillness:

(i)   *Physical feelings* are the result of feeling directly the values of the past. Density, repetitive sameness, and averageness of feeling tone are among its more obvious attributes. The realm of physical feelings is largely the same as the material realm. And indeed we feel it as largely the same, as impacted with the values of the past and as enduringly average.

(ii)   *Conceptual feelings* are the result of feeling forms of specific definiteness. They are therefore oriented toward the future rather than the past. Conceptual feelings feel what is possible for a situation rather than what has happened in the past. Conceptual feelings are the main avenue through which novelty emerges into the actual world. When conceptual feelings dominate an urban environment, then a certain transparent and fluid tone comes to the fore. It is as though the past has faded, the future is not quite here, and the actual value of the present has yet to be settled.

(iii)   *Propositional feelings* reflect contrasted unities of the actual and the possible. These contrasts will become all-important in determining the major dimensions of urban environments. For as shall be argued, the city is awash in propositions. Propositions can also be called lures, because they appear to favor certain possibilities and exclude others. They are suggestions anchored in concrete actual locations. Unlike conceptual feelings that feel possible forms of definiteness indifferently, propositions act as strong enticements to act or behave in a certain way. This is why Whitehead maintains that it is more important for propositions to be interesting than to be true. Propositions should be interesting, for their major function is to engage the attention of the subject who entertains them. In sum propositions contrast what is with "what could," "what should," or "what might be."

This contrast is carried out with a certain forceful intensity. Propositions literally propose a course of action to be carried out. In the act of entertaining such proposals, important future consequences for urban reality are set forth in a persuasive manner. All sorts of judgments of value are caught up in such propositional feelings. One consequence of the dominant role played by propositions in urban life is the need to move from a cosmological perspective to a semiotic one. As Part Two will make clear, propositions are felt as signs. In turn these signs provoke certain feelings, which is why the triadic character of Peirce's semiotics is so important for developing my argument. And as was the case with the category of pattern, propositional feelings also require enactment for their completion. Part Three, Urban Praxis, takes up this task. The very magnitude of city life demands that propositional feelings be tested in actual urban experience. It is the consequences derived from the use of propositional lures that tell us their meaning.

(iv) *Feelings of stillness* are the outcome of a certain sense of completed value. When feelings of stillness dominate an urban area, a mood of satisfaction spreads through the environment in question. Nothing seems to be needed. Everything is in place and a perfection according to its kind can be experienced. Feelings of stillness are rare, but the way in which they provide the sense that the ongoingness of process has been arrested is palpable and impressive. Stillness witnesses to the level of importance reached by the urban event in question.

This completes the analysis of the categoreal scheme. I now pass to the ways in which these feelings are expressed and felt in urban environments.

Urban Semiotics

The human body is the organ of amplification through which all the dimensions of urban value enter our being. The chief way the body does this is through the act of perception. Following Whitehead, I maintain that there are three main forms of perception: the two pure forms of causal efficacy and presentational immediacy and the mixed mode of perception in the form of symbolic reference. Each provides different levels of information in different ways. Once appropriately understood, these modes of perception go a long way toward establishing what I call an urban semiotics. The signifiers that fill urban spacetime are grounded in these distinctly different ways of urban perception.

Perception in the mode of causal efficacy is nonsensuous. It is not derived from any particular sense organ such as the eyes, nose, skin, ears, or tongue. Rather, it is derived from what Whitehead calls the "withness of the body." This is the immediate past stage of the body as it hands over its feelings to the next stage of its event history. Causal efficacy is therefore the way in which the legacy of the past is felt in the present. Since causal efficacy deals with the derivation of feelings from the past and these feelings are not specific to any particular sense organ, the outstanding characteristic of perception in the mode of causal efficacy is that it is vague, uncertain as to its origins and yet laden with important but dim emotions. We dimly feel the values of the past as a part of a background out of which the present is emerging. Causal efficacy is the feeling of continuity with the past. This withness is the gift of the human body as it functions semiotically in environmental fields. Causal efficacy locates us in the actual world. It alerts us to the reality of the past out of which we emerge. It informs us vaguely about the importances of the past. It establishes lines of worth and esteem throughout our existence. It is the primary way in which the heritage of past value is donated to the present.

Perception in the mode of presentational immediacy is what we normally mean by sense perception. The information it gives us about environmental events is the opposite of that derived from causal efficacy. Through the operation of the five senses it presents us immediately with a world that is objectively over there, standing against us. Unlike causal efficacy, this form of sense perception is very clear, decorated with vivid qualities such as colors, shapes, odors, aromas, and tastes. It is the world of objects spread out in space and time. While it provides us with sharp, clear-cut information about environmental objects, it tells us nothing about origins and derivations. Perception in the mode of presentational immediacy gives us the world as experienced through the five senses. That world is directionally straight-ahead, over there, and objectively present. This kind of perception does exactly what its name says: It gives us this world as immediately present but it tells no tales about the past or the future. It grabs our attention through the dazzling power of the senses. It organizes a world well proportioned to human experience but it can also be quite wrong about the objects it presents for our immediate attention. Opportunities for delusional experience abound in realms of experience dominated by perception in the mode of presentational immediacy. For one thing, presentational immediacy provides us with a clear picture of the world as systems and subsystems of objects strung out independently in space and time. But we know this leaves out at least two important facts about the environment. First, each of those "frozen objects" is a maelstrom of processive activity, and second, running all through the environment are lines of connections—all-important causal relations—that constitute contexts absolutely significant for the seemingly separated objects of our sense perception.

In sum, presentational immediacy is the mirror opposite of causal efficacy. It grants what causal efficacy holds back and it hides what causal efficacy provides. Now, what is at stake in all this is a very important dimension of human experience. I am referring to the truth quality of our sense perceptions, especially in regard to space and time. Spacetime forms the great backdrop of urban experience. Without reliable information concerning the past, the present, and the future our sense of urban value will be deeply flawed. Similarly, without a trustworthy sense of urban spatial dimensions the actual values of urban experience will elude us.

Perception in the mode of symbolic reference is called "mixed" by Whitehead. This is an accurate description because symbolic reference involves the transfer of information from one type of perception to another. Through the selection of an appropriate symbol the vague but important emotions derived from the past are transferred to a clear-cut object. The flag is raised. We salute its immediate presence and feel the patriotism settling through our somatic being. Alternatively, the flag is raised. We see it and repulsion at the swastika floods our being. In each case there is a transfer of emotion from the dimly perceived past to the immediately presented object. Sometimes the converse transfer can also take place. Victims of the Holocaust feel the pain and the fear and then transfer it to the skinheads marching in the streets. In either case what goes on is a unification of past experience with a present object. What happens in this mixed mode of perception is the bonding of the past, the present, and the future within the spatial presence of a clearly defined physical event. As a result, physical space and time become loaded with felt values. In urban environments this act of symbolic reference is at the core of our most important activities. From crossing a busy street, to participating in a community event occurring in a public plaza, to visiting special places, it is perception in the mixed mode of symbolic reference that is in operation. In

urban experience each act of symbolic reference is best understood
as the recognition of a sign. Now, the discipline of sign recognition
and interpretation goes by the term *semiotics*. Thus, an important
dimension of this study will be the effort to devise a fruitful urban
semiotics—one that yields valid knowledge of the values encountered, invented, discovered, uncovered, undergone, and experienced
in the city. Crucial to the development of such a semiotics is the
work of the great American philosopher Charles Sanders Peirce.

Before looking in some detail at Peirce's semiotics, it is important to underscore just what the connection between cosmology and
semiotics is in city life. In *Nature*, I made a distinction between three
levels of participation—the physical, the biological, and the cultural.
Nature is dominated by the physical and the biological. But while
continuous with the physical and the biological (urban dwellers still
live in a physical environment), the city transforms these levels
of participatory experience through an overwhelming emphasis on
the importance of meaning. This transformation also ties in with
another part of my argument from *Nature*. There, I stressed the
fact that when events enter into different environmental systems
changes happen to the character of the events in question. What is
H_2O in my kitchen faucet becomes a delicious way of slaking my
thirst when I swallow a glass of water on a hot day. On the smallest
physical level this kind of transformation is called achieving critical
mass. I have also called this an event's achievement of tensile
strength when it comes into being during its process of becoming and
perishing. Put simply, there are times when size does matter. Quantity can determine quality. This is precisely what occurs in city life.
Because a doctrine of normative measure demands that attention be
paid to both the level and the intensity of the forms of participation
at play in an environment, it becomes clear that in the city there is
need to take account of the enormous size difference marking urban
life off from other forms of social dwelling. A village is not a city because it is not as large. What is equally important is the fact that a
city's lines of communication become ever more critical. Meaning
(which is another term for the cultural) becomes the neural network
governing all forms of interaction. Because of its critical mass, communication becomes the primary form of energy transformation. In
fact, I argue that when one lives in the city, the category of transmission takes on ever-increasing vitality and therefore demands
ever-novel forms of propositional experience. These propositions are
the cosmological equivalent of the signs that dominate the urban environment. Thus, cosmology "naturally" turns toward semiotics in

order to do justice to the qualitative differences brought about by cultural levels of participatory urban experience. Therefore, what marks the difference between a city as opposed to a village is both the size of its semiotic system as well as the way in which space shrinks into increasingly smaller distances and time collapses into increasingly shorter durations. The adoption by the world of cyberspace of the concept of the "nanosecond" is but one measure of how infinitesimally small temporal measure has become in our urban environments. No village ever needed the forms of communication now spread throughout the great world cities. Thus, the logic that carries this argument is Platonic rather than Aristotleian. It seeks the continuities as well as the differences between events. It is grounded in the importance of relational rather than classificatory modes of thinking. That is why there continues to be a continuity between city and nature and other forms of social dwelling even as the differences assert themselves in culturally important ways. I am not talking about a way of thinking strictly based on genus and species. Rather, I seek the emerging organic wholes that mark the arrival of new modes of environmental participation. To stress semiotics in city life is as "naturally cosmological" as pointing out the value of the physical and the biological in nature. I seek threads of continuity that at the same time distinguish one way of being and becoming from another. As a Platonic naturalist I see transformational but relational modes of process rather than clear-cut *differentia* separating genus from genus. I have more confidence in *The Statesman*'s art of weaving than in Aristotle's *Prior Analytics*. What counts most in city life is the establishment of habits of interpretation that can identify both new and old meanings. Ultimately, the cultural level of participation is about weaving such nets of meaning. And what demands a shift from cosmology to semiotics and praxis is precisely the dominance of meaning as the most powerful agent in the city's physical and biological environments.

An outline sketch of Peirce's semiotics is now in order. For Peirce, every sign has a threefold character.[11] If any of these triadic features are missing, the sign immediately loses its sign character and becomes something else. This triadic character consists of (1) the object signified, (2) the sign itself, and (3) the interpretant. Let us take the sign experience "God." In this example the object signified is the being "God." The sign is the word "God" (including its capitalization). The interpretant is the theological system and symbols used to express the meaning of the term "God," or more simply put, the cultural effect the sign has on the interpreter's experience. If there is no object signified by God, then there is no sign. If there is no term God, then there is no sign. If there is no interpretant for the sign God, then there is no sign. The semiotics of the term *God* stands or falls on the interlocking copresence of these three dimensions—the object signified, the sign itself, and the interpretant.

It would be difficult to exaggerate the importance of this doctrine. It makes absolutely clear that a sign refers to a reality that lies outside the sign system used to interpret it. This triadic character stands in complete opposition to the more *au courant* semiotic structuralism of Jakobson, Saussure, and their followers Derrida and Lacan. These systems agree on one semiotic principle: that a sign always refers to another sign. This is the kind of dyadic semiotics that locks philosophy into what I call "the fallacy of the perfect signifier." It traps all future philosophical discourse in the tyranny of the text. Henceforth, it is the sign that is to be discussed, not the object it refers to, or the presuppositions of the interpretant system. In fact, in the canons of French structuralist theory, a sign can only refer to another sign. Human beings are locked into the sign systems of their culture and there is no way out. We are imprisoned in the unbreakable chains of the signifiers that make up cultural life. Furthermore, in this semiotics human destiny is caught up in the endless sliding and eliding of the chain of signifiers that make up our sense of reality. And just as there is no word to satisfactorily name the real, so also there is no way to satisfy our desires. We exist on the razor edge of the sign, which simultaneously defends and condemns us. It defends us from the horror of an unnameable reality. It condemns us to live ever a little bit askew, for our words, desires, needs, and actions never match up.

Now, Whitehead has warned against "The Fallacy of the Perfect Dictionary," by which he meant:

> That there is an insistent presupposition continually sterilizing philosophic thought. It is the belief, the very natural belief, that mankind has consciously entertained all the fundamental ideas which are applicable to its experience. Further it is held that human language, in single words or in phrases, explicitly expresses these ideas. I will term this presupposiiton, "The Fallacy of the Perfect Dictionary."[12]

Terming this philosophic attitude "the school of safety," he contrasts it with what he calls the school of adventure:

The fallacy of the perfect dictionary divides philosophers into two schools, namely, the "Critical School," which repudiates speculative philosophy, and the "Speculative School" which includes it. The critical school confines itself to verbal analysis within the limits of the dictionary. The speculative school appeals to direct insight, and endeavours to indicate its meanings by further appeal to situations which promote such specific insights. It then enlarges the dictionary. The divergence between the schools is the quarrel between safety and adventure.[13]

Now, adventure in philosophy is for Whitehead always associated with speculative thinking. It is in such a spirit of adventure that I have recourse in Part Two to Peirce's semiotics and metaphysical categories of firstness, secondness, and thirdness. For Peirce, all reality reflects in varying degrees the presence of these qualities. Firstness denotes the real presence of possibility. It is that which simply can be. Secondness is its opposite: It is the blunt actual presence of reality. Thirdness is the establishment of a certain generality or habit or law or custom in the texture of reality that binds together firstness and secondness.

This is a study of the city. Let us use New York City's Empire State Building to get a more concrete grasp of the ways in which firstness, secondness, and thirdness are felt. As a young boy, I stood at the base of the Empire State and looked up. What I felt was sheer secondness, for I encountered the shock of immense verticality. On the other hand, for many Americans the Empire State Building is an example of sheer firstness, the possibility of the greatness of city culture in twentieth-century America. Finally, for Andy Warhol the Empire State Building is an opportunity to explore thirdness through a single twenty-four-hour film shot. What is felt as one views the film is the alternating presence and absence of generalized interpretants for such a symbol of "Empire." Firstness is the presence of possibility, secondness is the presence of actuality, thirdness is the presence of continuity. All three qualities must be present to some degree in each actual event. It is the varying degrees of the presence of each quality that determine the actual constitution of the event. Firstness, secondness, and thirdness will form an all-important axis of interpretation as I move into different kinds of urban experience. These considerations bring my introductory remarks to a final topic—the normative dimension of human consciousness.

Normative Consciousness

Human consciousness has been defined as "the affirmation of a negation." By this is meant that we feel awareness as a factor of negation clinging to our experience. Thus, I can read along in a book seemingly without consciousness and then suddenly look up and say, "How can the author make that claim?" This is the affirmation of a negation. Consciousness says, "Is that it?" before it says, "That is it." To be aware that something is not there, is not the same as being aware of what is there. At best, one can only say what *might* be, *could* be, or *should* be there. This is the sense of the alternative that attaches itself to states of consciousness. It is precisely why I earlier defined consciousness as the experience of the contrasted unity of the feeling of what is with the feeling of what still might be.

This sense of the alternative at the heart of the experience of consciousness is the source of what I call normative thinking. This kind of thinking is the central activity carried out in this study. It also formed the argumentative ground of *Nature*. By normative thinking I mean that kind of thinking that seeks to identify, articulate, and judge the standards, measures, and ideals a culture uses to determine what is the best way for it to be. Normative thinking is therefore ethical to its core. It is also deeply concerned with the way in which the possible and the actual mix together in the real world. It takes seriously Plato's recommendation in the *Philebus* that all reality has four components: the limited, the unlimited, the mixed, and the cause of the mixture. The limited is what I have called the actual. The unlimited is the possible. The mixed is the real world of process. The cause of the mixture is the measure (or, more likely, measures) composing the proportionate relation that binds together into a unity the mixture of actuality and possibility ingredient in a real event.

Now, in terms of environmental contexts this implies that everything that comes to be has a structure. That structure is brought about by the relations established by the normative measures used to create that event. How something comes to be constitutes what it is. How it comes to be is the result of the appropriate harmony achieved between what is, what can be, what should be, what could be, and what might be. In sorting out these relations every event in a process world creates some form of harmony by which it measures up to or falls away from what is possible for it in this particular environment.

All this sums up from the perspective of consciousness what I called the metaphysical and ontological presuppositions of this urban cosmology. To be determinate is to be this rather than that. The this-ness, or *haeccitas*, of each event is determined by the way it measures out its possibilities and thereby actualizes them in the real world. A conscious awareness of this process entails a knowledge of the normative measures employed to distribute the actual and the possible in this particular situation. Platonic naturalism requires an exacting knowledge of the way in which the actual and the ideal combine in every process situation. To carry out normative thinking in a sustained manner is the task set for this urban cosmology. What must be established are the determinate ways in which the actual and the possible, the real and the ideal mix together in various urban environments. Urban value is the outcome of the limitation brought about by the measures used to structure the importances of city life.

This means that ideals, especially in the form of propositional feelings, are of paramount importance in city living. It also requires that Peirce's firstness, secondness, and thirdness play a leading role in the analysis of urban environments. For these characterisitics of reality constitute a very valuable shorthand version of the doctrine of normative thinking. Firstness names the possibilities available within a situation. Secondness names the situation itself. Thirdness names the worked out and generalized solution to the problem of finding a good way to be. Similarly, the triadic sign character reflects the normative dimensions of urban life (see fig.2). Every sign points to an object signified (a determinate value). Each sign presents the value of that object. Finally, the interpretants employed to understand the sign measure out the degree to which the sign accounts for the values achieved by the object signified. This close alliance between normative thinking, metaphysics, semiotics, and cosmology is precisely why Peirce singles out aesthetics as the discipline that underlies all forms of philosophic thinking. It is the aesthetically contrasted feeling of goodness achieved and goodness still possible that underlies all normative thinking worthy of the name.

This brings the discussion back full circle to the question of the difference between the logical and the aesthetic orders. Ultimately,

Figure 2:
PEIRCE'S *CATEGORIES AND SIGNS*

Firstness   Icons

Secondness   Index

Thirdness   Symbol

this essay is simply an attempt to understand the full import for urban experience of these compellingly cryptic words of Whitehead: "All aesthetic experience is feeling arising out of the realization of contrast under identity."[14]

Contrast, identity, and feeling are concepts that form the center of this study in urban cosmology. They also imply concepts like beauty, intensity, goodness, and consciousness. My thesis is straight-forward: The city is that region of value and experience wherein con-sciousness, goodness, and beauty join together to form exceptionally intense expressions of importance.

How I plan to demonstrate and defend this thesis concludes these introductory remarks.

Plan of This Study

The City: An Urban Cosmology has three parts. Part One deals with what I term "The Cityscape." It is an effort to articulate the spacetime values of urban regions. It also deals with the phenome-non of place, an experiential region at the very center of good urban experience. This leads to a concluding discussion of urban goodness. Part Two deals with various forms of "Urban Semiotics." It estab-lishes the essential continuity and major differences between the natural and the built environment as well as the moods, orders, and signs that distinguish urban regions.

Part Three takes up the theme of "Urban Praxis" and details the forms of intelligence, community, and justice normatively required for a fair and fitting city. I have deliberately not said much about Part Three. As the study of a normative urban praxis, it leans heav-ily on the insights and thoughts of G. H. Mead and John Dewey. Their discussions of intelligence,community, and justice flesh out the bare bones of the abstract doctrines I have been exploring in this in-troduction. Part Three establishes the applicability of the cosmolog-ical categories of Part One and the urban semiotics of Part Two. As such, it is to be experienced on its own terms as well as through the lenses provided by the earlier parts of this study. Part Three will show just how powerful is the concept of beauty as a guiding motif for studying the contours of urban experience.

In framing this plan I have kept in mind the unmet promises of *Nature*. Chief among them was the obligation to show how the cos-mological method can teach us to appreciate both natural and urban areas for what they really are rather than what we would like them to be. Only in this way can new forms of the good begin to emerge in our civilization. That we need such forms is a commonplace. As the millenium approaches, a return to Plato's concerns by way of the tradition of American naturalism suggests itself as a good path to follow.

I concluded my book on nature with the image of the child needing to retain its sense of wonder at the plenitude of nature even as it grows up and matures. Here in *The City* I offer the image of the adult sensitively aware of environmental circumstances, intellectually appreciative of what is, and responsibly prepared to create what should be.

Abbreviations

AI   *Adventures of Ideas* (1933). New York: The Free Press, 1967.

MT   *Modes of Thought* (1938). New York: The Free Press, 1968.

PR   *Process and Reality* (1929). Corrected Edition edited by David Ray Griffin and Donald W. Sherburne. New York: The Free Press, 1978.

SMW   *Science and the Modern World* (1925). New York: The Free Press, 1967.

S   *Symbolism, Its Meaning and Effect* (1927). New York: Capricorn, 1959.

CP   *Collected Papers of Charles S. Peirce*, Volumes 1–6. Cambridge: Harvard University Press, 1931–1935.

PART ONE

CITYSCAPE

The first challenge to urban cosmology is to make the city come alive. It is not sufficient to merely say that the city is a place where types of interesting life take place. That is to deny the city its own unique form. What must be done is to win for the city a radical vision of its living structure. Part One of this study attempts to express the vital character of urban regions by examining in detail the spacetime structures that embody its environmental processes. I will use the categories of inscape, contrast, pattern, and transmission to examine the tissues of the urban environment. This urban epidermis forms itself out of the spacetime configurations unique to urban settings.

What is more, this spatiotemporal skin also houses the joints, sinews, and bones that knit together to form the unique urban event that I call "Place." It is within the experiential phenomenon of place that the living form of the city first and foremost asserts itself. Also, these places are fundamentally forms of urban goodness. It is to place that we must look to understand the various theories of good urban form that have won attention in our age. Thus, the thought of Lewis Mumford, A. Doxiades, Christopher Alexander, and Paolo Soleri can be read as attempts to articulate the philosophical significance of place as it expresses itself within various urban environments. The

1

goodness of the city is the outcome of the interwoven realities that make up the special inscape of urban place.

What blinds us to this reality is the overwhelming cultural presence of forms of late capitalism, a habitual economic vision that makes the city only the sum of its mercantile and consuming activities. Just as scientific materialism is the major theoretical obstacle to coming to a true understanding of nature's value, so also in this volume late capitalism distorts the value of urban environments by turning them into arenas for the creation, transmission, and consumption of goods and services. While the city is all that, it is also much more. The greater burden of this study is given over to detailing just what that "more" actually is.

The first chapter of Part One begins with a categoreal analysis of urban space. It establishes the inscape, patterns, and symbolic perceptions residing in urban spatial experience. Chapter Two takes up similar tasks as it carries out an analysis of time. Space and time come together under the aegis of place and this all important region of urban experience is developed in Chapter Three. Part One concludes by examining several well known contemporary theories of urban goodness. In presenting these formulations of the goodness of the city, the need for a sensitive system of urban semiotics asserts itself. Part One therefore concludes with a natural transition toward the discipline of urban semiotics.

Chapter One

Urban Space

Space is one of the two great backdrops against which city life is played out. The other one is time. Because of the complexity of these issues this chapter confines itself to the problem of urban space. Time is taken up in the next chapter. I will follow the format of my earlier study by dealing in turn with the inscape, patterns, symbolic perception, and value of urban space. Such a procedure makes effective use of the categoreal scheme laid out in the introduction.

The Inscape of Urban Space

Urban space is continuous with natural space in that its inscape is always concrete, and creative.[1] It is also receptive to a variety of forms because it shares with natural space the character of extensiveness whereby a pliant character is an essential feature of its inscape. But here the similarity ends, for unlike natural space, which is always found, urban space is made. Its inscape involves the creation of three spatial characterisitics—sited directionality, access, and habitat.

Urban space exhibits the dipolar character of sited directionality. Both dimensions seriously affect the quality of access, which is the third dimension of the inscape of urban space. Natural space was distinguished by what I termed its shy openness to form. Urban space begins with an act of founding that already sets the direction of spatial possibilities within the selected region. To site is to locate in space (and time). Therefore, every city begins with a spatial mark. The creativity imprinted on urban space by the act of building sets forth continuing effects that reverberate throughout an urban region. Furthermore, every additional act of building establishes its mark on the urban landscape. What results is an interlocking matrix of spatial forms that comes to dominate urban spatial experience. This matrix is what allows urban space to create local values. The act of siting always sets boundaries around a region previously indifferent to spatial values. This indifference is the outcome of the trivial orders preexisting in the place in question. By drawing a track through natural space, urban space creates modes of order. These types of order then express both the patterns of urban space as well as their accompanying perceptual moods. Like natural space, urban regions exhibit an openness to form. All spatial regions (natural and urban) insofar as they are spatial must be part of the extensive continuum. Urban space shares in the agency to be attributed to space understood as the foster mother of all becoming. It is characterized by the capacity to accept extension. When this capacity is diminished, then urban space becomes jammed and occluded. As a result we can experience density as well as a definitive loss of spatial freedom.

The creative impulse of urban space is expressed as sited directionality. This dual character—the directional and the sited—is what shapes the spatial access definitive of various urban regions. Urban space is as concrete as natural space. It is the outcome of the events that make up its spatial character. Therefore, urban space, like natural space, is tied to the physical objects making up its particular inscape. But unlike natural space, human beings select both the site and the direction of the spatial events making up an urban environment. Whenever an urban spatial expression comes to be, it is the result of a selective process carried out by human agents.

It is a truism that the goodness of an urban environment is dependent upon the quality of its spatial character. What is not so clearly understood is that this character is first of all dependent upon the access afforded by the sited directionality inhabiting the space in question. Space is primarily about access. It is the open and the closed that mark the poles of spatial experience. What urban spatial creativity adds to this are the entwined facts of site and direction. Site sets forth the limits of an urban environment. Directionality influences its potential qualitative modalities. This directionality results from the type of mark left in space by the human builder. In the act of siting the human builder sets forth both an orientation and a scale that is decisive for the inscape of space.

Much of what will later be discussed under the themes of the beauty and goodness of the city originates in the primal inscape of sited directionality and access. This is because eventually the inscape of urban space must exhibit what I term "habitat." As the final dimension of the inscape of natural space, habitat names the quality of openness essential to all human dwelling. Urban space not only protects and shelters its inhabitants. It must also lay open for them potential domains of meaning. Urban space is the first creative impulse whereby layers of meaning emerge into city expression. This also will be the theme of later chapters. It constitutes the living tissue of semiotic richness that quickens urban experience. Thus, another important difference between the city and other forms of social dwelling is the hyper-rich system of semiotic activity needed for effective city life.

In sum, the inscape of urban space expresses a perspective that founds the many importances of city life. This act of orientation shapes the future flow of meanings throughout the community. Understanding this spatial shaping involves taking seriously the dimensions of the inscape of space: sited directionality, access, and habitat.

The Patterns of Urban Space

The analysis of urban spatial patterns has two parts. First I will discuss the primary spatial patterns experienced in city life. Then I will treat the four essential orders within which the primary patterns fall. The three primary patterns are the vertical, the horizontal, and the ambient. Vertical patterns are what most people associate with urban space. Looming skyscrapers, tall buildings, and massive rising walls are among the more obvious examples of such vertical patterns. In comparison with natural space, urban spatial events tend to cluster around the vertical. Part of this is due to the sheer economic pressure to make the most of the inscape of space. The higher I build, the more space I have. Some of it is also due to a certain narcissism sometimes found in urban founders and dwellers. But whatever the motivation, it is certain that the vertical brings to cities a great deal of what marks them out as special places. As soon as sited directionality is laid down, the possibility of upward verticality emerges as a genuine urban option. Just how much this pattern contributes to the quality of urban experience is a complex issue. Its potential for positive and negative contributions is enormous. Horizontal patterns are likewise a familiar dimension of urban space. Streets can stretch forward with decisive clarity. And whether they are leafy boulevards, tree-lined promenades, or stark neon-lit avenues, the horizontal both beckons and repels the city dweller. As a form of space that stretches straight ahead, the horizontal in both buildings and city arteries brings sharp geometric form to urban experience. In fact, when mixed with the vertical, these two geometries form the traditional pattern of the modern city. That pattern will be discussed at length when the symbolic perception of urban space and its qualitative weight are taken up. Suffice it to say, the vertical/horizontal axis forms the center of modern urban spatial experience.

Ambient spatial patterns are different in that they do not pull us upward or straight-ahead over-there in that direction. Rather, they embrace our urban existence and thereby provide shelter from the more starkly dominating vertical and horizontal patterns. Ambient space is like natural space in that its hallmark is a certain quality of environing intimacy that measures our body along a more human scale. The ambient surrounds us in a bath of spatial experience. It is all around at once and yet is never fully present in an ocular fashion. Rather it is sensed more through the "withness" of the body, a perceptual experience that brims with dim but rich feelings of importance. The next section deals directly with these types of perceptual experiences. For now, it is important to note that ambient patterns complete the geometry of the city. They provide for the curved, the spherical, and the circular dimensions of urban spatiality.

Whether the dominant spatial patterns be vertical, horizontal, or ambient, each such spatial expression is located within one of the four fundamental levels of environmental order: the trivial, the vague, the narrow, and the wide.[2] Trivial orders are those that suffer from an excess of incompatibility such that no important spatial pattern can be detected. As the lowest level of order, trivial patterns fail to single out any defining characteristic of a spatial region. One might think of an empty city lot as exemplifying this level of order. Vague orders mark a step up on the ladder of order. In a vague order a few aspects are picked out to stand in for all the potential types of order lurking in the web of spatial extensiveness. Such vague patterns suffer from an excess of identification, the opposite weakness

of trivial orders. Still, vagueness provides a level of massive averageness that marks the first step toward more compelling forms of
order. When we speak of "downtown" or the "neighborhood," the
vague is being identified.

Without some level of vagueness, narrowness, the next level of
order, becomes impossible. For vagueness provides the necessary
background of stability out of which select perspectives can emphasize their relative importances. Through narrow orders intense feelings are promoted within spatial regions. It is narrowness that
focuses spatial energies such that specific values are realized and expressed throughout an urban region. One may think of the force exercised by the Empire State Building. Its very presence compels its
surroundings to reflect its insistent dominance. Through narrow
spatial orders cities can give rise to expressions of intense individuality. Finally, where there is individuality, there is also the possibility of the richest form of order—width. When narrowness is woven
onto vagueness, then great width of spatial experience becomes
available. Width joins the intense individuality of narrowness to the
reach afforded by vagueness; as a result, space shows itself as simultaneously intense and congruent with a rich variety of values.
Individual expressiveness is wed to relevance such that intensity
and fitness become present at the same time.

Whether the primary spatial patterns are vertical, horizontal, or
ambient, their location within trivial, vague, narrow, and wide levels
of environmental order serves to enhance or attentuate their value.
It is the task of a cosmological study to set forth these vague normative measures so that the more particular arts and sciences can uti-
lize them in their respective analyses of urban environments. What
concretely grounds the effectiveness of these normative measures is
the way in which each of these primary patterns and each level of
order finds its resonance within the human body's sensorium.

The Symbolic Perception of Urban Space

Part One of this study is influenced by the speculative philosophy of Alfred North Whitehead. That philosophy envisions the world
of city and nature to be patterns of entwined events ever in the
process of becoming. It is by reason of the universe's creative advance into novelty that environments shift, alter, come to be, and
perish. Central to this event cosmology is the act of human perception. It, too, is an event that structures its world according to certain

defining characteristics. An understanding of the deep impact that
spatial experience has on human beings requires a review of Whitehead's theory of symbolic perception.[3]

Perception is the ultimate urban body event. Through perception our body acts as both a receiver and an amplifier of environmental processes. Human perception is always a mixture of two
more primordial ways of feeling the world, causal efficacy and presentational immediacy. Causal efficacy is the way in which human
beings feel the insistent pressure of the past as it impacts on their
being in the present. It is carried out largely through what Whitehead calls "the withness of the body." By this he means the largely
forgotten fact that I perceive the world through the immediate past
states of my body. It is through the chain of events that make up my
bodily events that I am most intimately connected to the environment. I feel remorse within my heart. I feel fear inside my bowels. I
sense the weight of the stone in my hand. Causal efficacy does not
give us sharp clear-cut information. That is the gift of the other form
of primordial perception, presentational immediacy. What I feel
through causal efficacy are the dim, throbbing impulses of the past
as they build up into the present moment. This perception does not
depend on any definite sense perception. In fact it is nonsensuous.
Antecedent states of my body feel the activity of the environment
and pass it on to my body unanalyzed and heavy with emotional
weight. Causal efficacy suggests the richness of the past without
specifically identifying it. Furthermore, it is weighted and freighted
by an enormous past that haunts the fringes of the present with its
looming sense of importance. It is the mode of process whereby we
sense most intimately the pressure of past spatial (and temporal)
values. What causal efficacy grants us is dim, inexact but impressive
access to the sense of the past that still clings to environmental
processes. Causal efficacy is the way in which the plenty of urban experience resounds through our bodies. Without this perceptual re-
source our sense of environmental value would be thin and poor.

Presentational immediacy is what we normally call the perception afforded us by the five senses. Its major contribution to environmental experience is the accuracy and sharp objectivity it brings to
our bodily awareness. We *see* that truck over there. We *smell* that
odor right here. We *touch* this stone at our feet. We *hear* that cry over
there. We *taste* this hot dog at this street corner. Presentational immediacy brings to urban spatial experience the clarity and sharpness
needed to negotiate such a busy world. As the words themselves
imply, through sense perception humans are granted "the immediacy

of a presence." All philosophical paradigms that take clarity, precision, and objectivity to be the signs of truth are derived from an exaggerated reliance on this form of perception. "True enough," I am given a set of objects over there in that direction that appear to be clearly and distinctly separate from other environmental events. But such perception tells no tales about the activities inherent in such events. Nor does it grant me access to the history whereby such values have been achieved. In presentational immediacy I am dazzled by the deliverance of my senses. But what I am given is an immediately present set of objects over there frozen in space and time and analyzable only through the abstractions of geometrical systems. I am cordoned off from the richness inscribed in the actual events making up that scene. Presentational immediacy is the converse of causal efficacy. It presents me with a sharp, clear-cut, and accurate picture of the environment. But that picture is thin and devoid of information. I can locate my world in presentational immediacy but I have little sense of its worth beyond that of the dazzle delivered by my senses. Causal efficacy, on the other hand, excites my interest in the active worth of events but it cannot locate them with any degree of accuracy. There is need of another form of perception that blends the opposing deliverances of these more primordial modes of perception.

It is perception in the mixed mode of symbolic reference that carries out this accomplishment. It marks the height of the human body's environmental participation, for it unites the clear but shallow objectivity of presentational immediacy with the rich but dim intimacy of causal efficacy. It makes symbols living factors in our environmental experience. When I perceive in this manner I transfer the experience of one pure mode to that of the other mode. A symbol quite literally is that which rolls together different levels of experience so that a certain depth of meaning is achieved. Thus the soldier's salute hails the dim but rich sense of patriotic allegiance transferred to the country's immediately presented flag. Or conversely, the immediate presented smell of liquor brings to the adult child of an alcoholic a dim but overwhelming sense of repulsion.

It is perception in the mode of symbolic reference that makes sense of our ever-changing environmental experience. Immersed as they are in the welter of events making up environmental process, human beings need the endowment of readily identifiable symbols to found an ordered pattern of meaning within an otherwise hopelessly chaotic environmental field. I say "within" because we literally exist inside this semiotic dimension of the urban environment. Human communicative praxis—the subject matter of Parts Two and Three of this study—depends in the most fundamental way on this mixed mode of symbolic perception. I could not negotiate the traffic of a busy street without the assistance of symbolic reference. It is the way in which I semiotically adjust to the most practical of urban activities. On a much more radical level, it is the artist who establishes new codes of symbolic reference that move against the accepted patterns of urban meaning and thereby open up new experiential realms.

For the most part it is the social order that educates us in the creation, maintenance, and interpretation of symbolic reference. That is one of the major tasks of civilizations. Nevertheless, revolutionary symbolic transfiguration is always possible within social systems. These, too, must be accounted for by an urban cosmology. Indeed, as just mentioned, an analysis of urban semiotics and urban praxis forms the greater part of this study. What must be remembered as those parts of this work take shape, is the somatic grounding of all these symbolic references. It is through the deliverance of our senses as well as through the "withness of the body" that the most abstract semiotic schemes originate. We are never removed from the rootedness of our bodily being. Far from being worldless subjects, the human body anchors our physical, living, and cultural participation in the urban environment.[4]

Perception in the mixed mode of symbolic reference explains both the positive and negative dimensions of urban vertical, horizontal, and ambient space. When the vertical is expressed within the city, it can be either inspirational or oppressive. To the extent that the vertical becomes the towering perpendicular, it diminishes the sense of human presence and alienates citizens from proper urban dwelling. This is caused by an unsuitable symbolic reference being embedded in the percipient body of the city dweller. In altering the scale of human dwelling, we shift the environment away from what is appropriate and diminish urban existence in favor of the monumental. Now, to some extent and in some degree the monumental has its place in city life. But too much vertical reference alters the plane of the human body and thereby skews our sense of place. Vertical space needs to be balanced against the symbolic perceptual limits of the human body. It is not just the sense of oppressive verticality that is felt within the body. Presentational immediacy in the guise of vision also comes into play. I see that looming building over there and towering over me. The resultant alienation is palpable. I sense the inhuman dimension of certain kinds of vertical space. This is one more reason why a city is distinct from other forms of social dwelling. The "habitat" of a village is limited to spatial structures so that forms of spatial openness take on a much different character. For example, the huts of so-called primitive peoples traditionally had a "smoke-hole" in the center of the roof. On the one hand, this was a practical solution to the important problem of dispersing the smoke. But on the other hand, it quickly became a symbolic reference for openness to transcendence and divinity. Even the top of the human head was seen to have such an opening, and various meditative techniques began their cultural emergence.[5] It would be difficult to find urban dwellings with deliberately placed holes in the centers of their roofs. Intense and vividly varied forms of semiotic transmission are a central identifying feature of urban life. Transmission across widely different vertical lines of communication defines a major urban dimension. The transcendent is in the city but it is felt more through the category of feelings of stillness than open verticality.

Horizontal space can also be both positive and negative. A sense of expansiveness exalts the strolling boulevardier. At the same time, horizontal space can so stretch out the sense of urban space within the city that a measure of immeasurable distance overcomes any sense of nearness and familiarity. What is at stake in horizontal space is the creation and maintenance of a proper sense of width. Too much width guarantees shallowness. Too little width brings about irrelevance. When horizontal space is only felt as far away and over there, a human scale of symbolic reference has been lost. Both vision and touch are affected, for we can only see what our horizon grants and we can only touch with our eyes what is appropriately near to us.

Similarly, the "canyon effect" felt in some cities results from a bad mixture of the horizontal and the vertical. When an overreliance on presentational immediacy is matched by a neglect of the more intimate and familiar effects of causal efficacy, the city dweller feels the gap separating her from the environment. Spatial distancing is one major form of urban alienation. Another aspect of the canyon effect is an overwhelming sense of diminishment in the face of the social institutions that are supposed to protect urban existence. When the body feels dwarfed, the heart can register little confidence. Communal existence is not encouraged by the gigantic objectivity symbolically felt in the canyons of the skyscrapers.

The major defect of this urban spatial form is an absence of the effective presence of ambient space. Spatial environments need not oppress human beings. What distinguishes good ambient space is the support it grants to those who dwell within it. Surroundings can nourish as well as oppress. Ambient space nourishes its inhabitants

when it provides a sense of security and intimacy.[6] A major reason
for this sense of support comes from the curved and circular dimensions of ambient space. Through causal efficacy my body feels the
surroundings as embracing me. This in turn is transferred symbolically to the immediately presented spatial locale. This is an important clue to what is missing in contemporary urban spatial values.
The insistent presence of the vertical and the horizontal leads to an
unfortunate overstressing of perception in the form of presentational
immediacy. The resultant distancing effect is what produces the
sense of separation, coldness, and oppressive objectivity so often felt
in the corridors of urban space. A later chapter on "Place" will
deepen and expand this theme. For now it is sufficient to note just
how sensitive the human body is to alterations in its symbolic perception of the three kinds of urban space.

The Felt Transmission of Urban Spatial Values

The inscape of urban space provides access to habitat through
sited directionality. To site is to establish limits. As the foregoing
analysis of urban spatial patterns suggests, these limits establish
habitats characterized by feelings that receive amplification or attenuation through the orders within which they sit. When symbolically perceived, these spatial values form the primary level of
creativity experienced in city life. Finally, as the categories of transmission indicate, these feelings are transmitted through the urban
environment in the modes of physical, conceptual, or propositional
feelings. In this way a world of urban feelings comparable to those
found in natural environments rises into being. This chapter concludes with an appraisal of these urban spatial values and the ways
in which they find expression in city habitats.

Physical feelings are the source of the material world of solid objects. These feelings reenact the past in such a way as to establish
stable patterns of conformity throughout an environment. It is these
physical patterns that lay out the underlying ground that provides a
city with its own sense of assurance through repetitive spatiotemporal structures. It is through the dominance of such feelings that important urban structures exhibit endurance. (Though it is a subject of
the next chapter, time also shows regular rhythms providing urban
dwellers with the confidence they need to build for the future.) All in
all, physical feelings provide the rock bottom sense of conformity that
is indispensable for city planning and prolonged urban existence.

   It is not just material structures that express physical feelings. All the more important levels of energy transmission in a city are similarly established through the stable repetition of conformal physical feelings. Various types of communication and transportation systems are among the more obvious types of such physically based feeling systems. The most important characteristic of such systems is dependability. Consider the sense of helplessess brought about by blackouts of urban electrical systems. Such consistency is made possible through the level of regularity occasioned by the massive conformation of feelings characteristic of physical systems. The truth of scientific materialism resides in its understanding of the repetitive character of physical feelings. The basis of the capacity of empirical science to predict accurately future events is in fact this repetition of the past. For in physical systems as well as material objects it is precisely the conformation of the present to the past that builds up spatial patterns. Put differently, the continuing presence of the past is what defines environmental regions dominated by physical feelings. It is this virtual absence of novelty that makes possible "the laws of nature." Since space (and time) are the fundamental background of all environments, the conformal dimension of these feelings is the reason for the immanence of such laws of nature. Without the repetition of the past no sense of an enduring stable environment could register itself. What we habitually take to be the static and unmoving quality of material objects is in fact the outcome of the continuing repetition of past spatial patterns within the events making up the present. Thus, even the most solid urban structure, object, dwelling, or system is a nesting of events. It is the process of these events that appears unchanging; in fact, each moment of urban experience is fresh, spontaneous, and novel, no matter how similar to the past it appears to be.
   Explaining the root of such novelty requires a brief detour into metaphysics.[7] The inevitability of such novelty is guaranteed by the creative advance that marks all forms of process. Nothing is ever the same twice for it is the new and the different (no matter how slight) that is always emerging from the womb of process. Now, the most direct way in which such novelty becomes available is through the agency of conceptual feelings. Unlike physical feelings, conceptual feelings feel the possibilities latent in a process environment. Conceptual feelings sense alternatives for they are sensitive to "what might be" instead of what already is. Furthermore, they feel not just mere possibility but rather "specific forms of definiteness." When actualized, these forms of definiteness account for the determinate

features of all environments. As such, conceptual feelings also mark
out incompatibles for the creative advance. A circle cannot be a
square. A red circle cannot be blue. At the same time, these conceptual feelings register a broad path of continuity stretching through
the realm of the possible. For example, a color implies space and
space implies figure and figure implies circle. The world of actuality
is made up of atomic events, each separate and distinct from each
other. This determinate character of actual events is what makes possible the identification of essential and conditional environmental
features. On the other hand, it is the presence of conceptual feelings
that provides a sense of alternative directions for environmental advance or decay. It is this mixture of the actual and the possible that is
"the stuff" of process, though there is no ultimate "stuff," only events
and their relations.

Returning to the question of the felt transmission of urban spatial values, conceptual feelings provide a sense of possible alternatives for city dwellers. When transmitted widely thoughout an
environment, these conceptual feelings embolden humans to try the
different and the new. Of course when they are absent, a certain desperate dullness permeates the urban scene. This is the difference between a dead-end slum and a growing neighborhood. Those who live
in such environments directly experience such feelings of hope and
despair. These experiences are the result of the real presence of conceptual feelings within an urban region. But pure possibility is rare
in any environment since its orders are for the most part already settled through previous processes. That is why propositions are far
more important as transmitters within urban environments.

Propositional feelings combine the actual and the possible
realms of process in special ways. They also elicit unique types of
feeling that are essential for meaningful urban experience. A proposition establishes a significant logical space within the world of city
dwellers for it creates a halfway house between the actual and the
possible. This space engages the interest of urban dwellers without
forcing upon them an immediate decision. Thus they allow urban
people to entertain possibilities without committing themselves to a
particular course of action. Propositions are the major source of
novel experience within urban areas. When later in this study the
semiotic dimension of urban experience is developed, propositions
will take on even more significance. What is important at this point
is to understand the structure of such feelings.

A proposition has three parts: a predicative pattern, a logical
subject, and a judging subject. The predicative pattern is the poten-

tial meaning awaiting realization in an actual environment. The logical subject is that group of events awaiting identification with the predicative pattern. The judging subject is that person or group of persons who affirm or deny the appropriateness of aligning the predicative pattern with the logical subjects. The resultant feelings are a contrast of physical and conceptual feelings. They are called "propositional feelings" because they can lure environmental beings into future choices. In spatiotemporal terms these feelings provide a sense of intriguing possibility such that real chances for novel experience begin to loom large as relevant and important possibilities. In sum, propositions are lures for feeling.

An example will make this discussion more concrete. Let us return to the Empire State Building, a classic urban structure. On the one hand, its form is quite simple. It is a tall building used for commercial purposes. But there are other possible predicative patterns lurking in the background of this landmark. Among these are the Empire State as a symbol of New York's prominence as a world city. Another might be its status as the first skyscraper proclaiming a new age of metropolitan architecture. Or for movie buffs, it is the site of King Kong's last stand. These predicative patterns hover over the actual steel, stone, and mortar of the Empire State Building. Those material entities have become potential logical subjects for the three predicative patterns just mentioned. Their environmental status has potentially shifted from conformal material events useful for their stability to a set of bare "its" awaiting the ingression of the predicative pattern, "New York" or "skyscraper." Stripped of their individual status as elements in a building, these material events are rendered pliable for fusion with the appropriate predicative pattern. But notice that the act of judging the fit between the logical subjects and the predicative pattern is carried out on two levels. The first level is whether or not the logical subjects and the predicative patterns have something in common. It would hardly be appropriate to entertain the Empire State Building as the propositional form of a Chinese dinner. The second level has to do with the capacity of the judging subjects to entertain the proposition in question. This introduces a decisive issue for urban life. Without citizens who have the capacity to entertain the propositions transmitted through the city by its multiform environmental events, much of the semiotic richness of the city is lost. Good urban dwelling is as much a matter of cooperation between dwellers and propositions as it is of gaining material advantages.

In sum, propositional transmission marks the bringing together of the physical and conceptual sides of the environment so that new

levels of meaning can be experienced. Each proposition brings together into a unity potential forms of meaning awaiting human entertainment. It is important to note that "entertainment" is the
requisite mode of dealing with propositions.[8] Another term for entertainment is "interpretation," and later chapters will deal extensively
with this profoundly important urban activity. For now it is sufficient to reassert the fact that judging propositions has more to do
with their ability to excite interest than with their putative "truth
value." As lures for feeling, propositions transmit through the urban
environment opportunities for discovering novel values. Novelty
that includes the spatial values dealt with in this chapter is an essential dimension of city life. Without the real presence of novelty in
urban environments, city existence collapses into trivial routines devoid of life and motion. Propositions are the most effective way of
transmitting such novelty through city spaces.

Propositions receive intensification or attenuation by reason of
the environmental orders within which they are situated. An underlying hypothesis of this study is that urban environments are regions
made up of events that fall within four fundamental orders. Each of
these orders registers its impact on city experience in distinct ways.
Different feeling tones are evoked by each of the four environmental
orders. As the previous discussion of spatial patterns argued, the four
orders are the trivial, the vague, the narrow, and the wide. When
trivial orders dominate city space, the accompanying mood is one of
indifference. On the other hand, vague orders provoke feelings of expectation. Narrow orders create feelings of intensity. Finally, orders
characterized by width evoke feelings of involvement. These moods of
indifference, expectation, intensity, and involvement affect the ways
in which urban spatial values are estimated.

The effects of this set of orders and their resultant feelings can
be best understood by identifying the ways in which they impact the
significant urban spatial patterns of the vertical, the horizontal, and
the ambient. Obviously any of the primary patterns that is set
within a trivial order will suffer from the reaction of indifference.
The excess of incompatibility that defines the trivial drains each of
the primary patterns of potential significance. Neither the vertical
nor the horizontal nor the ambient can reach a level of individuality
such that it can gain affective attention. The same is not true of
vague orders. The vague is marked by an excess of identification. Because some aspects of a vague order are singled out to represent all
elements in that order, the primary urban spatial patterns can stand
out with a degree of urgency. It is this level of significance that is felt

as a mood of expectation. Something vaguely compels attention. It is neither specific nor actual but it does call attention to potential expressions of importance. Vertical patterns established within vague spatial orders promote a sense of expectation that edges perpendicular space into a place of presumptive importance. But vagueness lacks specificity and therefore the possibility of nearness is slim. Vague verticality exhibits an inevitable distance between the perceiver and the particular spatial pattern. Likewise, a horizontal urban pattern set within vague spatial orders suffers from a lack of intimate connection. Something awaits our experience but sets itself at a distance. Finally, ambient spatial patterns placed in vague urban orders suffer from a similar lack of intimacy.

Still, expectation serves a purpose for it draws the urban dweller deeper into the environmental mix. This sets the stage for the role of the remaining orders, the narrow and the wide, in urban experience. It is when narrowness provides the requisite intensity that the primary spatial patterns begin to loom large in human experience. And according to its relation to width, great spatial experience can be had. The extremes for narrow verticality are feelings of great intensity that shade toward the experience of the monumental, the heroic, and even the transcendental. This positive spatial experience is negated by its opposite extreme when narrow verticality expresses looming perpendicularity within the urban environment. The resultant feelings combine a sense of diminishment with a sense of imminent threat. This is one side of the predicament faced by city dwellers—the sense of being boxed in by the environment. (Horizontal patterns are needed to complete the box.) The issue is scale, and it demonstrates how important the inscape of space as sited directionality really is, for human perception sets limits on what is environmentally healthy. When set within the order of width, verticality tends to fade into the horizontal since its primary expression is one of narrowness.

Similarly, horizontal space is felt as a proposition announcing either the positive feeling of opulent vastness or the negative sense of flat objectivity. When experienced as vastness, horizontal spatial patterns coax the city dweller into a sense of deep and profound involvement in a cultural matrix. This occurs when spatial orders are set into contexts that weave together the narrow and the vague. When negatively experienced, horizontal space feeds the urban citizen a steady diet of boredom that pushes experience toward trivial domains. Therefore unlike the vertical, which favors narrow orders, horizontal spatial patterns ought to emphasize orders characterized by the width that results from a weaving of the narrow onto the vague. At its best, wide horizontal space summons up feelings of intense involvement. Key to a wise use of urban space is therefore the right combination of the vertical and the horizontal. A failure of scale in either direction creates the sense of box-like doom described above. Just as there can be a canyon effect that overturns urban perceptual experience, so also the box effect profoundly alters the spatial goodness of the city. It establishes restriction as a way to be.

The last spatial pattern is the ambient. In many ways its effective presence is the very signature of great cities, and a proper treatment of its significance must await the discussion of urban place in Chapter Three.[9] Here I wish to stress the way in which ambient space concretely expresses all the dimensions of spatial inscape. The three features of spatial inscape are sited directionality, access, and habitat. Because it surrounds us without closing us in, ambient urban spatial patterns consistently offer engaging modes of sited directionality. It marks space with a sense of direction that is open and not confining. This is also why it grants access to generous volumes of space apt for the creation of what I have termed habitat. By establishing a pervasive spatial tone, ambient patterns send propositional lures echoing through the human body. These perceptions resound with the felt causal efficacy of the environment as well as the distinct spatial marks immediately sensed within the presented locus of ambient space.[10] When set in appropriate orders of vagueness, narrowness, and width, ambient space comes to take on the very definition of urban place. It softens the harshness of the vertical and the horizontal without compromising their essential strengths. It also is of major import for the building of public spaces suitable for urban experience.

This final summary of urban space and its inscape, patterns, and symbolic perception remains decidedly abstract. There appears within it little of the rush and bustle so characteristic of urban experience. In fact it appears lifeless, a caricature of city life. What is needed to add flesh and blood to these spatial skeletons is a sense of the drama of city time.

But before we leave urban space, let us try to experience it more concretely in itself. This means encountering "moving" urban space:

I, Homo Urbanus, emerge from the smelly bowels of the New York Subway System. I step out into the sun-dappled "Crossroads of the World"—42nd Street and Lexington Avenue. I will walk due west until I reach the Hudson River. Here I am on "Forty Deuce,"

*the pulsating artery through which flow the Big Apple's most out-
rageous forms of life. I have not gone five yards when I am knocked
off stride by four businessmen in their chesterfields and camel
hairs, striding aggressively (arrogantly?) toward some luncheon
rendezvous. But look! Here comes a madman tripping down the
Deuce, smiling at all and in no way trying to hide. Then along
comes a pack of teenagers bent on who knows what. To be followed
by three elegant ladies clicking their high-heeled way toward some
type of destiny. I come up to the corner of Fifth and 42. A man from
Senegal thrusts glittering gold objects for my inspection just as a
boom box plays Aretha singing "a little respect." Rhythms crash together, my ears pound, my eyes stare straight ahead, my body
crunches down to protect any exposed nerve endings. Entwined levels of moving space carried by endlessly novel events are flying at
me, through me, on top of me, within me, outside, inside, and side-
by-side me. Even as I swirl my head to check out Patience and For-
titude, The Great Lions of The New York City Public Library, more
spontaneous difference catches my attention. It is a game of three
card monte and the scam is on. Who will pay and who will play?
But before I can settle in, I am pushed west toward Sixth Avenue
by the tide of folk who just keep coming, from the east, the south,
and the north. Horns honk, drivers rage, pedestrians escape with
their lives (once more!). Two out-of-towners mess up everything by
gawking at the height of the buildings. Graduate students idly
lounge at the CUNY Graduate Center seeming for all the world to
be part of the scene, just taking it all in. Hot dogs are served, then
bananas are bought and pretzels swallowed whole. Sounds con-
found one another in the incessant arrival of immediacy as space
sweeps by bringing more and more spontaneity. I just make it as
far as Times Square. I am exhausted by the flush-rush hurry of it
all. Two homeless people block my path or am I stepping over them
and their threadbare humanity? All is intensely interesting in an
onrushing sweep of forms of value. There is no direction to take. All
lacks continuity and there is no clue as to what comes next. I head
back to Grand Central Station.*

It will take some time to sort out all this spontaneity. In fact, it
will take the semiotic metaphysics of Charles Peirce to make sense
of this plunge into immediacy. We have just encountered "iconic
firstness"—the reign of spontaneous quality experienced as moving
urban space. Part Two will deal with the ways in which this dynamic
of values can be fitted together into the texture of urban meaning.

■ Chapter Two

Urban Time

With the experience of urban time, this study edges closer to the semiotic domain. This transition from metaphysics to semiotics is due to the fact that the city is primarily a conversation and that conversation is primarily about time. But to understand this dialogue, it is necessary to control both its language and style. This is the reason why this chapter continues to follow the previous structure of inscape, pattern, and symbolic reference. However, the concluding discussion of urban time's value will explain why a movement away from metaphysical analysis and toward semiotics is inevitable when dealing with the city. In this way "place," the next chapter's theme comes quite "naturally" into our conversation about the continuity of nature and human meaning within urban life.

The Inscape of City Time

The inscape of urban time involves the two types of time to be found in city and nature. Both types of time are qualitatively rich but they are very different. In this section I deal with the inscape of time as epochal, while in the next section I deal with time as transitional.

Epochal time is concrete time that seals itself into drops of experience that are all-at-once, uniquely individualized, and totally whole. Transitional time deals with the movements between time's phases and is familiar to us as time past, time present, and time future. Both types of time are to be felt with immediate directness in the present moment but the quality of their respective feelings differs. This is one more reason why the semiotics of city life must ultimately be founded on the discipline of aesthetics. All other forms of time—even and most especially the physical time favored by scientific materialism—are derivative from these more concrete forms of time. As such, clock time or any "measured time" is abstract for it is dependent upon a nontemporal measure for its meaning. Later in this chapter a discussion of urban circulation and the speed of light will be employed in order to make this more evident. For now, it is important to insist on the primal concreteness of epochal time and to try to understand its significance.

What does it mean to call time epochal? There are four important aspects of the inscape of urban time.[1] Such time is always concrete, unique, a seamless whole, and of uneven flow. By concrete, I mean the fact that "time always takes time." This formula is at the heart of the epochal theory of time. It says in effect that before time there was nothing like time and that time itself is always only itself and no other. Strictly speaking time is not comparable to any other dimension because it is the way in which reality shapes itself so that a single unique drop of experience emerges as a spatiotemporal whole. As such it cannot be likened (except in a metaphorical sense or by way of imagistic thinking) to anything other than itself. It is called concrete because each drop of process is itself the outcome of the way in which each event assembles itself in the present by reason of its appropriation of the past and its appeal to and for the future. (Whitehead coins the far more active term *concrescence* to stress time's becoming in the world of the now.) Thus, epochal time is the way in which events come to be all-at-once. Such existential primes are indivisible because they have no parts. If they could be so divided they would not be epochs of time. All further possibility of existential division has been sealed off and forbidden. This is why epochs of time can be called quanta or occasions or events or even happenings. They constitute the way in which the process of reality breaks out into the open and declares itself as this right here and now and no other. Of course, in retrospect we may wish to divide up time into parts such as before or after, or earlier and later, but that is an intellectual analysis done for the sake of rational clarity. Concrete epochal time comes to be and then perishes. It does not change. Change is how we mark the differences between epochs.

Think of (and this is only an image) a drop of water forming at the end of a dripping faucet. The water congeals to a single whole and then drops. We hear the ping (probably to our annoyance) and then we wait for the next drop. That drop also comes altogether or not at all. Epochal time is the way in which the process of the world grows through the drops of real experience and thereby expresses different forms of value. Time is an event. An event is a value. A value makes a difference. The difference is wholly itself and no other. Change is the marking of the differences brought about by the emergences of value.

If epochal time did not come all-at-once and in an existentially indivisible manner, then reality would be infinitely divisible. At this point Zeno wins and we are plunged into the irrationality of his paradoxes. Or we can side with varieties of Indian thought that declare this world to be Māyā. Neither the option for the irrational nor the option for a phenomenal world of mere appearances is suitable for this study. Only a hardheaded realistic pluralism can suffice to make sense of the onward rush of time within a process universe. Now, the epochal theory of time may be difficult to understand and it may even harbor its own mysteries (consider Schrödinger's cat or some of the anomalies of subparticle physics or the "black holes" of astrophysics), but it does not invite an abandonment of reason at exactly the point where it is most needed. That point is the practice of ethical conduct in daily life. After all, the whole aim of this study is to enable us to prize the city and guard its goodness through such normative understanding.

The second character of epochal urban time is its uniqueness. Each and every drop of experience is different from its predecessor and its successor. If it were not, it would not be that predecessor or that successor. The uniqueness of the epochs of time is best expressed through the use of Duns Scotus's term *haeccitas*. Later on in this study I will argue that this irreducible quality of creative uniqueness is precisely what Peirce means by "firstness." Right now it is enough to simply note its consequences for the creative urgency embodied in epochal time. Each moment, no matter how repetitive and like its past or future, represents the emergence of a particular quality for only just this time in this universe. It is this *haeccitas* that forces Whitehead to recast the famous "time is like a river" analogy. It used to be said that one cannot step into the same river twice. Now it must be said that one cannot step into the same river once. The ineluctable freshness and spontaneity of realty that is witnessed by all attuned observers (be they Zen monks, Christian believers, or artists at work) is the outcome of this uniqueness. Without *haeccitas*, the reality of the city itself would dissolve into an altogether frightening dullness. Time and city would have lost their verve.

The seamless whole that also characterizes epochal city time guarantees that there will be many different kinds of time flowing in and through urban experience. This is due to the fact that each drop of experience, each event of value, each *haeccitas* cannot be reduced to something less than itself. The seamless wholeness of epochal time is the sign of its wholenesss. If such events, epochs, or occasions of experience could be so divided, they would thereby contradict their own epochal character. Epochal time comes to be but does not change. Time takes time. Time is what it is and no other.

This also means that epochal time must be discontinuous. For if each *haeccitas* is itself and no other, then there are many wholes and many unities in the temporal stream. Time does not stop all-at-once and then begin again. But rather time expresses very different types of modaliites at the same time. There is quick time and slow time, thick time and thin time, and many other kinds as well. Thus modes of time exist side by side as well as before and after each other. In sum, through its concreteness, its uniqueness, its seamless wholeness, and its uneven flow, the inscape of time spreads out to express varying patterns that evoke varying feelings. I turn now to an examination of those patterns.

The Patterns of City Time

The patterns of time are past, present, and future. Before turning to an analysis of each of these patterns, it is necessary to introduce the one remaining category of my cosmological scheme. I have already used the categories of inscape, pattern, and transmission. What remains to be deployed is the category of contrast. This category will be indispensable for understanding both the depth and the reach of time as well as place and its types of identity. Without contrast, the city would be a pale and sickly place. By contrast I mean the bringing together into a unity of that which is normally held apart. Thus, contrast is an aesthetic act whereby intensification of experience and width of understanding are simultaneously achieved. As Whitehead says: "All aesthetic feeling is the realization of contrast under identity."[2] Contrast is not to be confused with comparison. The latter holds things apart; the former puts them into a unity.

Now, the most fundamental contrast possible in a process universe is the contrast between the actual and the possible. This contrast is at the heart of all real events. I have already mentioned conceptual feelings as the outcome of feeling possible forms of definiteness. In addition, the physical realm has been characterized as the conformal feeling of the past as it repeats itself in the present. Finally, I have mentioned propositions as the contrast between the actual and the possible, which acts as a lure for feeling calling on human experience to entertain its potential realization in experience. The contrast between the actual and the possible is most fundamentally the bringing together into a novel unity "what has been" with "what might be." Therefore, one of the most important aspects of the category of contrast is that it demands a limit be drawn between the actual and the possible such that they can be brought into a unity.

To draw a limit is to establish a value as just this value and no other. The laying down of limits is precisely the act whereby identity and difference emerge from the crucible of process. All value in the temporal world of process is the result of such limitations: "Value is the outcome of limitation."[3] Furthermore, the very determinateness of the world of process is dependent upon such measuring out of the limits of existence and experience. It is not true that I can do whatever I want. Limitation and finitude haunt the edges of all urban decisions. It is precisely this sense of a boundary appropriate for all forms of existence that makes pluralism a viable metaphysics. Without limit there would be no final real things in any environment, natural or urban. The very price we pay for rationality depends upon finding these limits so that real being can emerge out of the welter of process. To have a definite form (and all forms are definite) means to have a limit set.

Now this concept of limit and finitude threatens to impoverish the world. If limit is at the heart of value, then it would seem that there is an inevitable boundary set upon creativity. It is just here that contrast can be of service as a cosmological category. Contrast lets us establish new limits between previous incompatibles. It widens and deepens experience so that a qualitative gain can be had. Likewise, it enables the many to become a more profound one by including the different in its self-formation. (Later in this study, I shall term this understanding of contrast the beautiful in urban experience.) A corollary to this metaphysics of contrast and limit is the idea of "acts of full temporal identity." For the achievement of a certain depth of identity and richness of experience is what is needed to make cities come alive. Such temporal fullness is also what makes a person real. Without the capacity to contrast many seemingly incompatible dimensions, human existence would never rise to a level of a conscious intensity worthy of city existence. This becomes even more apparent within the actual patterns of time and how they contrast with each other so as to achieve depth of temporal endurance.

Finally, the examination of each pattern of time—time past, time present, and time future—demands that each be viewed from its presence in the present. This follows necessarily from the inscape of time as epochal. Thus, even as time hurtles itself forward, it always does so within the limits of a determinate epoch. This is where contrasts must arise if humans are to move beyond a thin gruel of experience to a more robust urban menu. Therefore, this point in the analysis of urban experience demands the full utilization of all the cosmological categories: Inscape, pattern, contrast, and transmission come into massive effectiveness when the concept of urban time is explored. The yoking together of limit and value, finitude and importance, beauty and contrast may sound odd at this point; however, it is, as shall be seen, at the normative center of this analysis.

Time Past. There are many ways in which time past registers its presence in the life of the city. There is time that lays on "the heavy hand of the past." Such time is constrictive, demanding, and imposes an obligation on the present. Similarly, there is past time that acts like a vise choking off opportunity for novelty. But past time is not simply a form of restraint. There is also a kind of past time that functions to reasssure as in the repetitive seasonal cycles or the long endurance of a built monument. Such time grants us stability in the face of the onrush of the future. It steadies us by laying down a common ground from which and to which all citizens can appeal. Furthermore, such past time can serve to build up tremendous reserves of energy and value. This is what is meant by tradition and history.

All such forms of past time have their roots in conformal activities whereby the past is handed over to the present with a minimum of change. The best example of this kind of time is of course matter itself, especially on the mesocosmic scale. Within the midrange of material events that exist above the level of the subatomic and outside the level of the astrocosmic, there exist the buildings, streets,

machinery, and in general the everyday items of use within the contemporary city. All these material objects are formed from a repetitive temporal structure, Their endurance is bought at the price of
novelty. The less there is of change, the more there is of endurance.
Now, scientific materialism wants us to endorse the view that only
these forms of existence are real. But if matter is seen to be con-
gealed time, then there is much more at play in city life than the
mere shuffling of matter. City experience lays down strata after
strata of temporal regions, each one of which plays its part in the
present moment. The past is thick in the city. It carries its achievements with it and either closes down or opens up varieties of novelty.
Past time is therefore conformal, repetitious, enduringly stable, and
grounded. It provides the platform from which the present can push
toward the future.

Time Future. What does the future feel like in the city? It feels like a
concept. This is because the future is all about possibility. As the category of transmission points out, possibility is transferred around
environmental systems as forms of conceptual feeling: "Maybe this
will work ?"; "perhaps this is a better way ?"—each is a concept felt
as a form of definite possibility. In many ways time future is the opposite of time past. It lures instead of compels. It counsels entertainment of otherness rather than acceptance of the status quo. The
unformed and the inchoate stand opposed to the achieved and the
settled.

There are two types of conceptual feelings of the future. There
is pure possibility—anything might happen. This form of possibility
is largely ineffective except as a long-term stimulus for change. The
type of future found in the urban present is most effective when it
comes in the form of propositions. Recall that a proposition is a
halfway house between the actual and the possible. It deliberately
thwarts real decision in favor of encouraging entertainment. It
seeks to hold our interest rather than force action. As we have just
seen, it serves primarily as a "lure for feeling," inviting a normative
consideration of its potential value for the urban domain. Furthermore, given the recent discussion of the category of contrast, we can
see that a proposition is really a very effective instrument for advancing value in city life. This is because as a contrast and as a
proposition such lures for feeling suspend the need for immediate
action. They provide important breathing room within the cityscape. Citizens are allowed to entertain alternatives first and then,
if they so choose, enact them. In a phrase, propositional feelings are

the most powerful way through which the ground for intelligent, communal, and personal action is cleared in city life. Without a significant propositional dimension the possibility for good decisions and good actions disappear from the urban scene.

In sum, the future enters the present as an enticement. Its demand for recognition is both real and hypothetical; that is to say, the future is the propositional form enacted by citizens in their being with one another. The social dimension is enhanced or diminished by the presence or absence of appropriately forceful propositional lures. In fact, much of Part Three of this study, "Urban Praxis," is given over to a discussion of such propositions. It is precisely the advantage of speculative philosophy that it can, if bold enough, span the seemingly infinite distance between the cosmologist Whitehead, the semiatician Mead, and the pragmatist Dewey. This is because speculative philosophy demands that its major categories be directly applied to human experience.[4] The future comes into the present most effectively when social intelligence directs the ways and means of applying concepts. These concepts, in turn, must be entertained through and through by a judging public that takes the moral dimension as seriously as the political. Thus, the transition from urban cosmology to urban semiotics to urban praxis follows the actual structure of city experience. To understand the city one must see that its structure necessarily includes a "natural" transition from spatiotemporal structures to signs and their meaning to modes of effective action. This is one more reason why the city is both unique and continuous with other forms of social dwelling. Because of the change brought on by the city's shift in critical mass, an urban cosmology demands a necessary theoretical move to semiotics and praxis. While it is "like"a village, the city introduces new qualities derived from its unique spatiotemporal character. These shifts in quality are derived from overwhelming increase in the quantitative dimensions of urban experience.

Time Present. Many things go on in the present. There is the push of the past and the lure of the future. But most importanly there is the present itself. I have already detailed its inscape. The present is a concrete seamless unity that flows unevenly alongside its contemporaries. If the present is epochal—that is, all-at-once, then the central issue is how can the present make room for all the elements that jostle for a place within its presence? The answer, once again, involves the category of contrast. Contrast, properly carried out, gives to the present two overwhelmingly important gifts—depth and width. Recall that limit is a part of contrast.

At the beginning of this discussion of time, I spoke of the need for acts of "full temporal individuality." By now, the reason for such a need should be clear. Given time's epochal character, there must be some way to deepen and widen the temporal present. Otherwise, city life would be simply a series of temporal explosions lacking any enduring order or identity. Acts of full temporal individuality arise from two sources—contrast and the four forms of order. When the presence of the past and future are intense enough in the present, then the emergent value must make room for them if they are to be part of the ongoing character of reality. The emergent or concrescent present does this through the act of contrast—what was and what can be are joined to what is becoming real. The present moment thereby achieves great individuality that can be understood as richness of experience. Such wealth comes from the act of holding together in a novel unity that which never was before—in this case, the past with its achievements and the future with its possibilities. The resultant contrast deepens remarkably the texture of time present. What could have been ephemeral is now grounded in the present. What once had no future now enjoys some sense of continuity. The propositional dimension of contrast carries this out most effectively, for it yokes together the intensity achieved from contrast and the sense of a meaningful future dependent upon forms of conceptual entertainment. Acts with full temporal individuality arise from the effective use of contrast as a mode of categoreal behavior.

There is yet another way in which acts with full temporal individuality are encouraged and brought into being. I refer to the four orders whereby transmission transfers energy, meaning, and value around environmental systems. Recall that there are four fundamental ways in which the process of reality orders itself so as to establish levels of massiveness and continuity.[5] These orders are the essential ways in which city life manages its experience so as to to create what is important. There are four such levels of order: triviality, vagueness, narrowness, and width. Trivial orders die quickly due to the fact that they do not make much difference and are therefore pushed aside. Vague orders, on the other hand, establish the requisite minimum of generality required to gain and stimulate the urban imagination. They do this through "an excess of identification." Narrow orders select out a dominant perspective and pursue it with a vengeance. What results is a great gain in intensity as well as a loss of potential alternatives. Narrowness follows the law of limit but it is in danger of excluding too much. Lastly, orders characterized by width result from weaving narrow emphases onto vague backgrounds. This is the best way to transfer both depth of experience and well-integrated value throughout significant parts of the city.

It is through wise appropriation of one or several of these environmental levels of order that a sustained richness of experience begins to emerge as a real factor in urban experience. When this occurs with a frequency suitable to the environment, then it can be said that acts of full temporal individuality have emerged as an important feature of city life. Furthermore, when fully established, these modes of order transmit on a regular basis both a unique character and a richly intense experience throughout particular urban regions. It is therefore both true and interesting to speak of the flavor of a neighborhood or the mood of a block or the feel of a street. All these so-called subjective experiences are actually rooted in an awareness (dim but real) of the values being moved about city areas. This epistemological realism is the ground of the human capacity to perceive symbolically vastly different regions of value and experience.

The Symbolic Perception of Urban Time

The deepening of contrasts characteristic of city life gives rise to an enriched sense of the symbolic register. To review, symbolic reference is the way in which human beings bring together the deliverances of two more primal modes of perception, causal efficacy and presentational immediacy. Causal efficacy derives from the withness of the human body as it is existentially situated in the environment. It is not derived from the five senses but is rather nonsensuous, being the outcome of the way in which the body and its various organs feel when they are immersed in environmental activities. As such, it is a dim and elusive form of perception but at the same time rich in import and significance. Causal efficacy permeates our somatic existence as the present edges out of the past and into the future. Presentational immediacy, on the other hand, is derived from the five senses and is characterized by clarity and objectivity. It is the world as immediately present over there in that direction. It gives us clear-cut locations and is the ground of accuracy in our dealings with the environment. The information it gives us is the polar opposite of that derived from causal efficacy. Presentational immediacy gives us clarity but at the price of shallowness. The world of process with its throbbing creativity gets frozen in an immediately presented scene that appears to be both static and exact. In point of fact, we know that the world is, in James's phrase, "a buzzing, blooming confusion." But presentational immediacy gives us that scene "over there," that "solid" stone in our hand and that sound "right behind us." Finally, symbolic reference is how we refer the information derived from one type of perception to another. The transmutation can run either way: from causal efficacy to presentational immediacy or from presentational immediacy to causal efficacy. In city life both types of symbolic transmission occur, though obviously that derived from causal efficacy is much harder to locate and detect. (This will be the subject of much further discussion in the next chapter.)

Since urban time is perceived as deeply contrasted we can expect a polymorphic display of symbols at work in the ways in which we negotiate city experience. Still, there are certain general traits of urban time that can be singled out. The past is regularly symbolized as both a heavy constraint upon the present as well as the ground of a sure and solid foundation. Both symbols—the weight of the past and the support of tradition—can be seen daily in any European capital. The future, on the other hand, is felt as a lure and a set of expectations. It is symbolic of the impending presence of creativity. Any contemporary American city has places filled with the buildings of the future. Time present is symbolized by deep contrasts leading to a sense of full and genuine temporal individuality. This (along with space) is the ground of the polyvalent richness of urban place. When the contrasts are strong enough, experience is lifted to a whole new level of symbolic interplay. We are now "in the Bronx." What is actual is the present with its register of past history and the future with its propositional lures. The symbolic mixture leads to an experience of strong individuality (depth) with real possibility (width). Through the function of the integer (which is another term for contrast), the resultant power is exponentially increased.

There is one other major symbolic level of urban time that deserves attention. Natural time is tied to the seasons and is in general cyclical and routinized.[6] The very opposite is true of city time. This is because one of the great and grounding dimensions of city life is movement. The circulation of people, goods, information, and services is a defining property of city life. Now, the constant that measures motion is the speed of light. In nature we are not in control of that which travels at the rate of 180,000 feet per second. In the city we simply turn the lights on. So fast is motion in the city, that we can be said to have invented a new form of time, "city time." Urban time throws up a net similar to Indra's within which all the nuances of time future, time past, and time present glitter in each other's reflected presences. In Parts Two and Three this web of moving relations will be seen to demand symbolic breadth for its proper semiotic expression and political action.

This constant whirl of time plunges us into an experiential domain that even to this day still startles. In the symbolic perception of time the citizen has the past in front of him and the future right beside him and all of this occurs in a very intensely narrow, wide, and deep present moment. It takes a lot to be a city dweller. The sheer mastery of temporal dimensions (let alone spatial displays) is enough to exhaust even the most ardently energetic. Time moves through the city at the speed of light. The future beckons in the present moment. The past imposes itself in the present. And the present glitters with all these rich contrasts. What is the value of city time?

The Value of City Time

History is a real presence in the city. By this I do not mean a mere record of past events and accomplishments. I mean "presence" in a very literal sense. In the city the past is present. The future is also present in the constant rebuilding and restructuring that is so much a part of city life. Finally, there is obviously the presence of the present. The value of each temporal dimension deserves separate attention.

The Presence of the Past. The human body is a process of sedimentation whereby our contact with the city is governed by layers of responses that become habitual. There is a similar process at work in cities that preserve the past. When I walk the streets of Rome I walk through the rubble of the past. It is there for me to see and even touch. So also in Florence and Athens and many other cities. It is important to understand that this is not the mere preservation of the past. That is museum curiosity. I mean the living presence of the past that displays itself as part of the present texture of the city.

The display of the past in city life is a matter of nuance. Too much and the city calcifies and is turned into a graveyard. Monuments are often tombstones. On the other hand, a city without a past has no density. Modern Singapore is an excellent example, but so are the so-called "Edge Cities" that now spring up along the Eastern

Megalopolis. Their thinness summons up the superficial and surface appeal does not ultimately work for human beings. I suggest my reader spend some time in a modern airport in order to experience directly what I am talking about. We are through and through much too temporal to be left without a past. The mere toleration of the past as something interesting does little to help us sense the continuity that the presence of the past ought to convey. The sedimentation of the past in the present has to take on a much more mobile character. The past must be lived through in the performances of the city's citizens.

The past ought not to be used for nostalgia or sentimentality but for the sake of the present. When this occurs, the present is enlivened by the presence of the past. Instead of choking off change, tradition shows forth the strength of continuity. The past is useful but only in the present. The chief gift of the past to the present is to strengthen the time of the present. To know that the past is here is to know that human effort can establish a chain of worked reality such that genuine pride, respect, and hope can be felt and displayed.

In a similar way the presence of the past also strengthens the future. The phrase "we can do it too" suggests a joining with the past that guarantees identity in the midst of change. This is not nostalgia but human wisdom that sees the past as present in the future. Human temporality demands such continuity; otherwise, our life spans would be nothing but thins threads of triviality. Time is not the linear arrow of progress for, at our normative best, we back into the future by reason of the meanings of the past as seized in the choices of the present. In a city where history is thick, nothing could be more "natural" than the future's real dependence on the past.

From this vantage point the danger of transiency is evident. It is not simply a matter of no roots, though that, too, is there. The issue of transiency is the issue of drift. Transiency denies the reality of human temporality. It imagines that one can live in a "timeless present," but such thinking is sheer fantasy. Transiency is imaginary dwelling for it has no depth and saps a city of vitality.

The presence of the past takes on a singular concreteness when considered in the light of the restoration and reuse of old buildings. Whether these are intended for personal living or public use, the citizen feels the presence of the past as she goes about her own actions. This entwining of time zones results in a qualitatively different environment. Our eyes feel the past in the texture of ancient walls. Their symbolic weight is real. They support us with their presence in the present and this act of reassurance assures us of an effective sense of the future. The theme of re-membering ought to be understood literally. As scattered, we are not members but fragments. Remember-ed, we experience integrity with our past and our future. We stand whole in the penumbra of the past and are sheltered from the storm of the future. The ephemeral dimension of life disappears as we remember that we are part of a greater whole. That effort has gone on, is going on, and will continue.

In a city the three temporal regions—the past, the present, and the future—stand forth with extreme clarity. Time steps forward with a boldness and explicitness unmatched by nature. Temporal declaration is a significant element in the conversation of the city. The language of time past can be read in the city's buildings as well as its streets. It surrounds us with its leavings. The echoes of the past ring in our bodies, creating an unparalleled mixture of past and present. This commingling of history and our present being is one of the great glories of city life. The footfalls of the past reach right into the presence of the future.

The Presence of the Future. Nature is routine. The city is change. Here the future is upon us. It is alongside and all around us. The sense of haste so often felt in the city is not just the need to keep moving with the crowd. Its real significance lies in the dramatic presence of the future. This presence is so palpable in city life that it can be said with more than a degree of truth that the future is already here. This results from the essential meaning of "building." Building is already underway, it is developing before our eyes. It edges into the present, even though it is not-yet. There is nothing in nature to compare with this process of building. In the city the future burrows into the present so that creativity characterizes its being. Furthermore, this "principle of unrest " at the heart of city life lacks the steady rhythm of nature.

There is little predictability in the city, and surprise is commonplace. One leaves the house and there it is: Something has changed! It could be a lamppost or even a new building. My point is that the future does not announce itself in the city; rather, it intrudes, impolitely and without warning. The future throngs about us, continually uprooting our routines. If the past sediments itself in our bodies, the conceptual feelings that mark the presence of the future are always there to prevent the sclerosis of human value.

Surely, loss is felt when our constant environment is suddenly altered. What will replace the familiar scene? Will we enjoy it? Can we fit it into our bodily being? Has an old friend been lost because of an ugly upstart? The future slaps us in the face—not a very nice thing to do. Upset, dislocation, and disorientation are the very fabric of city life. It is the real presence of the future in the present. Place is difficult to maintain in city experience. Displacement is not confined to removal from one's home. The body's health depends upon a regular supply of nourishment from the environment. Displacement can occur when a favored stoop is suddenly altered. The city beats its presence into our body. Change endangers all the accustomed and "natural" rhythms of life.

But the anxiety attending change can also be leavened by hope. We do not see an abyss when faced with the urban future for it takes shape before our eyes. It may be disappointing but something is emerging. What falls is replaced. We can accustom ourselves to change and even say, "I can live with that." The need for patience is as real in the city as it is in nature. In a strange way, the crowding of the present by the future within urban domains is so intense that it acts as a kind of open-ended guarantee of continuity.

But before continuity can be gained, sight lines must be laid down so that some form of order emerges. I return to *Homo Urbanus* as he makes his way through Grand Central Station.

> *If my walk on 42nd Street was an exercise in experiencing space as a moving and ever-novel contiuuum that seemingly tolerates all kinds of difference, then one emotional result of all that spontaneity is surely confused exhaustion. I need some order, some form of purpose writ large. As I enter the tunnels leading down toward the subway and Grand Central Station, I immediately feel a change in mood. There seems to be just as much hustle and bustle, but patterns of force quickly emerge from the chaos. People continue to come at me but each has a direction. I find myself bobbing and weaving like a boxer, looking for an open space I can rush into. Here comes a man in a trench coat who looks just like George Raft. I sidestep him neatly but quickly fall into a footrace with an elegantly dressed business woman. But she leaves me in the dust. I am threatened by shoves, hit by bags, and pushed from behind, but I quickly take on the Big Apple "shuffle" and successfully make it through. Stop here, go now, pirouette. Watch out for those attaches. They are particularly vicious. Why so much force and why so much collision? Because there are signs that point. (Later each of these semiotic experiences will be called an index, for its sign value will be that of a pointer that indicates a way out of the strife, collision, and competition that seem to*

*mark a certain dimension of city life.) I have entered another do-
main. Here everyone rushes about but each seems to know where
she is going—except of course for the guy who just stands there
trying to figure out where he is and where he is going. In fact he
is so out of place that others collide with him. He is an obstacle
because he does not know which way the signs point. He has lost
track of the spatiotemporal indicators needed to negotiate this
level of experience. This situation is much more a temporal than
a spatial one. True, space is here but what the rush and directions are all about is time. As in: "After you go this far, then this
will be there." From past to present to an immediately looming
future, homo urbanus moves in a directional path made possible
by the indexical signs that show what is absolutely, positively
next. It is the pressure of an imminent future that shapes the
present. It is the pressure of an already committed past that
drives the pedestrian toward expected results. The break between
the past, the present, and the future becomes ever more narrow at
this level of urban experience. Later, it will be called, in semiotic
terms, the realm of secondness. Now we have two elements instead of simply the spontaneity so evident outside at the street
level of firstness.*

*   I look around and quickly determine the "right way to go."
Arrows, large-lettered signs announce that my goal is over here.
But this does not help much because others in the terminal are
seeking to go to different destinations. Over there is Track 10:
Greenwich, Old Lyme, and Stamford. Just ahead is Riverdale,
Yonkers, and Dobbs Ferry. There is a crowd of people milling
about in the center of the terminal. What are they looking at? Precisely the large board with the Railroad Timetable prominently
displayed. Now, this is the very sign of secondness. It points to the
collision that occurs when two differences are brought together
and a way to the second is sharply indicated. Then I spy my sign:
Lexington Avenue Subway, Trains 4, 5, and 6. I need the 6 because I am heading back to St. Jerome Church. I will take the 4
to 125th Street and then change to the local to get to Third Avenue and Alexander Avenue. That is my final stop on this indexical voyage. And given my plan, I have fallen in with the temporal
pressure characterizing secondness. From here I will go there, but
only in the quickest way possible. I now set out with determination for I know where I am going and how to get there. I slip
around others and follow the references for the quickest results.
Right here, left there, straight ahead for 100 yards, then down a*

flight of stairs. Check the sign for Uptown and for Express. I
stand there on the platform alert with triumph and wait for the
number 4.

All this directional force is what Peirce means by the collisions that mark the realm of secondness and its indexical mood. Part Two will examine in detail the ways in which an urban semiotics needs this semiotic domain in order to establish meaning. This midway point between the immediacy of firstness and the sense of continuity marking thirdness is absolutely required as the stepping stone to symbolic breadth of meaning. If two does not follow on one, then three does not happen. My discussion of urban semiotics will make sense of what at present appears to be a somewhat opaque arithmetic.

But to return to the presence of the future. How does the future show itself in the present in city life? Time shrinks in the city, especially in this age of instant news that arrives simultaneously with time future.[7] By this I mean the following. You are in the city and driving to work. You have your car radio on and it is 8:00 A.M. Suddenly the events of the day preceding and the day about to begin are read out to you. There is no pause in history. It surrounds you. You cannot break away. Everything that happened and everything that is about to happen are announced as done, finished, and now "news." Time has imploded and its density is palpable. The air is thick with time.

This implosion catches up the citizen in a whirling of time. What is past and what is future meld together in a single omnipresence. How does the citizen cull out of this temporal melange what is important? What are the normative measures for the important? More concretely, how does one even tell time? What was future is now past. What is past occurred but five minutes ago. Time collapses in on the city dweller, threatening to bury him in an avalanche of temporality.

Within such a temporal hurricane how does one act? Some people take the obvious way out. They simply ignore reality and cocoon themselves in a hidden interiority. Their impassive faces tell the tale. Others select out the significant, usually on a self-interested basis. What is important is that which has a direct connection with their lives. Still others drown themselves in this temporal soup. They are known as "trend-setters." They move effortlessly from fad to fad, embracing each as though it were a great discovery promising an end to life's problems. Much of the silliness, the vapid quality of

city life derives from such forms of behavior. Temporal confusion inevitably ends up in superficiality as citizens spend their days
scratching on the surface of time. The irony is that there where time
is potentially most thick, there time is most abused. The result is obvious when only shallow meanings emerge into city experience.

In urban life the present is not simply thinned out by such an attitude. It tends, quite literally, to disappear. The present becomes a
vanishing point between the past and the future. What has been and
what is not-yet dominate and the loss of the present moment becomes a constant threat. Human well-being requires that the present be present in the deepest and widest of ways. Once again the
importance of contrast can be readily seen. The present must linger
a while and show its gifts. For it is within the present that we most
concretely live. Failure of contrast in temporal terms means that the
citizen is condemned to either fruitless repetition of past glories or a
fantasy life based on dreams about the future.

The Presence of the Present. Halting time in the city demands deliberate human effort. So rapid is its pace, so throbbing is its pulse that
"occasions" must be found to stop the rush of time. The experience of
"taking time off" means taking time off its track toward the future.
What is distinctive about urban time in the present is that human
beings can actively help to create it. One cannot achieve such a feat
in nature.

What happens when we create the presence of the present? The
word *happen* tells the meaning of this creative act. When the present
is allowed to show itself in the city, an occasion emerges. If its meaning is known, even if in a peripheral manner, then its significance
can be expressed and participated in. Banners proclaim the streets
as now housing a different kind of time. "It is the festival of . . . ," and
suddenly we experience a time that is whole, separated from the
hustle of the city. We stroll in this time, breathe its air, smell its fra-
gance or pungence, feel its real presence. We give ourselves over to
it. We amble through the streets for only in that way can one's being
be open to the richness of this temporal experience.

Look at the human eyes as they gape in continual wonder at the
unceasing display of reality. Here in this present time there is no
judgment, only acknowledgment. We recognize ourselves and our capacities. Better yet, we re-member our bodies. Its separate parts
fuse and we become one flesh with others. The smiles, the leisurely
stroll, the warmth of others—all is an act of greeting. We are meeting our being-with-one-another and this act of recall sends its uni-

tive message through our body. The eyes smile, the hands open in gestures of welcome and acknowledgment, hearts literally beat to the same tune. The melody is not complex: It is the song of being alive in the city.

In the presence of the present we can celebrate the open region of space and time that lets us be fully human. Community emerges when we sing this song. Plato defines love in the *Symposium* as "something-in-between"—*Koinonia*—(the Greek word for community) shows that community only occurs when something is shared in common. Despite the presence of the past and the future (in many ways overwhelming presences), we can still carve out a present and, most importantly, share it. This act of communion is carried out by and through the body. What "happens" in this happening is that time floods our being and that of our fellow communicants. Why is it that a city can create time? As we shall see, the city emerges as the place where the human dimension asserts itself most creatively. The dominance of the human is such that time itself can be stayed—if only for a while.

There are other moments when the presence of the present becomes palpable in city life. These are not moments of community but of creative individuality. I think of Walt Whitman singing the praises of the Brooklyn Bridge. But such effort requires quiet and an absence of speed and noise. Somewhere in the city a form and place of stillness must be found. (The next chapter deals extensively with this issue.) This personal experience of the presence of the present is the outcome of an effort to make the hidden tangible and felt. It is the attempt to touch the recesses of our being. To carry out such a transformation of time (and space) demands that we be in the right place.

Chapter Three

Urban Place

My earlier work *Nature* maintained that life was the crowning achievement of the creative advance of nature. Place holds a similar position in this study of the city. Its creation is the sign of urban maturity and excellence. I begin with a presentation of the doctrine of normative measure as the ground of this inquiry into the value of urban experience. I then look at the inscape of place as the all-at-once unification of time and space. This leads to a discussion of beautiful place as the paradigm of urban excellence. The chapter concludes by looking at the ways in which feelings of stillness can well up in urban places.

The Doctrine of Normative Measure

Places are made up of events that contrast to an intensely high degree the cosmological extremes of possibility and actuality. Feelings of what is and what might be are felt at the same time. This unification of the ideal and the actual is grounded in what I call the doctrine of normative measure. Plato is the father of this way of thinking but family resemblances can be found in thinkers as different as

Confucius, Lao-Tzu, Spinoza, Leibniz, and Whitehead. In fact, anywhere philosophy acknowledges the real possibility of good, better,
and best, there also is present the experience of normative thinking.
To think normatively is to lay down a mark or measure that can be
used to estimate the goodness of some experience. This laying down is
a hypothetical gesture and not a stipulative act. Normative thinking
proceeds by vaguely suggesting what would pass for goodness in a
particular experience and then applies that vague hypothesis to actual experience. Thus, we vaguely hypothesize what would make for a
good philosophy lecture. Then we see how that hypothesis actually
works when enacted in a real classroom. The measure becomes a standard by which the experience can be judged. But note the different
possible outcomes for normative thinking. The experience may be
judged on or off the mark. Or what is often the case, the mark itself
may be judged as inappropriate for the situation. What is usually the
case is some mixture of both results. The measure is modified by
the experience and the experience is better understood because of
the measure.

As mentioned earlier, a *locus classicus* for this kind of thinking
is the *Philebus*, where Plato singles out four dimensions of reality:
the unlimited, the limited, the mixed, and the cause of the mixture.[1]
The unlimited is the realm of the possible. I have discussed this before under the category of contrast (indeed, place is the urban category of contrast par excellence). To be possible is to be an ideal,
something that may or might come about. It is unlimited because as
conceptually felt, there seems to be no end to its possible presences.
Nothing stops a circle from being a circle unto eternity. More cor-
rectly, nothing stops the possible except the actual. For the limited is
the actual. This realm is characterized by a sheer determinateness
so that what is actually experienced is some finite *this* which is de-
finitively different from *that*. The identity of the plural events that
make up a process world is grounded in this determinateness of actuality. I have also called this feature *haeccitas* after the great medieval philosopher Duns Scotus. Finally, wherever in this study I
have attempted to define the "inscape" of an event, I am also at the
same time seeking to determine its limits.

Several important corollaries follow from this concept of the
limited. For one thing, power and value come out of knowing limits,
not simply transgressing them. I underline the importance of this
doctrine for it runs against the temper of the age. In a postmodern,
post-Nietzschean world, we are supposedly charged with overcom-
ing limits. In my estimation that is exactly the problem with the

present age: We do not know the limits because we do not know what is value and what are the terms of its achievement. Grandiosity is not creativity. Furthermore, determinateness implies that every actual event has essential and conditional features as well as qualities of simplicity and complexity. Essential here means that which makes any event what it is and no other; conditional means that which hedges in or "conditions" such events. The essential is that which comes to be and the conditional is that environment within which *haeccitas* expresses its own uniqueness. Simplicity is the gift of the essential, for it is that which simply makes something what it is. Likewise, the conditional gives us the complex. For complexity is just how a determinate event orders its conditions so that certain things are kept and others are rejected. The conditional is the perspectival and the essential is what grants that unique angle of vision.

Returning to Plato, the mixed is what we encounter in reality: The mixture of the actual and the possible that expresses varying ranges of contrasts throughout a specific environment. What is brought together is done so under the aegis of a measure. This measure is the cause of the mixture such that just so much of this and not so much of that is granted access to reality. Measure is therefore another way of saying standard or norm. Normative thinking gets its name from the process whereby a community actively engages in the pursuit and utilization of appropriate norms for living. Some call this self-governance; others call it democracy. I call it normative because its central focus is on the goodness of any real event. Now, as soon as I say goodness, I imply two other concepts—better or worse. So therefore the doctrine of normative measure is a mere technical term for estimating the value of any situation. Thus, normative thinking is not just psychologically important as in the act of self-governance and neither is it just politically significant as in the process of undertaking social action. Rather, normative thinking is through and through ethical for it stresses the Platonic identification of value and reality. To know something is to know its importance. To appreciate and to prize are the foundational acts of knowing the mixture of the actual and the possible that makes up the really real. The cause of this mixture is the measure used to contrast essential and conditional traits and qualities of simplicity and complexity. In normative thinking it is never a question of either/or but rather always a matter of both/and. "Like the child we must have both."[2] The actual and the possible, the limited and the unlimited, the mixed and its measure all require each other.

Normative thinking is therefore an exercise in aesthetic composition and coherence.

Now, in the introduction to this work I argued that cosmology was the philosophical effort to assert hypothetically ideal normative measures and then apply them to reality in the hope of finding a good fit between the limited and the unlimited, the actual and the possible, the essential and the conditional, and the simple and the complex. As regards place in city environments I speculate that it is governed by all, some or one of the following normative measures: intensity, integrity, wholeness, and depth.[3] These are the same measures employed in my earlier study of nature and its goodness. If in fact they are also helpful in securing an appreciation of urban place, then there is additional proof that my thesis concerning the underlying continuity spanning city and nature is on the mark (see fig. 3).

Intensity. This is the measure used to estimate the value of any event in a process universe. Its essential feature is the degree of intensity it expresses by reason of how it contrasts the actual and the possible, the ideal and the real. Everything that achieves real existence does so by registering a difference in the environment. Where there is no difference, there is no novel reality emerging out of the past. Intensity measures the degree of tensile strength achieved by an event as it struggles to assert its own *haeccitas* in the midst of a welter of other environmental conditions. While intensity measures the inscape of any event, it is not to be thought of as a mere measure of more or less in the quantitative sense. Such a measure for intensity falls back into the metaphysics of scientific materialism. Intensity is always qualitative. Its degree is always measured by aesthetics rather than arithmetic. This is so even in the moment of achieving critical mass for that is when a novel form of quality

Figure 3:
SCHEMA OF IDEAL ENVIRONMENTAL NORMS

Intensity

Integrity

Wholeness

Depth

emerges from the tensions building up in an event. It is also essential for understanding how a city differs from a village. In these cases the critical mass of semiotic expression yields up a new form of quality. It is this that allows the transition from cosmology to semiotics to praxis to make logical sense. Intensity is a matter of how things fit together, not how they dominate each other.

Integrity. As the discussion of intensity suggested, reality is more a matter of composition than addition. Integrity is that measure whereby we judge the excellence achieved in the putting together of the limited and unlimited. Integrity is the very cause of the mixture, for the degree of integrity measures the degree of goodness achieved by an event. Integrity is another name for fitness and what fits is what is good. What is fitted together is the essential and the conditional, for without the act of integrating identity and otherness, there is no processive reality. When integration occurs, then a determinate balance between the actual and the possible expresses itself. This contrastive unity marks the place where a significant degree of otherness emerges with its own identity. In the metaphysical understanding of this process, what occurs is a happening of the one and the many. The environmental many is telescoped down to the emergent event's focus and another "one" is added to "the many." In Whitehead's well-known phrase, "the many become one and are increased by one."[4] Integrity is therefore another word for creativity, that ultimate ontological pulse that inscribes the rhythm of the universe.

Integrity also ushers in what I call "the factor of the integer." By this I mean that when different modes of being are housed together, the power of transformation is exponentially increased. For example, a person who seeks personal integration through soul, mind, and body is more likely to achieve progress than a person who confines her integration to the levels of body and mind. Obviously, integration is also a critical element in the creation of lasting forms of beauty. The importance of this aesthetic domain will grow as this study of the city develops. For now, it is sufficient to note that integrity advances creativity even as it introduces the aesthetic into the urban mix.

Integrity also fits together the simple and the complex. It needs must do so for the quality of simplicity is guaranteed by the presence of the essential and the quality of complexity is assured through the inclusion of the conditional. The event and its environment join forces to express seemingly opposed qualities throughout an urban region. It is a capital offense, however, to think that simplicity and complexity are opposed. Those who think so have not heeded Plato's warning that they must study the mathematics of proportion before entering the Academy. Simplicity and complexity are coherently contrasted terms. They are not merely opposed. This is to say, that it is not the case that simplicity automatically diminishes complexity and complexity automatically prevents the presence of simplicity. Rather, as terms of coherence, both qualities require a necessary reference to each other for their full understanding. Thus, it is perfectly possible that simplicity can be raised to a higher level even as complexity is similarly increased and vice versa. In fact, it is only through higher and higher contrasts of simplicity and complexity that rich intensity of experience is expressed within city life.

Furthermore, when simplicity eliminates complexity, the result is shallowness. Genuine simplicity is much closer to elegance "properly understood."[5] Elegance means maximum effect with minimum effort and is therefore one result of the factor of the integer. Properly understood, complexity brings about a measure of relevance not previously experienced. In the experienceable difference provided by the real presence of complexity, width of feeling is expressed throughout an urban environment. The many are broadened out and included within an increasingly elegant one. Therefore, wise normative thinking would seek a simultaneous increase in complexity and simplicity. But unfortunately we are seldom wise enough to be so creative. For example, the laptop computer on which I compose this book is both complex and simple at the same time. In fact, each quality complements the other to such a degree that the computer exhibits both elegance and relevance. The discipline of aesthetics involves the way things fit together: The actual and the possible, the essential and the conditional, the one and the many, and the simple and the complex fuse together and the beauty of urban place is simultaneously intensified and deepened.

Wholeness. This normative measure revolves about the concept of unity. There are many forms of unity, but most of them are deficient in integrity. These fake unities are better understood as aggregates, shallow sorites of events that disperse upon serious examination. Authentic oneness involves the bonding together of internal relations such that the many become a real and effective dimension in the unity of the one. In its turn the one embraces the otherness of the many so that an enlargement of experience takes place. Increase in width of application is one sign of the effective presence of unity.

Wholeness also suggests a certain measure of completeness. Now, there is no such thing as complete perfection in a process world. The rhythm of epochal time with its ceaseless becoming and perishing defeats all such simplistic thinking. Nevertheless, there can be a perfection suitable to the conditions and circumstances of its situation. Such perfection expresses a wholeness that includes maximum use of conditional features along with maximum essential simplicity. The resultant contrast sparkles with a sense of the complete, the whole, and the full. That glow of wholeness (often understood as health) is due to the massive conjunction of internal relations within the event in question. The environmental event swells with content such that it includes more and more without splitting open or being drowned in otherness. Wholeness is a sign of the addition of great vigor for it takes enormous strength to hold the many together in a complete environmental embrace. One must be healthy to endorse the presence of the many. It is often so much easier to turn one's back on difference.

Wholeness understood as real and complete unity takes hold whenever integrity has done its job. The internal relations that go into making up the essential environmental being of urban events registers a perfection according to its own kind. A mood of wholeness spreads over the city and, as shall be seen, great stillness emerges from such deeply contrasted urban regions. As is now evident, each normative measure relies upon the effective presence of its predecessor. Intensity, integrity, and wholeness are interlocked environmental measures because in the mixture of the limited and the unlimited, each such measure builds upon the gains of an earlier measure. In wholeness, the unlimited and the limited are mixed by a measure that establishes layers of environmental order which in turn guarantee depth of experience.

Depth. Wherever and whenever there is an affective presence of layers of order—especially when they are mixtures of the vague, the narrow, and the wide—depth becomes the measure of such mixtures. Various types of order stack up with the result that intense contrasts bleed through layers of environmental experience. What is felt is depth of space registering as sited directionality, access, and habitat. Also, feelings of significant temporal depth are expressed as the presence of the past in the present and the presence of the future in the present. This contrasted integration brings about a deepened sense of the present itself. Depth ushers in feelings of unplumbed and unthought novelty. It also compels a sense of wonder at the enduring presences of space and time. We speak of the age of mountains and the glorious possibilities of the future. The pitch of time and the well of space intensify, integrate, and make whole the depths of the urban region in question. In the nestings of space and time characteristic of the measure of depth, there lurks profundity. It is this sense of unknown and as yet unexpressed importance that is at the heart of the major form of beauty.

When depth is at hand, there also lurks the possibility of temporal acts of genuine individuality. These acts in their turn make possible feelings of consciousness. It is within the domain of consciousness that the four ideal normative measures of intensity, integrity, wholeness, and depth take root most effectively. I conclude this discussion of the doctrine of normative measure with a discussion of the form and structure of consciousness in a process world.

Consciousness feels like the affirmation of a negation. That is to say, awareness is more a matter of feeling what is not there, than it is one of feeling the presence of something definite. Consciousness is experienced when I feel the presence of an absence. Thus, I am reading along in a book silently comprehending what is being said when, all of a sudden, I remark, ". . . how can that be so . . ? "; " . . . did not the author just say. . . ?" Thus, I become aware of what is not there and confirm its negative presence. This is best understood as a corollary of the doctrine of normative measure. As was stated earlier, the doctrine of normative measure is rooted in the hypothesis that the universe is made up of two ultimate qualities, actuality and possibility. The contrast between these two regions of experience is what is felt in states of consciousness.

Thus, "what is" is contrasted with "what might be." Recalling the fact that a contrast is a form of unity we immediately see that awareness is the awareness of what is not there in contrast with what is there. But to know what is not there requires the presence of a standard or norm or measure by which the presence and absence of a quality can be affirmed. The doctrine of normative measure is made possible by this peculiar fact of consciousness: That it knows what is not there before it knows what is there. This "affirmation of a negation" is grounded in the existential presence of "what might still yet be." In turn, this knowledge is dependent upon the effective presence of normative measure.

Thus, the circle closes in on itself and demonstrates that consciousness demands normative thinking and normative thinking requires the affirmation of a negation. As was the case in *Nature*, "a

schema of ideal environmental measures" is also now available for
the examination of place in city life. The norms are the same: Intensity, integrity, wholeness, and depth summon forth powerful feelings
of value throughout city places. What is felt through these measures
are different configurations of space and time.

Space and Time All-at-Once

Place is that intersected region of ambient space and epochal
time that through sited directionality grants access to habitat as
well as significantly contrasted volumes of time. Each element in
this formal definition warrants attention: (i) By "intersection" I
mean the contrasted mixture of space and time expressing itself
throughout a significant urban region of value. (ii) "Ambient" indicates the element of the inscape of space that most powerfully brings
about a sense of the environment as a supportive surrounding. (iii)
"Epochal" is that form of concrete time that spills forth all-at-once
and is by definition indivisible into earlier or later segments. (iv)
"Sited directionality" is another dimension of the inscape of urban
space, and it here signifies the spatiotemporal axes through which
the place in question establishes its *locus*. When a place is hailed as
having a *genius loci*, it is the result of sited directionality. (v) "Access" means the quality of openness exhibited throughout an urban
place. Such access is usually propositional in nature. It lures the city
dweller into its embrace. (vi) "Contrasted" signifies the active unity
of actuality and possibility such that the ideal and the actual are intimately suggestive of each other within the ambience of place. (vii)
Finally, I use the term *volume* to express the open depths of spacetime all-at-once, which is the hallmark of urban place.

No thinker has provided a better explanation of the dynamics of
place than J. J. Gibson, whose *The Ecological Approach to Visual
Perception* remains the landmark work in the field of environmental
perception.[6] What Gibson terms "affordances" are sensory cues surrounding us and establishing massively and spontaneously perceived intimations of the spatiotemporal values inherent in a city
place. An affordance is really a symbolic reference, usually from the
visual field of presentational immediacy to the felt field of causal efficacy. But the opposite can also occur, especially when the perceiving instrument is the generalized body presence of the perceiver and
not any specific sense organ. We pick up the ambient array of a place
by reason of the access to habitat and temporal value granted us by

affordances. The body accesses place and renders its value in terms of the presence of space-and-time-all-at-once. Places become the most concrete way in which spacetime is experienced in city life. By bringing together into a unique unity different modalities of space and time, place clears a ground for meaning within the cityscape.

Vision, touch, and hearing are the more familiar ways in which the locus of place is specified, but there is also what can be called the general "feel" of a place.[7] Such a feeling begins with causal efficacy but is then raised to a quite sophisticated level of conscious experience by appropriate forms of symbolic reference. Affordances make sense of what is the most salient characteristic of urban places— what I term *synaesthesia*, the all-at-once fusion of causal efficacy, presentational immediacy, and symbolic reference within a spacetime event in an important moment of city life. Places arise by reason of their textures. And what is texture? Gibson tells us that texture is: "the structure of a surface"; and furthermore, "the terrestial world is mostly made up of surfaces and not bodies in space."[8] Now, there is substantial truth in this but Gibson does not go far enough in his analysis of the visual field.[9] He sees vision only under the guise of presentational immediacy. He fails to reckon with the somatic fact that seeing is also "touch at a distance." Now, touch is the mode of presentational immediacy closest to causal efficacy.[10] This is because touch echoes through the antecedent states of the body and brings forth the type of dim but rich perceptual information found in feelings of causal efficacy. It is therefore necessary to add to Gibson's definition of surface by saying that while vision brings us into contact with the surfaces of place and their textures, it is the accompanying sense of touch at a distance provided by body memory that enhances and deepens the sense of profound "surround" so characteristic of urban place. Thus, place is the entwining of textured surface and depth. As we shall see later, this is precisely what happened to me on an October afternoon in 1951.

Place is experienced all-at-once within a region demarcated by ambient space and voluminous time. It is accessed through the symbolizing power of the human body, which renders the locus of place thick with meaning. All such meanings are the result of dwelling in a human habitat as well as rich involvement in the aesthetic orders of vagueness, narrowness, and width. What place creates is a world of feelings sculpted out of space by time and out of time by space. The resultant relevance and elegance is exactly what renders place so important a human event. It nourishes us when we are weak and sustains us when we are fatigued. It enlivens us when deadness surrounds us and it motivates us when we are wrapped in meaninglessness.

The types and kinds of places are indefinite. This cosmology does not try to name all of them. What is important is that a speculative account of the essential dimensions and factors of place has been hypothesized. One reason for the indefinite number of kinds of places is the fact that ontologically a place is nothing but its relations. A brief excursion into the Kyoto School of Zen Buddhism in general and the philosophy of Nishida Kitaro in particular is helpful here. This "nothing but" is what Zen calls Bashō, the place of emptiness where absolute suchness can come into being.[11] This nothingness which is also a suchness (*sunyata*) allows what is in place to take place. It is the spacetime in between (*ma*) characteristic of place (*bashō*) that provides the nothingness (*mu*) that in its turn is the emptiness setting free "the nothing but" of place. Bashō is the poetry of nothingness.

This recourse to another culture for an understanding of place is doubly important. First, it shows that there is a commonality across cultures concerning the inscape, contrasts, patterns, and transmission of place. Second, this use of the language of Japanese philosophy underscores the vague generality of our categoreal scheme. It indicates that the cosmological project is on track, for my vague categories receive finite specification within the limits of another culture. If all value is the gift of finitude, then it should be such wherever human beings build cities. What this points toward, is the ineluctable structure of *haeccitas* underlying all forms of civilized process. And in its turn this inscape of *haeccitas* is always and everywhere nothing but its relations.

It is precisely because "place is nothing but its relations" that the schema of ideal normative measures is so useful in identifying the value of place. Nothing gets in the way of intensity when it is really there in its suchness. Likewise, integrity receives full play because of the emptiness of place. Wholeness can move toward an essential completeness according to the perfections of its kind of place. Finally, depth is maximized because of the suchness of its profundity. Because of the presence of nothingness, the suchness of each of the four ideals can reach its own limit within place.

All-at-once means synaesthesia. This form of perception is a field of sensual and causal relations bound together in the intimacy of a determinate place. It could be Tiananmen Square, St. Mark's

Plaza, Madrid's Plaza de Mayor, or the floating place of the Staten Island Ferry. What is felt in genuine places is the fusion of space-time. But space has its own inscape and so does time. This is another reason why there can be no definitive accounting of all possible mixtures of space and time. The variables are too rich to itemize. But space does have a determinate inscape and so does time. It is therefore possible to single out the generic traits of place insofar as it entails a wise mixing of the spatial and temporal fields of city life.

I begin with space. The space of place must assemble through sited directionality an access to habitat. In terms of human dwelling this essentially means a city place charged with meaning. Humans do not live by bread alone. They require meaning. Now, Part Two of this study specifies the kinds of meanings to be found in city experience. For now it is important to note that the inscape of space is precisely calibrated to carry out the act of meaningful dwelling. A space is opened by the orientation of place and this in-between is filled up with the suchness of the environment. Depending on the fortunate interplay between space and suchness, the nothing but of place can be one, beautiful, good, and true. (I deal with these "transcendentals" of place later in this chapter.) The field of space characteristic of place is always one of emptiness, relational suchness, and a diaphanous tone of nothingness.

Time, on the other hand, is layered through varying orders of the past, present, and future. This sequence is made solid and causally effective through the aesthetic orders of intensity, vagueness, and width. The concrete pitch and timbre of time is determined by the relative weight granted the patterns of time in its fusion with space. A place dominated by the past can feel solidly traditional and strong. At the same time it can breathe forth the stink of nostalgia. Time can be as easily a place of relics and fossils as it can be one of rich and supportive history. Kitsch always lurks around the next corner. Stressing the future brings into play the creative advance of civilization, but here again an overplay means steady deterioration toward a mindless form of "progress." Lastly, the right amount of present time is necessary if a vibrant sense of being human is to be felt. The process of reality still only occurs in the present. But, again, too much present lets the city dweller flail about in immediacy. A philosophy of *carpe diem* is disastrous for city existence. I am now talking about balance, which means the normative measure of harmony that is the ground of each beautiful place no matter how various and different it may be from its fellow places.

A Beautiful Place Is Always One and True

Place abounds in lures for feelings. Because it is always a contrast between the spatial and the temporal, place is the region where
propositional feelings demand entertainment. Indeed, a place that
does not evoke propositional feelings is no place at all. But is there a
normative measure that can be used to measure all urban places despite their concrete differences? In other words, is a cosmology of
place possible? I argue that the most appropriate cosmological measure of the mixture for place is beauty. What then is beauty? How
does it become a proposition and what is the appropriate reaction to
the perception of its presence in city place?

Beauty is the harmony that composes the different aspects of
place into a unitary spacetime moment that includes both identity
and difference and elegant adaptation toward an end. In a beautiful
place the essential as well as the conditional, the simple as well as
the complex, and the actual as well as the possible are always made
one. This stunning unification is brought about primarily by acts of
human consciousness that introduce new levels of symbolic reference into city place and thereby summon up ineffable resources of
creative unity from the depths of the urban process.[12] But there is
also another ingredient essential to what Whitehead calls "the Major
Form of Beauty."[13] I call it significant individuality, by which I mean
a symbolic reference that transforms the passing parade of process
into acts of great spatiotemporal significance. Inscribed in the
beauty of every place is the signature of strong individuality. Human
consciousness and individuality of place work together to secure the
beauty of city place. One without the other prevents authentic
beauty from taking place.

Obviously such beauty cannot take place unless it is unified in
some way. As the previous discussion showed, the ideal normative
measures of integrity and wholeness are needed if the full intensity
of beauty is to be felt. The unity that place provides is always the
unity of a contrast. It is never merely an additive unity that piles up
aggregates. Beauty is not a heap of disconnected items. The unity
that binds together a beautiful place is a qualitative unity that
makes a difference in the actual form of place. The unity of beauty—
that which makes it one—is always a matter of better or worse
rather than more or less. In fact, one definition of the ugly is that
which is out of place. The ugly is out of place and therefore does not
fit. What does not fit cannot partake of the *genius loci* of a place. A
beautiful place is therefore always one.

But consciousness can be mistaken and individuality can be a superficial facade running along the surface of process. How can beauty be anchored in the real? What makes a city place sparkling with beauty a true place? What is truth in a process universe? Certainly, it must be more than a mere correspondence between appearance (the deliverance of consciousness) and reality (the meaning of process). Nor can it be just mere coherence. For Beauty to become Truthful Beauty and thereby anchor itself in reality, there must be "a carryover of value" from the past through the present to the future such that the truth of the past receives massive consolidation in the future by reason of an enlarged present moment.[14]

This enlargement of the present moment—both in spatial and temporal terms—is brought about by the two factors noted above, consciousness and individuality. Through consciousness the process of reality is plumbed to a depth greater than usual and the "might be" grows alongside the "can be" in importance. The place opened up by this contrast between the actual and the possible is filled with propositional feelings that suggest alternative ways to feel the present moment. This intense sense of the alternative provides the opportunity to entertain the possibility that more and more experience can be had with less and less conflict. Elegance arises in the locus of place and is entertained as a genuine option for human being-in-the-world. The major form of beauty transmutes conflict into contrast and makes diversity a living option for those who would risk it.

Individuality, the other factor, is what grants relevance to beauty. Individuality is akin to truth in that it draws attention to what is actually there. Strong individuality claims our attention, and consciousness goes out to meet it in an aesthetic embrace. The feelings of a process universe that would ordinarily be scattered throughout an environmental region are narrowed down to a single focus. As already said, intensity is the result of narrowness. The combination of aesthetic awareness and intense feelings of a real individual presence work together to establish the power of a place. Place forces itself upon human awareness, not as a compulsion but as a lure for consciousness. For what place whispers is, "here is something for you." What beauty adds to this suggestion are dimensions of relevance and elegance. What unity brings along is integrity and wholeness. And what truth provides are the steadiness and endurance of values of space and time carried over from the past into the future by way of the present. Truth provides depth even as beauty calls forth new forms of value from the well of process.

Unified truthful beauty makes three important differences to city place: It provides rich individuality and uniqueness; it makes a place true and authentic; and it widens and deepens experience so that new alternatives for value emerge as a regular rhythm of place's creative process. Without uniqueness a place is not a place. Failing an important degree of *haeccitas*, any place is just that—"any place," and therefore no place at all. All place is local in the sense of the locus of its particular spacetime. The unity brought about by the oneness of beauty is a guarantee of the emergence of significant novelty in a specific place. At the same time, the difference brought to a beautiful place by its truthful character is exactly a feeling of the presence of genuine authenticity. A place that lacks a sufficient truth character is not a real place. The difference between Disneyland and other places is not a difference in beauty or unity but a difference in truth. From the standpoint developed in this chapter Disneyland is a fake. Finally, a beautiful place has a certain gracious openness to it. It welcomes because it is generous due to its width of order. It presents genuine alternatives to routine process and thereby pushes the creative advance farther into the future. This ends my discussion of beautiful place, but before moving on, I conclude by offering two definitions of aesthetic experience that will grow in importance as the arguments of Parts Two and Three develop.

[1]   All aesthetic feeling is the realization of contrast under identity.[15]

[2]   Aesthetic experience is the awareness of the possibility of meaning, that is, the awareness of recognizable feelings.[16]

The great American philosopher John Dewey also helps us understand the profound experiential dimension of urban place:

> In such [aesthetic] experiences, every successive part flows freely, without seam and without unqualified blanks, into what ensues. At the same time there is no sacrifice of the self-identity of the parts. A river as distinct from a pond, flows. But its flow gives a definiteness and interest to its successive portions greater than exist in the homogeneous portions of a pond. In an experience, flow is from something to something. As one part leads into another and as one part carries on what went before, each gains distinctness in itself. The enduring whole is diversified by successive phases that emphasize its varied colors.[17]

As a concrete example of how experience transforms an ordinary
place into one unified by truth and beauty, consider the following
autobiographical account of place.

*It is October 3, 1951, I am eleven years old and living on
136th Street in the South Bronx. The Brooklyn Dodgers are leading the Giants as the last and final playoff game goes into the
eighth inning. A true Giants fan, I am broken-hearted but know
enough to leave the scene of the disaster (listening to my radio in
my apartment) to see if I can find my way into a basketball game
at the 136th Street Playground. Better to get active than to merely
"offer up" the pain of such a disappointing loss. I race down the
stoop and start up 136th moving west towards Willis Avenue. My
eyes downcast, still I look for bright shiny objects in the street.
Who knows I may even find a nickel. I find one and quickly run
back to Jake Kazigian's store where I purchase a Yankee Doodle.
In those days they only cost $00.05.*

*As I wander up 136th my ears catch the vague sound of ex-
cited voices coming from the radios that are perched on win-
dowsills or turned on in autos. I step over the metal grate covering
the basement entrance to Burke's bar and grill. As I do so, I reach
out to touch the stone carved with the face of an ancient Roman
woman. Who is she? Sometimes I think she is Medusa; other times
Diana comes to mind. I near Burke's and the sounds grow louder.
I reach its doorway jammed now with a crowd of people. Burke's
is one of the few places that has a TV. You can watch the baseball
games there. Men and women are crowding into the narrow entrance, baby carriages are left outside (near the "Family Entrance"), their occupants uncared for during these precious
moments. But I can't see over anybody and besides the smell of
stale beer is making me sick. The closest I can get is to see where
the sawdust begins and the entryway ends. After that it's all noise,
shouting, booze, and cigarettes. I can't see a thing.*

*I turn away and head across Willis Avenue, still moving west
and headed toward the playground. I race two cars to the sidewalk and get the thrill of winning back in my blood. Just as I
clear the curb, a shout wells up behind me and cars begin to honk
their horns. The shout is from Burke's and all the cars with radios are adding to the noise that now fills 136th street and Willis
Avenue. I can't go back to Burke's. There is no room for me there
anyway. I move forward and farther west. In fact I am now approaching Eddie Hermann's house. He has got to know what is*

*going on. He is a flaming Dodger fanatic. I approach his stoop.
He lives on the first floor and I see that his window is open.
"Eddie"—"Eddie"—I yell. He won't answer me and yet I know for
sure that he is there. How come? This is very fishy. I continue
westward and cross under the Third Avenue "El" just as it begins
its grand serpentine over the Harlem and East Rivers. Now I am
in sight of the Playground. I can see through the wire fence that
nobody is playing any basketball. Instead there is a large crowd
surrounding the "Parkie's" house. Everyone is straining to get
their heads as close as possible to the wide open doorway. Those
inside the house relay information to those standing outside and
they in turn pass it on to others in the crowd. Eventually, it stops
at the far edge of the excited group and then fades back in toward
the inner circle of listeners.*

*I am about a half block away and I begin to run toward the
scene. It's hard to keep the scene in sight because I am running so
fast my eyeballs jerk up and down. "I gotta learn to run smooth
like Willie Mays," I say to myself. But speed is more important
than sight at this moment in city life. I run through the handball
courts, dodge around the swings, race pass the monkey bars, and
cut through the basketball court. Breathless now, I begin to slow
down and walk toward the swirling noise being generated by the
crowd. I stop to catch my breath. I am walking very slow now and
trying to figure what the noise is all about. Suddenly I realize
that my Keds are filled with water. I remind myself to stop at
Greenburgh's and get more tape so that I can reattach the rubber
sole to the canvas upper. All the guys in the park did that. It
saved good sneakers and even made you look like a pro (either
Dick Maguire or Carl Braun, or even Sweetwater Clifton). I did
not know why it did that but everyone insisted that it did and
therefore it did. Meaning arises from group identity.*

*I stop at the edge of the crowd and listen. Lockman, Irvin,
Mueller are some of the names I hear, along with "Branca coming
in for the Dodgers." The words are passed slowly at the fringes of
this snarl of people. Each one is like a gift coming down from on
high. It might even be from the Holy Ghost (mostly Catholics in my
neighborhood). I finally get some info that helps. It is the bottom of
the ninth, two out and the Giants are trailing by two runs. Bobby
Thompson is up and Willie Mays is on deck. Branca is taking his
warmup pitches. Russ Hodges is doing the play-by-play. To this
day I don't know precisely how I got that information or even if it
was correct. What I did realize was that the game was not over, the*

Giants were still at bat and had a chance to win the National
League Pennant. My earlier grief left and was immediately re-
placed by a mind-numbing, heart-stopping anxiety that moved
through my arteries and veins like a freight train. All was now ab-
solutely silent. Then a murmur from the crowd. I can't tell whether
it's the guys around me right here on 136th Street or the Polo
Grounds fans. Thompson steps in and Branca begins to pitch.

An awesome quiet falls upon the playground. In that space-
time place I can see and hear things like never before. I see the
scattered white pebbles mixed into the asphalt that makes up the
surface of the basketball court. I hear the traffic humming on
Alexander Avenue and the occasional shouts that rip through the
neighborhood. Something real big is about to happen. I know it
because I can feel it. This is the consummatory moment that
began way back in the first inning when I was still at 447 East
136th Street, listening to the game in the kitchen. Surely it is an
enduring experience. It has now gone for more than three hours.
Then suddenly I hear Russ Hodges screaming: "The Giants win
the pennant! The Giants win the pennant! The Giants win the
pennant! The Giants win the pennant! The Giants win the pen-
nant! The Giants win the pennant! The Giants win the pennant!
The Giants win the pennant! The Giants win the pennant! The
Giants win the pennant! The Giants win the pennant! The Giants
win the pennant! The Giants win the pennant!"

Those in the know say he screamed it thirteen times. I believe
them. I spent the rest of the day celebrating. An ice cream soda at
Klees. A slice of pizza at Vaccaro's. A chocolate donut at Beck's. All
"freebies" donated by the shop owners. By the time I got home the
shock of unexpected victory had worn off and I was reviewing the
day, but this time minute by minute and hour by hour. What else
could one do with such an experience of beauty had all at once and
truthfully? What was most evident was that I would never forget
this day. Never forget where I was and what time it was when all
these events occurred. Now, space and time all-at-once is the very
definition of place and it is also the reason why place is not bound to
merely material structures, no matter how monumental or historic.
Place is continuous with beauty which in its turn is never authentically separated from space and time.

And so we come back to the factor of the integer. It is this force
that binds together separations and differences and makes of aesthetic experience a continuous flowing whole that consummates di-

mensions of human life. These regions of experience can only be fully appreciated when known in the goodness of their spacetime and place elements. Sometimes it is better to speak of its harmony; at other times beauty is the proper word. Also, consummatory experience is useful when understood in Dewey's way. In Part Two I will take up the meaning of these experiences when undergone with an appreciation for the semiotic web in which they find themselves embedded. For now it is enough to have given a concrete example of such a process and to have reexperienced once again the intensity, integrity, wholeness, and depth created by the power of exceptional places.

A Still Place

Stillness is the last undiscussed topic in the categoreal scheme. It is one of the ways in which feelings are transmitted around environments. Places may be filled with feelings of stillness, and this chapter concludes by pointing out why this must be so. The ideal normative measures of intensity and integrity have already been extensively used in the discussion of beautiful place. Here what matters most are measures of wholeness and depth. This is because stillness implies a certain completeness and rest.

Recall that feelings of great stillness are transmitted throughout an urban environment whenever a massive degree of completed importance is expressed throughout a particular place. The satisfaction sensed in such an environment is due to the attainment of a certain qualified perfection according to its own kind. The feeling of peace that settles over a place when it has finished its tasks exemplifies this notion of stillness—for example, a hushed church late at night on a ghetto street in the South Bronx. In fact, feelings of stillness are better understood through ostensive definition than through the kind of formal definition I provided for the concept of place itself. I therefore conclude this discussion of "A Still Place" with a description of a midnight visit to such a place of stillness. Wholeness and depth are felt all through this place, which is in fact set in the most blighted urban area in New York City. By wholeness I mean the sense that an intense integrity has already been achieved, and rest and appreciation is what is required in this particular place. And by depth I mean that the layers of history—personal, social, racial, ethnic, religious, and cosmological—are all somehow present in this extraordinary place. The place I choose is St. Jerome Church on the corner of 138th Street and Alexander Avenue, down where the Bronx

begins, separated from black and Spanish Harlem by the confluence
of the Harlem River and the East River. I was born, baptized, and
raised there a half century ago and John Grange, my twin brother,
has been its pastor for the last fifteen years. I have returned there
many, many times since moving to the state of Maine in 1970. In
fact, it is "at," "in," and "around" this place that this philosophical
journey began.

SAINT JEROME CHURCH. SOUTH BRONX, NEW YORK. *It is quiet
and it is dark. The only lights are supplied by a few flickering
candles and whatever illumination there is, is cast by the reflecting lights of automobile headlights playing off the darkened and
aged stained glass windows. This place has a center. In the middle of the nave some sixty feet from the floor, a great blue eye
watches over the silent church. Around this cosmic eye is written:
"Our Father who art in heaven" and "his eyes are upon the ways
of men." Just as the present parishioners (mostly hispanic and
black) have to forgive the eye its color in order to move beyond it
to the still place, so also feminists must forgive the unrelieved
maleness of this church built by Irish immigrants some 150 years
ago. This eye sees everything.*

*And everything it sees is still. Why is this so? Time past is
completed and fused with time present, here at the midnight hour.
Time future is wrapped in the embrace of a day about to begin
again. The sound of gunfire outside in the streets assures me of
this fact, as do the police sirens that go off with regular rhythm
from the 40th Precinct diagonally across the street. And even so
all remains hushed inside this place. Is it just because I am here
alone in the dark by myself? I think not, for I am not alone.*

*I am surrounded by the past and its people. Each of the mag-
nificent stained glass windows has a name attached to it—a real
family that lived here. Up in the choir loft four Latin Doctors of
the Church, Ambrose, Augustine, Jerome, and Gregory stand
watch telling me about an even more distant past. And the light
that dimly and occasionally scatters itself into the church discloses massive windows on the side naves—Jesus and the Widow
of Naim; Jesus and the Feeding of the 5000. I fall even farther
back into history. I notice the statue of Melchisedech high above
the Main Altar and at the same time I see Gabriel preparing
to blow his horn. And all the while a much more eternal presence watches from the skylike dome.*[18] *All this occurs in the
epochal present, which is intensified by both the darkness and the*

silence. In these volumes of space and time I can sense the presence of the past and its overwhelming depths of dignity. Causal efficacy shoots through my body. In the absence of sensory cues derived from presentational immediacy, I feel the symbolic weight of the past. It is still here in the stillness of this still place. This is city place in solido. The internal relations binding me to the past lurk in the penumbral corners of the place. They lure me and I dimly sense their rich importance. Pressing in on me, these ambient spaces let me access a usable past even as I face a future about to begin. I dwell in a habitat of meaning built out of space and time.

What of the future? Does it find a place in this place? The past roots me in this present place which, some say, is New York City's meanest ghetto. Outside in the projects and the broken down apartments left over from the prewar era, the love, the joy, the pain, the sorrow, the poverty, and the sense of futility continue to go on and on. And I also know there are crack houses around the corner and down the street—in fact, right down on Brown Place near where I used to play stickball—evil born of desperation preys on goodness and its intentions. Destruction seems everywhere. How can I go on about a still place in the midst of such pity and terror?

It is here that the future asserts itself as a "might be," an ideal alternative that is as frail as it is powerful. Place brims with propositions but still place creates a particular kind of proposition. Call it a proposition of stillness. It is best understood as a contrast characterized by the prominence of the remaining two ideal normative measures of wholeness and depth. Once effectively contrasted, they lure the feeler into entertaining a double "might be." First, there is the possibility of real wholeness; that is to say, a healthy way of life that is integrated, complete, and intense. Second, such propositions of stillness bring into unity with wholeness the real possibility of depth. Now, depth here means profound sources of power and transformation. It is the unification of wholeness with depth that allows the parishioner of St. Jerome to go forward despite the pain and the agony.

But all such hope is vain, if it remains an abstract normative measure. Such an outcome would indeed be Marx's "opiate of the people." No! Marx's "sigh of the oppressed" must be made local through ritual and political action. This will be done tomorrow, Sunday, at the liturgy and all during the week through the political actions undertaken by the parish's local chapter of South Bronx Churches. It is not enough to pray, nor for that matter to meditate on still place in the Church at midnight. Propositions are lures for feelings, which, in their turn, ought to promote thoughtful action. Anything less is a falling away from the inspirations of still place.

So wholeness and depth show themselves as hope in the darkened pews of Saint Jerome. Pews I myself knelt on more than fifty years ago. Pews more than 150 years old. Past and future contrast to grant rest and action at the same time. This is a great paradox. How can action be restful and rest be active? The answer to this question lies in the quality of the experience being undergone in still place. Only a still place that is also one, true, and beautiful will promote such peaceful action. So the analysis ends with an appeal to the goodness of place. But that should be expected. Of the four great metaphysical transcendentals of Western philosophy we have seen three—one, beautiful and true. Goodness remains to be examined.

Chapter Four

Urban Goodness

This chapter examines the idea of urban goodness. It begins with an examination of Kevin Lynch's classic work on city forms. It then analyzes three normative measures for urban goodness. I move from there to a discussion of the work of Christopher Alexander. The chapter concludes with an acknowledgment of the need for a much more radical approach to city experience if we are to do justice to its rich layers of value.

More specifically, this chapter acts as a hinge between Parts One and Two of this study. The first part has examined the spatiotemporal forms of city life. Through this structural analysis of forms the city can be seen as a vast network of events, moods, and orders of feelings. What is required is a model of city life that will move the discussion closer to the heart of city experience. I attempt such a hypothesis at the end of this study of the cityscape.

Kevin Lynch and Normative Measure

In 1981, Kevin Lynch published his classic work *A Theory of Good City Form.*[1] In this study he offers a compelling argument why there cannot be one single normative form of goodness for the the city.[2] The many interrelated objections he examines are all derivative from the customary one that there is too wide a gap between the general and the particular, the abstract and the concrete:

> The linkages of very general aims to city form are usually incalculable. Low-level goals and solutions, on the other hand, are too restricitve in their means and too unthinking of their purposes. In this dilemma, it seems appropriate to emphasize the goals in between, that is, those goals which are as general as possible, and thus do not dictate particular physical solutions, and yet whose achievement can be detected by and explicitly linked to physical solutions. This is the familiar notion of performance standards, applied to city scale. The proper level of generality is likely to be just above that which specifies some spatial arrangement. Neither "a pleasant environment" nor "a tree on every lot" but "the microclimate should fall within such and such a range in the summer" or even "some long-lived living thing should be visible from every dwelling."[3]

Now, this is a laudable approach, even quasi-cosmological. But it is my thesis that it does not go far enough. There are two reasons for this judgment: (1) There is an overreliance on the physical dimension of spatial form, and (2) "performance" is restricted to material activities.[4] I do not wish to be negative about Lynch's work. He along with Christopher Alexander are major inspirations for my own efforts to plumb the depths of city goodness. Nevertheless, Lynch does here commit at one and the same time "the fallacy of simple location" and "the fallacy of misplaced concreteness."[5] This is because he does not have an adequate metaphysics of events as units of feelings. In other words, there remains the residue of scientific materialism even in so humanistic a thinker as Kevin Lynch. Instead of seeing matter as the spatiotemporal spread of happenings that are really orders of aesthetic feelings, Lynch falls back on the myth of quantifiability so beloved by empiricists.

This is all the more regrettable since his discussion of these performance standards relies heavily on aesthetic language. He lists some six domains of performance: vitality, sense, fit, access, control, efficiency, and justice.[6] In dealing with each of these regions of experience and value Lynch underscores the need for a humanistic language that will concretize abstractions. In fact, this section of his work is a classic statement of the cosmological method *sans* an appropriate metaphysics. Thus, along with the problem of a residual scientific materialism, Lynch also confuses the cosmological project. Recall that cosmology is meant to arrive at "vague" hypotheses concerning the value of urban experience. Lynch confuses the general with the vague. It is not a universal we are after but rather a sense of what is common yet in need of further specification. In Peircean terms, Lynch lacks an understanding of the importance of abductive reasoning. I shall deal with this at length in Part Two, Urban Semiotics. For now it is sufficient to define abduction as "felt intelligence"—that mode of thinking that yokes together the aesthetic, the ethical, and the logical in a single embrace. Of course, what makes such a unification of human experience possible is the metaphysics underlying the reality in question. Also, the cosmological understanding as well as its application to concrete experience depends entirely on the concepts and terminology employed. This is why Lynch's thinking can only take us so far. He remains stuck in the fallacy of simple location even though he repeatedly stresses the interrelatedness of all urban events. This is further complicated by his commission of the fallacy of misplaced concreteness. By confining city form to the spatial he replaces the living concreteness of the city with the dead abstractions of space.[7] In conclusion, Lynch's theory of good city form starts us on the way toward a more concrete grasp of cityscape, but something more is needed to fill out the picture of an effective method at work. That method, I submit, is cosmology.

Three Normative Measures

Lynch provides a clear analysis of the three most evident normative theories of cityscape so far developed by the human race. Actually, he calls them metaphors, not normative measure, but at this point the identification of measure with metaphor is entirely acceptable.[8] The three normative measures are : the cosmic city, the city as machine, and the city as organism.[9] Each represents a summing up of a cultural epoch and its root metaphors as to quality, fact, and continuity in city life. Therefore, the ensuing analysis also represents a brief history of the city in human experience.

The cosmic city is the model for all those city forms that replicate a culture's understanding of the ultimate cosmic dimensions and traits of the universe. This form is often associated with religion but need not be confined to that realm. Indeed, the city of Jerusalem has its origins in sacred texts and understandings of the Covenant between Yahweh and his people. But it should not be overlooked that some of the so-called "new" cities of the former Eastern bloc also exhibited their own cosmic form of socialist realism. This city form emphasizes the defeat of chaos and its replacement by forms of order. A single comprehensive view is deployed so as to arrange the city as a replica of the divine plan of creation and salvation.[10] Encircled enclosures, clearly demarcated zones of the sacred and profane, city officials charged with keeping the rites pure, the themes of taboo and pollution—these architectual and social forms are evidence of the dominance of the cosmic city form.[11] In Lynch's words:

> The cosmic model upholds the ideal of the crystalline city: Stable and hierarchical—a magical microcosm in which each part is fused into a perfectly ordered whole. If it changes at all, the microcosm should do so only in some rhythmical, ordered, completely unchanging cycle.[12]

The second model is that of the machine. Major advocates of this notion include Soleri, Le Corbusier, and Miliutin.[13] The machine model involves the idea of interchangeable parts destined to carry out efficiently (and, hopefully, even forever) certain assigned tasks. The machine is the blunt force instrument of the technological revolution. It exerts its will on urban environments and attains its goals with a cold efficiency that is altogether remarkable. As the Roman *castrum* attests, this form of city structure was most popular among colonizers. Thrown up quickly and totally functional, its grid of streets remains a staple of city planning.

A machine is merely the sum of its parts. It is not less than its parts and it is not more than its parts. It simply is what it is and this is why cities built along these lines take on the aura of "explicit rationality."[14] Machines grow by addition, and various types of "add-ons" are characterisitc of the machine city. Insistence on the functional, the efficient, and the determinable are also inscribed on the face of this kind of city. All is clean, well lit, and as smooth as stainless steel. In fact, it is precisely a streamlined urban existence that the machine city endorses and encourages. Indefinitely interchangeable and expandable, this is the prototype of megalopolis, the great Babylon of modern times. Its virtues are real enough. Babylon is capable of great transmissions of goods and services. It is the consumer city par excellence and the final last great achievement of advanced late capitalism.[15] Not much more needs be said about this form, for its day is waning even as last ditch efforts to build yet one more great megalopolis continue.[16] The age of the machine city is ending but what will take its place appears open to question.

The last city form is that of the organism. With this form we reach the contemporary age and encounter a powerful symbol for future city planning. The organism is a living, autonomous agent directing its own growth, regulating its own environment, and reproducing itself in a rhythmic manner. Organisms are made of internal relations and, unlike machines, are always more than the sum of their parts. What counts in an organism is the supervening form that animates the parts so that an entirely novel entity arises where before there were only parts. Organisms are spontaneous and respond to their environment in creative and free ways. Their form is their function. How they become constitutes what they are. As self-regulating they have a degree of control over their environment decidedly more powerful than that of the machine model. Organisms depend upon cooperation and community. Their forms stress openness and access, a quality embedded in the sinuous curves and radiating patterns of growth. Lastly, organisms manifest heterogeneity and diversity. For them the sameness and homogeneity of the machine spells doom. An organism's ability to adapt is in direct proportion to the degree of otherness it is able to house within its own form.

Now, all this sounds very much like the cosmological scheme I have been laboring over. And to some extent that is true. Shades of the major form of beauty, the propositional lure for feeling consequent upon heightened contrast, and the idea of feeling as the major structural element in urban environments are all closely related to organic forms. But a complete identification of organism and city does not work.[17] Unlike an organism, a city is not an autonomous entity, nor does it automatically regulate itself. It is far too complex and tied into the general civilized environment to be mistaken for a self-determining being. Despite the important work carried out by Geddes, Mumford, Doxiades, and Olmsted, the simplistic identification of the city with organic functioning is not on the mark. One reason why the "Garden City" failed is that the city is not a garden. As a metaphoric measure the organic metaphor works to some degree but in the end it falls short as a cosmological category. Think, for example, what would happen if democracies took seriously this organic rule—an organism is characterized by a strict hierarchy among its higher parts. In the normal organic functioning of the human body, the head tells the feet where to go. Such hierarchical power would spell the end of democracy. Also, organic entities know more or less how to regulate their growth and size. There is no agreed-upon "perfect size" for a city. Neither is there any literal sense in which a city can be said to be alive. And yet it is precisely "life" that most especially defines an organism. Lacking self-autonomy and life, the city cannot be shaped according to the dictates of organic functioning. It just does not have the talent.

Still, there is great value in the metaphor of the organism. Its principle advantage for city life lies in the way in which it demands a holistic view of urban structures and experience. The really important urban questions revolve about how things fit together and how they work to create a greater whole. The organic metaphor reminds us constantly of the innate power of organic life. But cities are more than places for growth and reproduction. They are also the places where human beings learn to adapt themselves to the onrush of creative process. Learning and holism must somehow be brought together if the full sense of the city is to be given its due.

Alexander's New Theory of Urban Design

It is precisely the project of learning to grow as a whole while at the same time dealing with powerful environmental stimuli that distinguishes the work of Christopher Alexander.[18] In a seminal work entitled *A New Theory of Urban Design*, Alexander makes three important moves: First, he explains "the idea of a growing whole"; then he develops "the overriding rule"; and finally he provides detailed rules for sustaining this growth. Alexander has a great talent for clear expression. I will, therefore, content myself with citing his own words:

> In each of these growing wholes, there are certain fundamental and essential features.
> First, the whole grows piecemeal, bit by bit.
> Second, The whole is unpredictable.
> Third, the whole is coherent.
> Fourth, the whole is full of feeling, always.[19]

Now, these essential features of the growing whole are identical with the theory of urban cosmology I have been developing in Part One of this study. The very cityscape analyzed in this first part of my study can be read as an expansion and commentary on this vision of a growing whole. As epochal, spontaneous, integrated, and full of feel-

ing, the foregoing cityscape of urban cosmology reflects the central
idea of Alexander's new theory of urban design.

This theoretical basis is operationalized through Alexander's
overriding rule:

> Every increment of construction must be made in such a way
> as to heal the city.
>   . . .

Most simply put, the one rule is this:

> Every new act of construction has just one basic obligation:
> It must create a continuous structure of wholes around it.[20]

This rule insures a neverending drive toward wholeness as the
very signature of the healthy city. Alexander sees the effort to learn
how to create wholes to be the primary tasks of the city planner
and the citizen. He makes this even more specific in his seven detailed rules:

> (1)   It is necessary . . . that the idea of piecemeal growth be
> specified exactly enough so that we can guarantee a mixed
> flow of small, medium and large projects of equal quantities.
> (2)   Every building increment must help to form at least
> one larger whole in the city, which is both larger and more
> significant than itself.
> (3)   Every project must first be experienced, and then ex-
> pressed, as a vision which can be seen in the inner eye (liter-
> ally). It must have this quality so strongly that it can also be
> communicated to others, and felt by others, as a vision.
> (4)   Every building must create coherent and well-shaped
> public space next to it.
> (5)   The entrances, the main circulation, . . . its daylight
> and the movement within the building, are all coherent and
> consistent with the position of the building in the street and
> in the neighborhood.
> (6)   The structure of every building must generate smaller
> wholes in the physical fabric of the building, . . . in short, in
> its entire physical construction and appearance.
> (7)   Every whole must be a "center" in itself, and must also
> produce a system of centers around it.[21]

I wish to highlight just a few of these rules. Rule # 2 insists on
the importance of learning to make wholes. Rule # 3 binds that rule

to the creation of visions that are realizable. Rule # 7 demands that centers become evident throughout the city. Now, in the terminology of this cosmology, Alexander requires the city to exhibit continuing wholes, provide intense lures for feeling, and establish "places" as centers of meaning. There is a exceptionally fine fit between his design vision and my cosmological scheme. Nevertheless, there are differences. Like Lynch, Alexander remains too tightly bound to the metaphor of the organism. He does not seem to realize that the goodness of the city resides in something much more than spatial form. Or perhaps this is merely the *déformation professionelle* of the contemporary urban planner. Philosophers have their flaws. Why exempt the design master?

What is missing in Alexander's treatise is a sense of the art of learning how to read the signs of wholeness.[22] He does not show just how human beings become aware of wholes and signal their presence (or absence). In short, despite the genius of Alexander's work, he does not make explicit the connection between the goodness of the city and the discipline of semiotics. This is most unfortunate because before anything else—before space, time, and place; before beauty, truth, wholeness, and depth—the city is primarily a continuing conversation about signs and their meaning.

Lynch saw the city as a process of learning to adapt, but he did not see the importance of sign reading in that process. More so than Lynch, Alexander sees the importance of wholeness as a guiding normative measure for good city experience. Yet he, too, does not see the relevance of semiotics to the goodness of the city. I conclude this chapter with a brief transitional discussion of that connection.

The Goodness of the City

In its emphasis on value and the terms of its achievement this urban cosmology stands opposed to the reigning orthodoxy of scientific materialism. The world of urban design is infected with this kind of thinking. Its hallmark is an absolute insistence on quantitative measurement as the guide to goodness. My urban cosmology opposes this doctrine and insists on the importance of aesthetically grounded normative measures for prizing the value of an environment. It stresses quality over quantity. Scientific materialism also sees the world as a continuum of facts devoid of purpose and meaning. This urban cosmology asserts that the world is full of feeling and this feeling is best understood as an expression of value. Scientific materialism insists on the reality of matter as the base line of all discourse about the meaning of the city. I oppose this doctrine by working with the speculative thesis that process is reality and that events in structured processes of becoming are more fundamental than matter. Finally, scientific materialism is content with a vision of the universe as a fully determined field of vacuous facts. My cosmology stresses freedom and spontaneity as more nearly accurate measures of the universe's ultimate creativity. It also insists that each event, no matter how minute, is a value in itself, for others and for the whole.

In pursuing this alternate line of thinking I have taken my reader on a long journey. It is helpful to glance backward at where we have been. I began with a categoreal analysis of space. In setting forth its inscape, contrast, pattern, and transmission, I argued for the concreteness of space as against the empty container theory of scientific materialism. Space is concrete and makes its presence felt through sited directionality, access, and habitat. Furthermore, this spatial habitat is potentially charged with meaning, for it is in structuring itself according to the four aesthetic orders that space expresses levels of meaning that are trivial, vague, narrow, and wide. Learning to sculpt space in horizontal, vertical, and ambient patterns is one aspect of learning how to cultivate the habitat of meaning that is the city's spatial dress. In its drive toward wholeness ambient space smooths out the sharp edges of the vertical and the horizontal and thereby offers to city dwellers their best chance for a consistently holistic experience of space.

Similarly, time was also seen to be concrete; in fact, so concrete that in its epochal form it could not be torn apart or further analyzed. Thus, time is itself a sign of wholeness. In its all-at-onceness time brings a wholeness to the present moment derived from its own measuring out of the place to be accorded past and future. Insofar as time can be contrasted so as to promote width and intensity, it gives rise to a full temporality that threads its way through city life. This sign of individuality marks out an essential ingredient in authentic value—the coming to be of real unity and wholeness within the unique *haeccitas* of urban events.

Various mixtures of space and time constitute the fabric of place. Through the doctrine of normative measure I argued for an understanding of place that stressed its intensity, integrity, wholeness, and depth. Place can be experienced as one, true, and beautiful. In its beauty, place brings together all the themes of cityscape so far developed. It shows that the cityscape shines with value. Finally, it demonstrates that this value is the outcome of limits imposed through normative measure and that limit is best widened through the experience of truthful beauty. An example of moving place was offered as a good representation of the texture of urban place. The normative measure of depth was also introduced to explain the category of feelings of stillness often felt in beautiful places. This sense of a perfection according to its own kind is the analog of a type of completed wholeness. Thus, despite the onward rush of urban process, some rest and at least a partial peace can be experienced in the cityscape. Place is to the city as the arrival of life is to nature—a supreme and crowning achievement of value.

This brings us to the present chapter, where various theories of good urban design have been enlisted in order to examine the concept of urban goodness. From Kevin Lynch we learned that the history of city form has culminated in an organic model with both advantages and disadvantages. The advantage is that the organic model stresses what this cosmology calls oneness, truth, and beauty. The drawback is that such a theory of urban goodness appears to go against our democratic sensibilities since it demands hierarchical authority. Lynch concluded his analysis by suggesting that living in a city was really about learning how to learn. This is also the ground of humanity's most distinguishing evolutionary feature: its exceptional adaptability. This makes the city itself the result of learning and also humankind's primary evolutionary vehicle. From this perspective, Alexander's insistence on the overarching idea of wholeness as the guide to good city form takes on concrete meaning. More than anything else, the goodness of the city resides in its capacity to let human beings learn about wholeness.

But how do we learn? Until this question is given a satisfactory answer, all appeals to wholeness are empty, vain, and futile. Is human learning simply a matter of trial and error? Do we merely lunge forward through happy or unhappy learning experiences? In a sense we do, but in the course of evolution two factors have impressed a unique character on this human process of experimentation. We have already discussed the first factor. Through the wise use of propositional feelings we can put distance between ourselves and experience. We can exhibit a directed intelligence that is more likely to hit the mark than other more impulsive ways of behaving. But propositions hold up experience by creating a halfway house between the actual and the possible. How do we return to the really real? What ways do we have to measure the mixture of the ideal and the actual so that satisfactory responses to life can be a consistent part of our experience? This is where the second factor plays a crucial role.

It is the thesis of this study that city life is best understood as the creation, maintenance, and transmission of signs of understanding. All human learning takes place through signs. These signs in turn are the outcome of evolutionary habit made real by hard-won experience. Signs can be true or false, because they constitute the ways in which we engage reality and its values. Thus, signs do not merely refer to other signs. Such is the effete doctrine of various forms of European structuralism. Nor are we enmeshed in a web of language and unable to penetrate to the real world. Signs are neither dyadic (referring only to themselves or to other signs) nor are they confined to language (verbal or written). Every sign is a gesture of meaning that has a triadic character. A sign is composed of itself, its interpretant, and its object and therefore has a necessary reference to the world outside itself.

Urban Semiotics, Part Two of this cosmology, is given over to explaining and expanding this definition of a sign. Now is not the time to begin that task. I confine my comments to the question of the relation of semiotics to urban goodness. In one sense signs are good in terms of their pragmatic consequences. What difference does the sign of a handshake make in a community? In this sense the quest for the goodness of the city deals with very practical issues like justice, community, and social intelligence. Part Three, Urban Praxis, deals with this dimension of the goodness of the city. But like Peirce, I would not have my doctrine smeared through an easy association of truth with "the cash value of an idea." Truth, beauty, oneness, and goodness are more complex than that unfortunate Jamesian remark. I see goodness and its relation to signs as part of the normative fabric of reality.

In fact, one can map the four elements of urban goodness—space, time, place, and growing wholeness—onto the semiotic system to be introduced in Part Two. The category of space is the semiotic equivalent of firstness for it stresses ever-flexible openness.[23] Likewise, urban time is allied with secondness since it emphasizes the importance of directly experienced otherness. Time in its strict epochal sense is always the happening of a difference.[24] The collisions that mark secondness and its indexical signs are the semiotic mirror of the temporal cosmological features of a cityscape. The meaning of the continuity and growing wholeness that Dewey calls aesthetic experience (and Alexander sees as the one essential rule for good city form) echoes the role of thirdness and its emphasis on continuity.[25] Consequently, space is to firstness as time is to secondness and as place is to thirdness. Urban goodness spreads itself throughout the city and its neighborhoods when there are enduring modes integrating these components into significant aesthetic processes. I call this fusion the achievement of "symbolic breadth."[26] It becomes an established part of the cityscape whenever the form of urban goodness is consistently maintained. Viewed from another perspective, goodness is best understood as truthful beauty and, therefore, it expresses with symbolic breadth the contrast achieved whenever the factor of the integer successfully spreads itself throughout an urban environment. Symbolic breadth brings together in novel ways both the form and the content of significant harmony. Thus, urban goodness is beauty endowed with truthfulness and experienced as continuity. What emerges from these forms of human creativity are novel expressions of important depth and wholeness (see fig. 4).

In the same way the four normative ideals of intensity, integrity, wholeness, and depth play a defining role in understanding the symbolic breadth expressed by urban goodness. Goodness is a complex affair depending upon what is done as well as where, when, and how it is done. That is why I have argued that beauty is the best measure for the good, since it measures out what is fit, fair, and appropriate in a process universe. Consequently, there is a definitive relation between the elements of urban goodness and the four normative

Figure 4:
FEATURES OF THE CITYSCAPE, SEMIOTIC EQUIVALENTS,
AND URBAN GOODNESS

Dimensions of Urban Goodness	Semiotic Domains	Semiotic Qualities
Space	Firstness/Icon	Spontaneous Value
Time	Secondness/Index	Collision
Place	Thirdness/Symbol	Continuity
Goodness	Symbolic Breadth	Wholeness and Depth

Figure 5:
URBAN GOODNESS AND THE FOUR NORMATIVE IDEALS

Normative Ideals	Urban Goodness
Intensity	Goodness
Integrity	Truth
Wholeness	Beauty
Depth	Continuity

ideals. Intensity understood as the immediate felt experience of qualitative value echoes the presence of goodness. Similarly, integrity with its insistence on the relation between value and its forms of expression resonates with truth, which is the carryover of value from the immediate past through the immediate present to the first edge of the looming future. Wholeness vibrates with the truthful appearance of beauty. Finally, depth with its promise of ever-more powerful displays of symbolic meaning brings to the understanding of goodness a level of continuity that is unmatched in semiotic excellence. Thus, the understanding of urban goodness requires recourse to both the cosmological and the semiotic parts of this study. Also, Part Three will revisit these themes from the perspective of an urban praxis. The intelligence-in-action demanded by such issues will find concrete expression in certain lived forms of communal human praxis (see fig. 5).

Therefore, the goodness of the city depends on the normative excellence of its signs, for it is through their propositional lures that we engage the concrete reality of city life. Semiotics is to be understood as a subdiscipline of the art of normative thinking. The quality of our signs will either lead us into fruitful contact with the real world or lead us away from such experience. Truth, beauty, and oneness are the outcome of a good semiotics. The city is the great place of signs. It is to the understanding of this hard-won insight that I now turn.

PART TWO

URBAN SEMIOTICS

The City! What images it conjures up!

City of God	City of Sin
Metropolis	Gotham
Heavenly City	Eternal City
City on the Hill	City of Light
El Dorado	Camelot
City of Life	City of the Dead

Happy, laughing cities. Cities drowning in their own offal. Cities of pilgrimage. Fortress cities and cities up the sides of mountains. Cities that float on water. Cities made of iron. Cities of brick and stone. Cities bejewelled in their own light or slumbering in darkness.

Cities whose stench overpowers you. Cities whose beauty astounds us. Cities where evil is a palpable presence. Cities radiant in their presence. Cities teeming with human flesh. Cities abandoned with bones bleaching in the sun. Dreary cities and cities alive with grace and power. Brutal cities preying on newcomers. Cities that eat their children and cities that nourish them. Cities one never wants

Figure 6:
AESTHETIC ORDERS AND CORRESPONDING MOODS

Triviality	Indifference
Vagueness	Expectation
Narrowness	Intensity
Width	Involvement

to see again and cities one must return to. Cities that crush the human heart and cities that elevate it.

Big cities and little cities. Vast sprawling thickets of cities now called megalopolis. Unique cities and cities that are the same. Impenetrable cities and cities magnificently open. Confusing cities and cities easy to move around in. Cities that choke off breath and cities that invite the stroller.

Wealthy cities—so rich that only a chosen few can live in them. Cities so impoverished their bleakness overwhelms. Commercial cities. Transportation cities. Cities made of money. Cities where no one is poor and cities that corral their poor behind ill-concealed facades. Cities where everyone works and cities where there are no jobs.

Babylon and Jerusalem. Athens and Rome. Paris and New York. Extremes of every sort rise up when we think of cities. How can we ever describe them all? Is there a cosmology that can do justice to their individual uniqueness as well as what they share in common? It is an essential part of my hypothesis that a city ought to be understood as a semiotic field whose signs knit together the fabric of urban experience. This is a vague hypothesis that can be applied to city life in order to specify what is the same and what is different in urban environments. Part Two therefore begins with an analysis of the connections between mood, order, and sign. It will be necessary to provide a compact statement of the philosophy of Charles S. Peirce, for, above all others, he provides the type of semiotic thinking needed to make sense of the city.

At this point in my study of the city, three themes stand out with a certain clarity. First, there is the continuing relevance of the aesthetic orders of vagueness, narrowness, and width along with their accompanying moods (see fig. 6) and their ideal normative measures. Second, these orders are reflected in the three types of cities so far expressed in human evolution: the cosmic city, the city as machine, and the city as an organism. Third, the goodness and excellence of a city can be measured by the kinds and degrees of wholeness established in its important places. Part Two, Urban Semiotics, is given over to an articulation of these themes through the metaphysics and semiotics of C. S. Peirce. It will be shown that vagueness, narrowness, and width are what qualify the triadic structure of all signs. Furthermore, it will be argued that the value, the facticity, and the continuity characterizing historical urban orders are best understood through Peirce's metaphysics of firstness, secondness, and thirdness. This means that the act of interpretation is at the foundation of effective urban praxis.

■ Chapter Five

Mood, Order, and Sign

This chapter marks a transition from the urban cosmology of Part One to the urban semiotics of this second part. I argue that the city is primarily a place of learning and that this learning is what the city is basically all about. I see this learning activity as the evolutionary key to the survival of the human race. Furthermore, this learning takes place through sign activity. I therefore view semiosis (the study of sign activity) as an indispensable tool for studying the city. I do not wish to enter into a detailed scholarly examination of Peirce's semiotics.[1] Rather, my goal in this chapter is to tie together the themes of human survival, habit, and growth with the act of felt intelligence required to read signs within urban experience. Such an interpretation sets the stage for using Peirce's semiotics to discuss the essential and conditional features of urban culture.

Survival

Cities are among the chief means through which human beings have evolved. Despite all their limitations, they are a consistently important instrument for human survival. The central reason for the importance of cities is the fact that in them language develops rapidly through intensification and frequency of use.[2] Just as one cannot imagine a city without language, so one cannot conceive of human beings without language. Granted this fact, then the act of making, using, and understanding signs becomes the cement that holds all forms of urban experience together. Therefore, as a means for understanding city life, semiosis (sign activity) is the most important subject matter. This is not to deny the importance of economics, architecture, defense, religion, statecraft, and so forth. But it is to say that before any of those activities can take place there has to be semiosis.

Language is the source of humankind's most important survival skill: adaptation through learning. And learning takes place through language. How can this be so? We are used to thinking of evolution in terms of the opposable thumb and the acquisition, development, and spread of tools. This image of *Homo Faber* has its importance, but human technological growth could not have occurred without the use of language. Showing, pointing, indicating are primary ways in which adaptation is shared. Also, even the act of recognition whereby one's fellow humans are brought into association with one another is entirely dependent on language. How could one human join forces with another if sign acitivity were not present? Even more tellingly, how could one human being know her own being without its recognition by another? Language makes possible social grouping, technological advance, and self-identity.

Semiosis is therefore the ground of human survival, self-development, and social gain. Humans beings survived because they could group together and share resources and experience. In so doing they elaborated a vast network of signs that ranged from primitive signals announcing the nearness of danger or opportunity to the most exquisite techniques of information sharing. In the course of establishing this network of signs, they also came to differentiate themselves and their needs from other animals. They began to understand the environment in a different way. What semiosis allowed them to do was to move from environmental experience to "worldly" experience.[3] They survived by adapting to the environment through a shift in the way they understood their surroundings. This great transformation took place through the power of sign activity. Semiosis allowed human beings to carry out two projects at the same time. First, they were able to distance themselves from their immediate environment and thereby gain the critical advantage of reflective intelligence. Instead of reacting entirely in a stimulus/response

manner, humans were able to exercise judgment and organize themselves in more favorable spatial and temporal patterns. Second, this
gain in response time allowed for the emergence of a novel set of feelings. Sheer physical feelings and their conformal harshness were
softened by the presence of more and more conceptual feelings.
"What if" began to replace "what now?" Eventually, propositional
feelings of great intensity became the currency of group life. As the
importance of plans, strategy, and group sharing came to the fore,
sign activity grew in tandem. We became "smarter" by sharing, not
by the actions of a few isolated geniuses.

Furthermore, by adapting together we began to recognize our
fellow humans as more and more important for our survival. This
sense of mutuality grew to become a form of recognition. We greeted
each other through signs. What was once merely noticed in passing
now became an object of curiosity. The "other" was now of interest to
us and through this process of acknowledgment self-consciousness
grew more intense. Hegel has already told the story in his classic
"Master/Slave" dialectic in the *Phenomenology of Spirit*. Each needs
the other to recognize the other. But this can only be done by granting the other the freedom to recognize one's self. Social life and
growth in self-consciousness go hand in hand. I cannot be myself
without letting you be your self. Something like mutual respect
began to be felt. And as Part Three shall argue, this need for the
other's recognition is one essential ground of community.

All this did not happen suddenly. It took long hard work, especially work of a semiotic kind. I wish now to explore Charles Peirce's
understanding of semiosis. Sign activity is always a triadic affair. It
consists in bringing together into a relation a sign, an object, and an
interpretant. The object is the event, state of affairs, person, or
whatever that is to be signified. The sign is what stands for the object. The interpretant is the effect that the sign has on the interpreter. Notice that there are three items here and not two. Semiotics
is not a dyadic process consisting only of a dialogue between sign
and interpreter. There is always a third that mediates between the
sign and its object. Δ is a sign for God which is the object that the
sign signifies. For Δ to function as a sign for God it needs an interpretant to convey the meaning of God for that particular sign. Now,
in this case Δ is a traditional Christian symbol for God. So the Christian theological formulations used as interpretants of Δ are what
convey to the interpreter the meaning of God in that tradition. A
similar process would take place if other symbols for God had been
used. The sign and the interpretants would change but the object

signified would not. Now, the importance of this triadic sign structure cannot be exaggerated. For it does two things at the same time. First, it secures for reality a leading place in the sign process. As object, "God" functions dynamically to lead the interpretants on to, hopefully, richer and richer uncoverings of the meaning of God. Studies of Moslem, Jewish, Christian, and types of Asian theologies serve to plumb the depths of the sign for God without turning the object into a mere sign itself. To do so would be to fall into the effete style of contemporary semiotics, which sees signs as referring only to each other in an endless and futile play of *différance*. God is no longer an object in the real world. Rather, God is just a word backed up by sets of references to other words. What Peircean semiotics achieves is the preservation of an extramental sphere wherein real objects continue to exert a dynamic influence on the meaning of our sign activity.

The second effect of Peirce's triadic semiotics resides in its power to explain the process whereby cultures manage to convey the shifting meanings of its important concepts. By varying both signs and interpretants, an immensely wide field of potential meanings can be developed without ever losing sight of the primary object so signified and interpreted. Thus, "God" remains "God" in the Jewish, Moslem, Christian, and Asian traditions despite its different interpretants. Whether it be Δ or YHWH or Allah, or Brahma, "God" is still "God." Also, the triadic scheme of semiosis serves to distance the human signer from the object in question. This distance encourages what I earlier called directed intelligence. By providing necessary breathing room, a triadic semiosis allows both learning, meaning, and adaptation to grow apace of each other. This is a vital contribution to evolutionary survival. It lets a "world" of propositions grow in place of the do or die struggle occurring in natural environments. What is lost in immediate experience is compensated for by a growth in meaning. Semiotic deliberation replaces reactions built on stimulus/response mechanisms. Thought can come into play, sometimes falsely, sometimes successfully. Reflective experience replaces automatic answers to life's problems.

From this perspective, the concept of truth takes on a much different significance. Similarly, learning and adaptation change their customary meanings. And the same can be said of beliefs and certitude. Meaning itself, the very outcome of sign activity, is also altered. Finally, the idea of survival is radically changed. For survival shifts from a desperate attempt to escape from an endless series of crises to a very long project of adaptation through growth in meaning. The experience of securing such growth can be called living in a "world." Suddenly, everything changes as we move from desperation to exploration and from life and death to depth and wholeness. The normative measures selected to mark out value become exceedingly important. The right word and the right method loom forth as urgent questions. The question of how to secure life now becomes the question of how good that life is going to be. Humankind has finally reached the stage of ethical reflection, and philosophy as the love of wisdom is now an important cultural concern. While I am not saying other forms of social dwelling have no ethical core (that would be ridiculous), I am maintaining that the critical mass achieved in large cities is such as to transform and recreate in a novel way the form of social dwelling. More and more, as the city develops, its citizens in their maturation become entwined social realities. Each either adds to or detracts from the possibilities for goodness present in the urban environment. Once within a city, we are confronted with a different social reality—one based on the possibility of massive and intense communication.

It is at this point that, once again, semiotics becomes so important, for it is by our signs, their objects, and their interpretants that the good life will be measured. In the hurly-burly of city life questions like truth, justice, and beauty are no longer the idle sport of the leisure class. In a democratic society much depends upon how the society will come to understand such vitally important matters. Language has made directed intelligence both possible and necessary. What is at stake is the development of habits that will bring us into touch with the good, and these habits will be largely semiotic ones.

Habit

Survival is secured through the establishment of habits that successfully interpret the meaning of human interactions with the environment. Inevitably, a discussion of habit entails an exploration of Peirce's metaphysics.[4] Peirce maintained that the generic traits of reality can be summed up in three categories that he called quite simply: one, two, and three. Before examining firstness, secondness, and thirdness it is important to establish certain characteristics of Peirce's metaphysics. In the first place, Peirce, like Whitehead, is a process metaphysician.[5] He sees reality as an advancing system of events that move toward ever-greater generality and truth. These events are constituted by their relations with each other. It is from these interacting events that the structures of reality as we most generally know them emerge. Furthermore, he maintains that there is a direct connection between the semiotic categories of sign, object, and interpretant and the three metaphysical categories because sign activity reflects the processive character of the real as it grows toward greater and greater generality. Also like Whitehead, Peirce sees metaphysics as an attempt to form vague but testable hypotheses about reality, which in turn should allow us a richer and deeper contact with reality. Thus, metaphysics retains its essential character as an investigation into the most general traits of the real. Once again, we are looking for vague but specifiable traits of the real that can then be tested in actual situations.

For Peirce the process that is reality exhibits a triadic structure that he calls firstness, secondness, and thirdness. The next three chapters will be given over to a detailed examination of each of these categories; therefore, the task at present is to gain an overall view of these categories and how they relate to each other and reality. There is a threefold character to this categoreal scheme. It is monadic, dyadic, and triadic. As a system, firstness, secondness, and thirdness express the most general ways in which real events interact with each other. Thus, any event has a character of firstness, which simply means that which stands alone without relation to any other thing or event. Secondness signifies that which is in relation to another. Thirdness is the way in which two events previously opposed are brought together so that they combine to form a third. "One" means to be alone, "two" means to be in relation with another, and "three" means to be part of a process wider than either one or two. The triadic structure signified by the signs 1, 2, 3 therefore represent in the most general way the processive character of reality.

Let us imagine any environmental region whatsoever and ask in an objectively vague way, "what is going on within its boundaries?" From Peirce's perspective the region in question exhibits a triadic character that moves asymmetrically toward the future in three distinct but related phases. Category one names the initial phase of reality termed firstness. Within this category there is found an immediate experience of undivided qualitative wholeness. It is entirely original and not to be compared to anything else. In terms of my categoreal scheme this firstness names the utterly unique *haeccitas* that is at the heart of the inscape of every environmental event.

Firstness is the category that expresses the uniquely irreplaceable value that emerges from the womb of process. But emerging value is not the whole story.

Simultaneously with this emergent inscape of value, there are also other existing values expressing their importance throughout the environment. This elementary conflict is expressed through the category of two. Secondness involves the ways in which these separated and independent values jostle for existential place. Thus, the environment moves from an initial feeling of stability derived from the felt wholeness of firstness to a jarring tension characteristic of the struggle entailed in the category of secondness. The resistance of two to one is what establishes an element of brute force in the process of reality. This secondness is what is responsible for the sense of energy and effort to be found throughout an environment. The intensity of feeling that builds up through the opposition of inscapes is what is responsible for the sense of importance that surrounds all such existential conflicts.

The sign of three represents the mediation of one and two. It establishes a healing tone of continuity throughout an environmental region. It does this through the power of mediating contrasts that bring intelligible relations into the oppositional force field of secondness. Continuity, growth, and habit are the signs of the effective presence of thirdness as a metaphysical agency. Thirdness is a real presence in the universe of value that drives parts into forms of wholeness. Viewed from the perspective of my categoreal scheme, contrast and pattern represent the triumph of thirdness as well as the way in which transmission moves values throughout the environment.

Now, what does all this metaphysical speculation have to do with habit? Habit is thirdness achieved. When $1 + 2 = 3$, then human beings have arrived at a settled belief that lets them learn in an uninterrupted rhythm. Such consistent success is what turns environmental interaction away from a struggle for mere survival toward patterns of steady growth. Vital to this process is the learning of successful signs, by which I mean signs that provide regular achievement of value within a selected environmental region. For the farmer it may be the recurrent cycle of rain that marks out the planting season. For the city dweller, it could be as simple as learning about traffic lights or as complex as using a transportation system. In terms of evolutionary survival nothing is more important than the establishment of habit. It allows for an element of pragmatic reasonableness to become part of the daily routine. In fact, habit is routine itself. Humankind cannot live by surprise alone. We do need to know where our next meal is coming from.

In sum, Peirce's metaphysical categories, understood in the light of this study's categoreal scheme, let us fill in the gaps between metaphysics and semiotics in city life. As we shall see, habit is made real by signs and successful signs lead to stable interactions with the urban environment. In their turn, such signs make growth possible.

Growth

All growth comes out of a successful combination of firstness, secondness, and thirdness. When 3 is the sign of 1 + 2, there are present all the important dimensions of the process of reality. Quality, fact, and continuity are united. A true sign engages us in a selected environmental field by making the value of its objects present through rich interpretants. Meaning assembles more meaning. Value builds on value. In terms of city life the environment overflows with significance. Randomness has faded and a sense of probable success fills the air. Habits of growth are now routine. What thirdness has achieved is an effective synthesis of feeling, willing, and knowing, which are the human counterpart to the metaphysics of 1, 2, 3. Self-control is now a matter of course, for the act of waiting is characterized by what I called earlier directed intelligence. Growth is not simply a matter of obtaining good results through the effective use of tools. Rather, growth in the richest sense of the term is a semiotic achievement—a set of fruitful signs—that properly represents the real presence of firstness, secondness, and thirdness within a city region.

All such growth is primarily a normative activity. Growth demands selecting the right ideals for various situations. This kind of normative thinking is carried out in and through signs. Thus, mind is itself a sign and the ultimate interpretant for growth is a successful habit change. Reality is a process unfolding in fits and starts and according to a rhythm not entirely at our disposal. Growth means the acquisition of habits of interpretation that fruitfully engage the process of which we are a part. Effective ideals serve as signs marking out human participation in the real world. When signs are transmitted throughout a city environment, the question to ask is, "What difference do they make?" In this way the pragmatic maxim and the semiotic network meet to establish a reliable set of norms for engaging in real tasks that are important for the community and the human person.

Normative measure and the pragmatic maxim unite to secure growth that has significant possibilities for future success. This sense of a secure future is the social equivalent of the major form of beauty discussed in Part One. Through thirdness effective thought spreads to include as much difference as possible. In fact that is the very meaning of 1 + 2 = 3. Thirdness is the synechistic resolution of the monadic, dyadic situation. Growth therefore is a result of what Peirce calls the spreading of thought. This act of growth is the natural destiny of thinking insofar as thinking in signs is characteristic of environmental participation. The sign itself is what unites the object and its interpretant so that a smooth transition toward the fixation of effective belief is secured:

> The real, then, is that which, sooner or later, information and reasoning would result in and which is therefore independent of the vagaries of me and you. Thus, the very origin of the conception of reality shows that this conception essentially involves the notion of a community without definite limits, and capable of an indefinite increase of knowledge.[6]

For Peirce, there is an indissoluble bond between community, truth, method, and reality. Just how this enables us to take a richer view of city life is the subject of later chapters. For now, I wish to stress the fact that growth is part of a communal act of coming into the truth and signs are the vehicles whereby such truth is communicated. Sharing and recognition take on deeper and deeper significance, for without recognition there would be no real human selves, and without sharing there would be no striving toward truth. Growth is the sign of a continuity between selves, others, reality, and truth. The bond between truth, self-identity, and social recognition is greatly transformed in city life. It becomes one more difference between a village and a city.

Growth becomes predictable when supported by appropriate forms of order. Once again the four levels of order—triviality, vagueness, narrowness, and width—serve to secure the basis of growth. More than that, when growth is tied to certain forms of order, the urban environment begins to exhibit certain moods as signs of its solid growth. An objective sense of what is reasonably possible in terms of value achievement begins to spread through various city regions. One can, as is often said, "feel it in the air." The unification of mood, order, and sign is the groundwork of all effective forms of city growth.

Trivial orders remain trivial orders within the limits of the city. The incompatibility of factors that issue into feelings of triviality prevents any strong expression of value. What grows is a steady sense of indifference. Boredom and loss of hope arises from the conjunction of signs and triviality. So much of contemporary political discourse is so ineffective because it is so trivial. No one wants to listen to it any more, for it strikes the hearer as merely the ramblings of experts or the empty rhetoric of politicians. Talk of the "vision thing" is the pale contemporary equivalent of the struggle with triviality. Community cannot be built on triviality. This is the tragedy of contemporary liberalism, which raises individual liberty to such a level of importance that it trivializes all forms of communal existence.[7] The building of solid community is essential for growth. Thinking takes place in signs and not in some putative private space called "the mind." This public realm of thought, constituted by recognizable signs, depends upon the kind of mutual interaction that is the very stuff of community itself. Moods of indifference reveal a double problem. Triviality is infecting the signs of a city region, and preoccupation with private concerns has obliterated the public sphere.

The order of vagueness helps growth by providing a certain level of seriousness within urban regions. Vagueness helps the many stand as one and thereby promotes a mood of expectation. As opposed to the incompatibility infecting triviality, vagueness offers a form of order that is a first step toward unity. Its boundaries are still inchoate, for vagueness requires specificity for its full functioning; nevertheless, a vague unity offers a level of unification far superior to triviality. When signs of vagueness dominate an urban region, then opportunities for habit formation and its companion, growth, begin to suggest themselves. There is about vagueness a certain enticement that leads the interpreter of its signs to think that something major is about to occur.

Growth is expected and signs of vagueness promote a sense of importance throughout the urban community. When vagueness qualifies the sign structure of a city, the dynamical object compels a loose but lasting interest in acquiring signs and interpretants that can push the communal quest for truth forward. Vague orders are indispensable for gathering up the kind of social energy and intelligence required to begin major community projects. When the many begin to count as a one, then great force can be brought to bear upon issues of concern. By focusing issues, vague signs point toward real solutions. Expectation can fuel the desire to resolve issues in a way worthy of the truth. A mood of expectation settles over urban experience. Communities of inquiry always form with the expectation that something can be achieved, but it is of overwhelming importance that something specific be done. Otherwise, once again community intelligence will dissipate in the toxic vapors of political rhetoric or the jargon of experts.

The required specificity is brought about by the order of narrowness. Here selective emphasis knows what it is about and ruthlessly eliminates every element not directly associated with its goal. Narrowness is the opposite of vagueness for it picks out one aspect to the exclusion of all else. This results in the storage of an enormous energy. This energy fosters the mood of intensity found in all orders of narrowness. Feelings are directed toward a single end. What does not fit is cast aside and what does fit is seen only in the light of its instrumental value for achieving the goal in question. The dynamical object insists on its presence with a radical urgency. The sign, too, must be unequivocal for there can be no mistaking its meaning. This in turn requires interpretants of absolute clarity. It is precisely this sense of intensity that characterizes all social movements bordering on the fanatical. Be it ideology or dogma, narrow orders create narrow semiotic networks. For all its value in shaping up the contours of the vague, narrowness by itself rarely allows for sustained and productive growth.

What is missing in narrowness is width. Wide orders are brought about by weaving the narrow onto the vague in such a way that alternative signs and interpretants are not necessarily eliminated. Width fosters a mood of involvement, which is exactly the prime requisite for healthy community. Tolerance is wedded to direction and relevance takes on broad significance. In wide orders, generality of expressive value has been achieved. As a result, object, sign, and interpretant are richly interlocked. Thought, feeling, and action spread out to include wide interests. There is nothing cheap or narrow about the thought that goes on in such regions. It is distinguished by the full participation of its members. The mood of involvement is entirely general and no item of experience is neglected. Width is the order closest to thirdness. Its stability and continuity are the earned results of efforts at semiotic inclusion.

The triumph of thirdness requires the effective presence of the ideal normative measures of intensity, integrity, wholeness, and depth. Without intensity signs could not generate the kind of energy needed to foster full inclusion of experience. Narrowness is really a kind of laziness for it convinces us that no more need be said. In a process universe such a mood spells disaster. Growth demands inclusion and that means width is the sign of the great community. Similarly, width must present a balance between the extremes of vagueness and narrowness. Now, the measure of balance is integrity—the quality that seeks to give each dimension of experience its due. To be integrated is to experience what I called in Part One the power of the integer. Through integrated growth, a whole much more than the sum of its parts is established. Now, wholeness is the third ideal normative measure. As we have seen, growth in wholeness is the very sign of good city form. In like manner, its semiotic structure should also reflect a similar capacity to express wholeness as a distinguishing feature of its regions. Finally, a thirdness without any depth is a contradiction in terms. The wholeness characteristic of the sign of 3 includes the depths of process itself. Thirdness experienced in the present brings about a thickness of experience that calls for signs and interpretants worthy of such depths. That is why thirdness and beauty are at this level of analysis one and the same.

My reference to beauty serves as a conclusion to this discussion of growth. I take seriously Peirce's insistence that aesthetics is the primary normative discipline of philosophical reflection. I also take seriously Whitehead's injunction that it is to aesthetics we must look if we are to fathom the ultimate mysteries of the cosmos. For Peirce, logic is grounded in ethics and ethics in turn is grounded in aesthetics. Aesthetics itself has no need for a further ground since beauty is itself the *summum bonum*. In working out this comparative study of Whiteheadian orders of process and Peircean categoreal and semiotic postulates, I am consciously trying to push the tradition of American naturalism farther along the road of philosophical inquiry. One test of its adequacy ought to be the power of its instruments for understanding city life. The next three chapters attempt just such an application of this speculative system. But before advancing to that task a final dimension of Peirce's thought needs exploration. He calls it "abduction." I term it "felt intelligence."

Felt Intelligence

This chapter has as its title the words "Mood, Order, and Sign." I conclude with a summary of the interrelations between these three concepts. The key to bringing them together resides in Peirce's idea of abduction. Abduction is distinguished from deduction and induction by reason of its lack of formal rules. Abduction is a guess at an answer to a problem. The abduction suggests itself because the inquirer has achieved a certain level of intimacy with the problem. This is as much as to say that the inquirer has lived with it for some time and is familiar with its general contours. The abduction consists of an inference from a specific set of circumstances to a more general hypothesis. What prevents this from being called either a deduction from universal principles or an induction from many empirical observations is the fact that the abduction represents a concrete effort on the part of the inquirer to get a handle on the situation and set the direction for further inquiry. Unlike deduction, abduction does not involve a necessary deduction from prior principles, and unlike induction, abduction does not involve the systematic application of observations that characterizes the empirical sciences.

In what then does the persuasiveness of abduction consist? It cannot be strict logical deduction nor the rigors of the scientific method. I characterize it as an intelligently felt reaction to a situation that demands a solution. It is intelligent because our mind has been at work for some time digging around the edges of the problem either directly or by way of community participation. It is felt because it is a concrete stab at reasonableness arising out of our participation in specifically particular circumstances. Here is Peirce describing the purpose of abduction:

> Its end is, through subjection to the test of experiment, to lead to the avoidance of all surprise and to the establishment of a habit of positive expectation that shall not be disappointed. Any hypothesis, therefore, may be admissible, in the absence of any special reasons to the contrary, provided it is capable of experimental verification, and only insofar as it is capable of such verification. This is approximately the doctrine of pragmatism.[8]

Abduction, therefore, is the first step toward establishing successful habits of engagement with the environment. We shall soon see just how crucial such a skill is for negotiating city life. Right now I wish to stress both abduction's character as felt intelligence and the way in which it precisely binds together mood, order, and sign in city life. Abduction is a short cut to habit. Habits begin as successful responses to survival situations. They then grow through sign activity into general ways to deal with critical issues. They are thirds seeking to resolve the problems of life. They are the practical down-to-earth solutions created by humans in the course of evolution. As

such, habits bear with them the authority of the past and the reasonableness of the community. They do not, however, always work.
Whenever the failure of a habitual response becomes evident, there
is great danger to the community, for what was once settled is now
in doubt. Surprise rules where regularity was once the order of the
day. What is needed in the immediacy of city life is not a long tedious
deductive or inductive procedure. There is no time for that in the
present state of doubt. Abduction serves as a quick response that
turns the community in the direction of a solution. It marshalls the
resources of the community's intelligence and sets forth a provisional course of action. It is a leap but not a leap into the dark. Some
things are known and that heritage of fact is brought into play when
abduction takes place. Also, the collective intelligence of the community is not totally disabled. There remains in the storehouse of intelligence resources that can be brought to bear on the issue at stake.

What abduction is about is trusting one's "feel" for a situation. It
is not a blind trust but it is a sense that one knows more than one
can say and that a particular response may prove pragmatically effective. I say "feel" because that is precisely what is going on:
Through the advocacy of signs we "feel" the potential rightness of
certain kinds of actions. As we might expect, Peirce maintains that
there are three kinds of signs. Each of them is geared to represent
what is going on in one of the three dimensions of reality. The sign of
firstness is an icon. The sign of secondness is an index. The sign of
thirdness is a symbol. This set of signs is rightly called "the unveiling triad."[9]

What is unveiled by each member of this triad is a different level
of the world of signs. Icons reveal the existence of quality lying at the
base of reality. This quality is another term for what Whitehead calls
"value." An icon participates in the feelings of quality that it stirs up.
It is a copy or simulacrum of the reality in question. Its relation to its
object is brought about by an embodiment or likeness that summons
up the feeling of the quality in question. Icons are images that seek
to stir up felt reactions to the object being signed. Here is Peirce's
definition:

> [An icon is present} where the dual relation between the sign
> and its object is degenerate and consists in a mere resemblance
> between them. I call a sign which stands for something merely
> because it resembles it, an *icon*. Icons are so completely substi-
> tuted for their objects as hardly to be distinguished from them.
> Such are the diagrams of geometry.[10]

They provide a likeness of the object and suggest an identification that may or may not be there. Like all imagistic activities, icons engage our attention and pull us toward the reality in question. They can, however, be quite deceptive, since they share only some features of the object they stand for. However, on the positive side an icon makes real the category of firstness. It therefore shares in all the evanescence of this most ephemeral of categories. The vanishing quality of firstness is due to its embodiment of possibility. Therefore, icons may or may not be successful in unveiling the quality in question. And yet they are crucial for an urban semiotics. Without effective iconic activity, the feeling tone of an urban environment flickers unsteadily and possibilities of guessing at the feelings at play within the region are decidedly lessened. This is why the four levels of aesthetic order are so important for urban semiotics. As the next chapter shall argue, it is when icons are situated in orders of narrowness and width that they are most efficient in bringing about habitual responses. It must be remembered that the ground of this cosmology is its thesis that the interlocking sets of events making up city existence are all alike in this way: They are expressions of felt value. What is unveiled by each member of the semiotic triad is a different level of value. An icon reveals the existence of quality lying at the base of reality. Its relation to its object is brought about by an embodiment or likeness that summons up the feeling of the quality in question.

An index points directly to the object in question. It is fact laden and there is no hesitation in finding the relation between the object signed and the index that unveils it. Peirce defines it as follows:

> [An index] signifies its object solely by virtue of being really connected with it. Of this nature are all natural signs and physical symptoms. I call such a sign an *index*, a pointing finger being the type of this class.[11]

The felt intelligence engendered by an index is blunt, indubitable, and direct. An index points and the interpreter sees. There should be no guesswork, for indices are concerned with real facts existing in the real world. This is because an index unveils secondness. The dyadic relation of secondness consists in the straightforward existence of something that is in direct relation to another. The index points directly at this second and a causal relation is established between the sign and the object signified. Spots appear and measles are understood to be the cause. The index is the relation between the object and its interpretant. Indices are felt immediately and with vivid force. They grab our attention in an undeniable way. Obviously, indices are crucial for effective city living. What would happen if the stop sign did not gain our immediate attention? An index functions as a sign that something real is present and must be acknowledged as such. The denial of indices anesthetizes felt intelligence and renders experience dumb and blind.

An index also finds its expression helped or hindered by reason of the aesthetic order in which it finds itself. Narrowness is the natural habitat for indices. Vagueness does not help at all but width can be of some service. Of course a trivial index is a contradiction in terms. I shall have much more to say about this sign of secondness in a later chapter. Here it is only important that we gain a sense of what an index is and how it functions to stir up felt intelligence. Directness, necessity, and compulsion describe both the feeling tone and the semiotic action of an index.

A symbol is the sign of thirdness. It therefore carries with it all the weight already associated with survival, habit, and growth. Its act of unveiling concerns the way the third dimension of reality mediates between the other two in order to establish regular rhythms of value within the city. Peirce's definition is as follows:

> A sign is a conjoint relation to the thing denoted and to the mind. If this triple relation is not of a degenerate species [icons and indices], the sign is related to its object only in consequence of a mental association, and depends upon a habit. Such signs are always abstract and general, because habits are general rules to which the organism has become subjected. They are, for the most part, conventional and arbitrary. They include all general words, the main body of speech, and any mode of conveying a judgment.[12]

A symbol smooths out the rough relations expressed through secondness and stabilizes the fleeting quality of firstness. It is the primary way in which mind registers itself in the city. Through symbols the stable takes center stage and provides a platform for further inquiry and experience. The great gain brought about by symbols lies in the sense of control it grants to those who employ them. Through symbols, the reasonableness of the city asserts itself. As the sign of 3, a symbol is the most up-to-date representation of the fullness of city experience. And yet it remains abstract. Therein lies the negative dimension of symbols. Peirce stressed that generals tend to generalize. Such movement away from the *haeccitas* of the icon of 1 endangers the concrete particularity of urban experience. We can be dragged away from rich encounters with the quality of city life. In addition, the straightforward directness of an index of 2 can be inappropriately identified with symbols of thirdness and thereby misdirect experience. This is why the value of urban experience is dependent on the kind of symbol used to express it. Inadequate symbols wash away the vividness and intensity of the values achieved. Our consciousness, insofar as it depends on the medium of symbols to do its work, is also at the mercy of symbolic representation. Just as symbols can summon up great integrity, wholeness, and depth of experience, so also can a symbol dilute the very process it seeks to signify. All symbols are double-edged swords. Will they deliver experience full, rich, and entire or will they choke off vital dimensions of the real? Once again, the pragmatic test shows its fruitfulness as an aid to metaphysical speculation. The question to be asked is: "What difference does the symbol make in the life of the city?" An answer can only be had by also retrieving the firstness of the icons and the secondness of the indices of which the symbol is a third. And that is the precise task of the next three chapters.

This chapter has tried to introduce the major, salient elements of Peirce's metaphysics and semiotics in order to understand more precisely the interplay between mood, order and sign (See fig. 7). I needed the help of Peirce's categories and semiotic system in order to make useful and applicable the categories of my own speculative scheme. By "mood" I mean a certain tone of feeling that pervades a particular urban region, structure, or event. This mood has been established because certain processses have reached a level of consistent repetition. In so doing, they establish habits of interpetation suitable for the particular region under analysis. These moods receive intensification or attenuation by reason of the aesthetic orders

Figure 7:
CATEGORIES, SIGNS, ORDERS, AND MOODS

Category	Sign	Order	Mood
Firstness	Icon	Vagueness	Expectation
Secondness	Index	Narrowness	Intensity
Thirdness	Symbol	Width	Involvement

within which they sit. Peirce's firstness, secondness, and thirdness supply an excellent tool for identifying what expressions of urban value are going on in a particular region. Their instrumental value is doubled by their association with different kinds of signs. Thus, this urban cosmology adds icons, indices, and symbols to the already rich speculative system set forth in the introduction and elaborated at length in my earlier study, *Nature*.

I now pass on to a more detailed investigation of each of these signs and the various ways in which they express themselves in city life. Cosmological speculation needs to be applied, and with the assistance of Peirce's categories and semiotics, such application can make specific what heretofore has only been objectively but vaguely outlined. The next three chapters deal with the urban presence of the icon of one, the index of two and the symbol of three. This task demands a heightening of aesthetic sensibility. Although the moods signified by signs are often difficult to detect, appropriate training can advance our capacities. Just as my earlier book *Nature* concluded with the need for a foundational ecology, so also I am hoping that the next three chapters can lead to the development of an appropriate urban praxis.

Chapter Six

The Sign of One/Qualitative Value

This chapter begins the application of Peirce's metaphysics and semiotics to city experience. My aim is to use these tools to enlarge and deepen the understanding of the city as a unique human creation. As already seen, Peirce developed a categoreal scheme and a system of signs that correlated firstness with icons, secondness with indices, and thirdness with symbols. What follows concerns itself only with the realm of firstness and its iconic representation. Also, my employment of Peirce's metaphysics is confined to the task of gaining a general grasp of the shape of urban regions. Likewise, the iconic semiosis derived from firstness is restricted solely to urban experience.

I begin with a discussion of the importance of firstness in the present age. Next I examine the iconography of the city. A concrete example of city firstness is then offered. Finally, the preeminence of feeling as a reservoir for the human experience of value is made evident. Throughout this discussion (as well as the next two chapters) I avoid the thorny issues still surrounding the interpretation of Peirce's thought. My goal is to make his philosophy fruitful by applying it directly to this grand instrument of human evolution, the city and its regions of value and experience.

The Importance of One

It is scarcely possible to overestimate the importance for the present age of feelings of firstness. In this study, as well as my earlier work on nature, I have stressed the negative effects of the dominant world view of scientific materialism and advanced capitalism. When facts replace feelings as the touchstone of experience, then human consciousness suffers an outrageous deprivation. All that is rich and worthwhile in human life revolves around states of feeling as genuine indicators of the value of reality. To scorn such feelings as merely matters of private concern is to dismiss humanity's capacity to interact meaningfully with its environment. Given its origins in rigid empiricism, scientific materialism necessarily confines its attention to that which can be communicated through the quantitative analysis of sense data. What cannot be measured is at best purely subjective reactions to the dynamics of matter in motion. No reliance and certainly no credence can be given to such ephemera as moods and feelings. For the sake of objective knowledge, scientific materialism rules out of bounds precisely those dimensions of human experience most intimately bound up with the discovery and articulation of levels of value. Civilization is left with a world laden with facts and devoid of importance, and advanced capitalism provides the motivation for carrying out such a project on a transnational scale.

In opposition to such a viewpoint, this urban cosmology seeks to guarantee a primary place for feeling. In fact, it makes feeling the very foundation of all process. Everything we encounter as human beings is a result of the weaving of feelings onto each other. The city is really a great conversation about the meaning and status of feelings. One reason why sociological examinations of city life often seem so sterile and off the mark is the fact that they seek only facts. I contend that a feeling is a fact and some way must be found to locate and express such felt facts. It is precisely here that Peirce's category of firstness becomes so useful.

What is firstness? It is above all else that which comes first. It is the origin of every process and the beginning of all expressions of value. It is the cradle of reality. It has no equal for it is always first. Nothing can be compared to it and nothing can be substituted for it. It is an indispensable one, pure and simple. It has no rivals, for nothing comes before it, beside it, or after it. Firstness is the primordial issue that marks the birth of the really real. To be a one is to express monadic being. One could call it absolute suchness for it is completely itself such as it is. Overwhelming in its simplicity, firstness declares itself as itself and no other. In terms of my cosmological scheme, first-ness is *haeccitas*. The inscape of every event, natural or urban, is an expression of firstness. Unique and never to be expressed again, what is first cannot be mistaken for anything else. The importance of one lies in its own quality. It is what it is and is no other.

How then can firstness be experienced? It cannot be as a comparison for that would turn it into a second. Neither can it be experienced as a general thought for that would make it a third. Only a feeling can convey the immediacy, freshness, and originality of one. For a feeling is just that—a feeling and no other. One cannot get behind a feeling to something more primordial. Neither can one describe it by comparison with another feeling. What is felt is the feeling itself. As Peirce puts it:

> Stop to think of it and it has flown! What the world was to Adam on the day he opened his eyes to it, before he had drawn any distinctions, or had become conscious of his own existence,— that is first, present, immediate, fresh, new, initiative, original, spontaneous, free, vivid, conscious, and evanescent. Only, remember that every description of it must be false to it.[1]

Firstness is the bedrock level of reality from whence grow all other dimensions of the real. Without a one there could be no two or three. Manifestly, feelings of firstness are crucial for a normative appreciation of reality. One is the starting point for all estimates of the value of reality. For quality is another name for value, but it is aboriginal value having the character of immediacy, wholeness, and unanalyzable totality. In terms of city experience, if feelings of firstness cannot be felt, then any type of axiological study becomes impossible. It is sensitivity to the now, the immediate moment in all its *haeccitas* that grounds this urban cosmology. And yet it is precisely this sensitivity to the immediate quality of urban experience that is so sorely lacking in contemporary accounts of urban form. When it comes to feeling quality, scientific materialism would have us believe that all such efforts are vain attempts to make what is private public and what is subjective objective. But that is only because contemporary culture lacks a metaphysical vision capable of rendering such feelings of quality normative for human experience.

What is most characteristic of our culture is a prevalent neglect of habits of aesthetic appreciation. We can scarcely locate the place of value, let alone feel it. An aesthetic deprivation grips our sense of city life. In its insistence upon the significance of faceless privacy as the touchstone of individuality, modernism has made it impossible to take the issue of intensity of feeling as anything more than aberrant subjective poetizing. A public anaesthesia befogs our immediate relation to the environment, natural or urban. There seems to be a culturally induced inability to feel the presence of value and to mark its expression. While I assign the greater part of the blame for this to the unfortunate dogmas of scientific materialism, the situation is made all the worse by the rampant presence of forms of late capitalism (Part Three deals with this issue directly). As a result, human consciousness is impoverished and unable to connect with the normative presence of value in urban life.

It is to challenge this anaesthesia that I bring Peirce's metaphysical semiotics into the discussion. Firstness marks the emergence of value, for within its boundaries feelings of quality are directly experienced. What is meant by the term *quality*? A quality is an achieved form of value. And it is what comes first. This means that reality is to be understood as the constant emergence of forms of value. Now, I have already employed such an understanding of process as the ground of this cosmology of urban experience. Peirce's category of firstness adds a double advantage to my metaphysical scheme. First, he makes clear that feelings of quality (in my scheme, feelings of value) are directly experienced in everyday life as forms of freshness, spontaneity, and wholeness. These forms of value achieved are felt as unanalyzed totalities incapable of further analytic discrimination within the domain of firstness. Value is directly given in epochs of temporality that resist being broken down into more concrete instances of value.[2] This is entirely in accord with the category of inscape. Therefore, there is agreement between Peirce and this cosmology on the fundamental meaning of reality: All reality is the creative passage of events expressing irreducible forms of value. Second, Peirce also provides a way in which we can locate these instances of value or firstness. The sign of one is an icon, and therefore within the iconography of city life we can locate the emergence of forms of value as they express the normative presence of urban value. Now, it must be remembered that "every description of it must be false to it"; nevertheless, there remain within the semiotic traces of urban existence likenesses and similarities (icons) of these values. If ever there was a direct challenge to the nihilism of the present age, it is this speculative hypothesis—that the world of city life is already brimming over with the normative presence of real value.

The importance of one is now evident. Through the category of firstness a space is cleared for feelings of value. These feelings are direct, immediate, and not to be reduced to any other category. Inscape always marks the presence of value in city as well as in nature. This metaphysical hypothesis directly confronts the anaesthesia of the age. It asserts that forms of value are felt within the environment. It thereby makes aesthetics primary for any application of the categoreal scheme. In fact, it is firstness that makes aesthetics the ground discipline of all the normative sciences. It is by being sensitive to the felt quality of various environments that their authentic value can be located and expressed. This brings the study to a discussion of the iconography of city life.

The Iconography of the City

What is an icon? It is primarily a likeness of the object signified. Through this likeness a certain kind of feeling is felt. This iconic feeling can only approximate the original value, for that has already gone by in its immediacy and spontaneity. Still, an icon can recover some dimensions of the felt values of the category of firstness. It works through resemblance. In terms of the semiotic triad an icon stands for its object to an interpretant that is largely imagistic. For example, Peirce speaks of the diagrams of geometry as iconic signs for the geometric relations themselves. So a drawn replica of a triangle resembles the actual relations of a three-sided figure whose angles add up to 180 degrees. The unveiling power of an icon resides in its capacity to provide a simulacrum for the object in question.

At this level of the world of signs, there is an identity established between the reality to be signed and the sign itself. An icon therefore participates in the feelings of quality that it stirs up. It is a copy or simulacrum of the reality in question. Its relation to its object is brought about by an embodiment or likeness that summons up the feeling of the quality in question. Insofar as they function as "stand-ins" for their objects, icons suggest an identification that may or may not be there. Like all imagistic activities, icons engage our attention and pull us toward the reality in question. They can, however, be quite deceptive since they share only some features of the object they stand for. Resemblance is not identity.

Nevertheless, an icon signs the presence of the category of firstness. This category is above all else fleeting since firstness is the realm of possibility. Due to its ephemeral character firstness is always slipping away. In this sense icons are never stable unveilings of the realm of firstness. They come and they go, and what is a powerful image for one generation can be largely ignored by another. Therefore, icons may or may not be successful in unveiling the quality in question. Still, icons are critical for the initiation of an urban semiotics. Effective iconic activity stabilizes the feeling tone of an urban environment. It makes possible the further semiotic development of the region in question. The category of one necessarily precedes the unfolding of the other two categories. My thesis remains the same: The interlocking sets of events making up city existence are all expressions of felt value. A failure in iconic representation inevitably leads to further abstractness at other semiotic levels. As the foundation of a concrete urban semiotics, icons begin the process of engagement within which the meaning of city experience grows and takes on deeper values.

Firstness stands alone in all its monadic power and so also does its sign. To be effective an icon must express a quality of singlemindedness. It must be a copy of that which it represents. This sense of replication is in line with the general meaning of firstness; that is, a first is without a comparative dimension. It is a direct immediate feeling of a value that is unquestioned in its authenticity. Icons must seek to duplicate this direct expression of value. And of course they cannot. For every icon is already a copy and therefore not an original. This is simply part of the price to be paid for living in a process universe. Time and its occasions of value move on. There is no perfection that is the sum of all perfections. What comes to be perishes and becomes part of the creative advance. The firstness of the present has already moved on even as its icon seeks to represent it.

The upshot of this temporal situation ought to be the recognition that no icon exhausts the value it attempts to express. There is always something askew and something missing. It is not the nature of iconic representation to be exactly what it signifies. This fact, of course, is at the bottom of Borges's conviction that a perfect description of the world would make it disappear. Likewise, it is at the heart of the sense of uneasy fantasy caused by the so-called magical realism of Latin American novels. No icon is equal to the firstness it expresses, and yet somehow it should evoke the felt sense of the experience in question. It is around the question of the power of evocation that a fruitful discussion of urban iconography must revolve. How can that which is inevitably off summon up a "true" account of the value in question?

The answer to this question involves the pragmatic definition of truth and meaning. For Peirce as for all the pragmatists, the meaning of any sign resides in the consequences that it brings about. Look to results and aftermaths to find out the truth of a sign. Truth is not found in the correspondence of an idea with the reality it represents. Rather, the truth of a sign is demonstrated by the effects it brings about. Does the geometric drawing of the triangle evoke the value of the triangle? If so, it is an effective icon. To the degree that an icon summons up feelings similar to the value it invokes, to that same degree its truthful meaning is established. There is therefore a certain "all or nothing" dimension to icons. Either they immediately call into being the value to be felt or they do not. Such is the monadic nature of firstness. An element of instability always clings to iconic representation. It is this evanescence that makes the four aesthetic orders so important for stabilizing the iconography of the city.

Narrowness, vagueness, and width are the types of order most valuable for creating a richly stable iconic evocation. Vagueness is already set within iconic representation by the very fact that an icon is a simulacrum, a likeness of the quality to be represented. Even an "exact replica" is only a likeness of the object to be signed. Also, in a vague order the many count as one; that is to say, the salient feature of such an order is similarity. Now, similarity is not identical to sameness. It is for this reason that icons are always vague; nevertheless, there is an indispensable benefit bestowed on urban iconography by the order of vagueness. It will be recalled that the mood attending orders of vagueness is expectation. Nothing could be more important for the establishment of effective icons than the alertness brought about by vague aesthetic orders. There is need for an antidote for the fact-obsessed thought of scientific materialism as well as the pursuit of private gain promoted by capitalism. Expectation brought about by the dominance of vague orders of feeling helps to correct the unfortunate numbness that affects our culture. In a similar vein, a narrow aesthetic order serves to enhance the power of iconic representation. Since narrowness is accompanied by intense feelings, an icon set within a narrow range of meanings exhibits a force that is most likely to capture our attention. In this sense vagueness and narrowness are required aesthetic fields for the proper functioning of iconic signs. But as I have already argued, it is when narrowness is woven onto vagueness that genuine width of feeling is produced, and it is the character of width that is most useful for icons. Because they operate through similarity and likeness, icons function through forms of feelings that spread widely through specific urban regions. Not every feeler feels the same way but each can have in common feelings similar to their neighbor. An icon exhibiting great width of representation casts a wide net that embraces many interpreters. Iconic forms built up out of narrowness woven onto vagueness provide the requisite width for effective social communication. In and of itself a vague iconic form is as likely to be misinterpreted as it is to be authentically understood. Such is the danger of vagueness. Narrowness, on the other hand, confines the sign activity to a selective emphasis that may be defective in similarity and therefore is inhibited in its proper functioning. It is only when narrowness intersects with vagueness that feelings of involvement come into play. Again as argued in my earlier work, involvement is precisely what occurs within orders of feeling characterized by great width. A social order that does not manifest width of iconic representation is a contradiction in terms. The very meaning of the social is that which bonds individuals together. Now, the act of urban semiotic bonding is carried out through networks of meaning within which citizens can participate. It is through these participatory networks that the quality of firstness becomes available to city dwellers. Involvement through wide orders of feeling is the very signature of the vibrant city.

Now, iconic involvement differs from indexical and symbolic participation in at least three ways. First, the act of participation must be immediate and nonreflective. There ought to be a directness to the level of involvement. This is entirely in accord with the essential quality of firstness. The social group must feel the value in question with a direct urgency. It ought to stir up the intended feelings in an almost instinctive manner. Thus, all urban iconic activity should evidence an undeviating force of feeling. In effect, this means that the icon should be immediately recognizable by wide sections of the populace. Without such effectiveness, the unveiling power of the icon is seriously diminished. Its very being as an iconic sign is thrown into question.

Second, the icon ought to lead the city dweller into an active engagment with a value. Icons are not just informative. Neither are they discursive. Rather, they are likenesses of the value in question. An icon must be able to carry significant axiological weight. If it is trivial, the value of firstness will not be felt with any vivid power. If it is merely vague, the quality will fade with the continuing utilization of the icon. Vague icons cannot stand up to the task of direct participatory activity. If it is excessively narrow, entire segments of the interpretive community will be excluded from participation. Since the category of firstness is the level on which value begins to emerge into urban experience, inadequate iconic representation spells disaster for a city dedicated to the enhancement and enrichment of its citizens' lives. There is no such thing as a "value-free" icon.

The third aspect of iconic participation flows from the other two. Icons must always embody a degree of freshness such that upon being experienced there is always a sense of encountering them for the very first time. The freshness of firstness must be matched by the freshness of its iconic semiosis. This criterion of permanent originality can only be met by having recourse to the doctrine of normative measure sketched out in the concluding chapter of Part One. There I made a case for the establishment of some four ideal normative standards by which the value of types of experience could be measured. Those normative measures were intensity, integrity, wholeness, and depth. Freshness and originality of iconic representation is made possible through wholeness and depth. What is provided by wholeness is a sense of fullness whereby the icon in question is guaranteed an almost overwhelming sense of immediacy and directness. There is a feeling that nothing of importance is being left out. (This of course is a metaphysical restatement of Alexander's theory of good city form.) Similarly, through the presence of authentic depth the finite human feeler is drawn into a network of meanings suggestive of a sense of inexhaustible novelty. More and more ample representative power can be drawn up out of the level of firstness signified by the icon in question. What is immediately felt is the rock bottom creative urge at the base of city life. Through its fortunate unveiling power the icon summons up new resources of feeling from the axiological ground of the urban environment.

With this discussion of wholeness and depth, I am of course introducing the themes of beauty and creativity so central to this study of the the city as a region of value and experience. Part Three will deal directly with these topics. For now, I only wish to underline the fact that the category of firstness and its iconic semiotics is intimately interwoven with this cosmology's concepts of feeling, value, beauty, and creativity. Just as the cosmology needs Peirce's genius to flesh out the concrete activity of city life, so also does Peirce's semiotics need the cosmology's normative dimensions and categories to articulate the full reach and power of his insights. It is time that a concrete example of iconic activity be offered.

The Street

or
"Where did you go?"
"Out."
"What did you do?"
"Nothing."

When I was a boy, I lived on the fifth floor of an apartment building in the South Bronx. "To go down" to the street was always a special occasion. It had a sense of adventure to it. It promised surprise and it offered an entirely different inscape than that of my home. The street is the great icon of city firstness. The street in urban life is the likeness of the convergence of space and time. Each mode of the inscape of space and each mode of the inscape of time find expression in the phenomenon of the city street.[3] The result is an urban experience filled with surprise, expectation, and potential value. To go down to the street is to welcome the presence of firstness in all its freshness and authentic value. I have already, in Part One, provided a provisional sketch of urban firstness when I described a walk down 42nd Street. It is time now to discuss in more detail the semiotic dimensions of the urban iconography.

The three dimensions of the inscape of urban space are access, situated directionality, and habitat. The street lets the city dweller onto a radically volatile scene. There is a swiftly moving stream of environmental events that the citizen must literally "jump into" if real urban participation is to take place. To hang back is to become a spectator distantly removed from the action deeply characteristic of urban firstness. This spatial stream has no beginning and no end. It is just the street itself in all its active modalities of process. Like firstness, the street is just itself and no other. As an icon the street is the place where uniqueness comes to meet the city dweller. Suddenness and amazement are among its major features. In fact, access to surprise is as good a description of street life as can be had. This quality of surprise is the result of the street's situated directionality. A city street is open to experience for it allows that which is, to become part of its process. The street is situated such that life comes strutting down it in radical openness as well as in all manners of forms and guises. It is this continual openness to experience that makes the street a place where permanent habitat is impossible.[4] One cannot dwell on the street in any meaningfully human way. There is too much openness and not enough shelter. Part of the dread experienced when meeting "street people" is just this sense of the nomadic, but even nomads bring their homes with them. The homeless of the street are caught up in a whirl of firstness that never lets either the actualizing power of secondness or the sheltering ground of thirdness come into real play within their lives. To live out on the street is to be absorbed into a din of excitement that threatens one's sanity. For all its importance as an origin for value, iconic intelligence is not enough for full human experience. I doubt that humankind could have survived this long if its cities were merely places where the face of first-ness was continually encountered.

The presence of time within street experience demands a similar conclusion. Time in the street is the continual collision of the past and future with the present. There is no time to stop and recollect the past. It simply "comes by." The future streams into the present with such immediacy that it could be said to implode into the present. There is barely enough time in the street for all its modalities to take place. This sense of a pell-mell rush enveloping the street is the temporal counterpart of the sense of homelessness noted above. With so much happening at once, there is little time to savor any full time. Even as it invites surprise and participation, the street squeezes out any real opportunity to feel the depth and width of value. All is excitement and buzz.

Is it therefore any wonder that the typical icon of the city dweller is the pedestrian walking head down, headlong, and headstrong into the grip of the future as it impacts the present moment, the very icon of transience and speed? It is the effort to avoid any delay that marks the progress of the pedestrian. In fact, much city street action is precisely a dance of avoidance. The best one can hope to do within the icon of the street is to carve out small segments of value within which one can linger. Look! Here is a stickball game. Look! There is a delivery of beautiful flowers. But the traffic, speed, noise, and action of firstness within the street blunts all real chance for healthy temporal dwelling. Humankind does not live by firstness alone.

This sense of haste and quickness infecting urban street life is a reminder of the importance of the epochal theory of time as the most concrete understanding of the true meaning of temporal urban experience. For each event that comes sliding down the street is in itself a world unto itself. Seamless, not reducible to further analysis, street scenes must be jumped into if they are to be experienced. To delay for a moment is to be swept up into another, alternate world of unique and inevitably distracting values. This suggests why the pedestrian invariably keeps her head down. Distraction does not just mean a loss of focus. It signifies absorption into an entirely different world. Such is the power of iconic semiosis on the level of the city street (see fig. 4, p. 74)

But I wish to be more concrete.

I, Homo Urbanus, return once again to my youth. I am in the apartment located at 447 East 136th Street and situated on the top floor. It is four o'clock in the afternoon. I am getting ready to go out. School ended at 3 P.M. It's good to relax in my home for a while. I know where my clothes are, my sneakers, my baseball glove, my basketball. It is the mid-50s and I am not allowed to make any phone calls because they are too expensive. Only emergency calls! In fact, there is a lock on the phone. So to see where my friends are, I have to leave the building and walk to certain places where the guys hang out. Even if no one is there I will find something to do. So out I go. I make sure to take my baseball glove with me—a Marty Marion "Mr. Shortstop" special model that I still have and still use.

I walk down the five flights of stairs and suddenly I am on the stoop facing "the street." It is late April, so the sun continues to shine with that Spring brilliance so dear to humans young and old. Down the street comes the "knifesharpener" clanging his bell and carrying his equipment slung over his shoulder. A mysterious character who shows up in the neighborhood randomly. The housewives hear his bell, throw open their windows and shout that they are sending their children down with knives to be fixed. He speaks little, bends himself to his task and sends the kids back with the knives and a torn and soiled piece of paper with a handwritten bill for his services. After him comes the "the vegetable man" and his horsedrawn wagon. He yells some totally incomprehensible words and again the housewives yell down their orders and children pick up the goods. I pause on the stoop taking in all this vitality, this urban creativity. It is the street that shepherds down its ways ever-changing forms of life. It itself is alive—an urban icon of freshness and originality

I skip down the steps. Four in number and I can do it blindfolded. On the sidewalk I am faced with a big decision. Which way do I go? If I turn left, I will be heading toward the school yard at P.S. 41. That way lies stickball and the mysteries of Brown Place. If I turn right, I head toward Willis Avenue and the 136th Street playground. That way offers basketball pickup games. Maybe I can even get into a game with the big guys. I pause to consider the matter.

I realize that I have enough change to buy a soda, so its down to Jake Kazigian's store where a soda costs $ 00.12. While there I meet Jake's Mikey (Jake's son). We chat for a while and he tells me he is going to Taft where he will take courses in "shop." This means that he has not been able to get into the academic program and has been scheduled for life as an industrial worker of some *kind. This does not seem much of a big thing to him but to me it is a frightening piece of news. Suppose I too wind up in shop? The brothers in Saint Jerome's were always threatening laggards with a future devoted to "shop." Too dreadful to think about on a nice spring day. Jake's Mikey was never much for sports so we leave it there and I return to my stoop.*

What to do? What to do?

I decide to make the great circle. I will head toward Brown Place and the schoolyard and if nothing is cooking I will turn up 137th at Brown Place and make my way to Alexander Avenue and then the Playground. This way I double my chances for a game of some kind. I start down 136th (actually I am moving east toward the River and the Triboro Bridge, but the street slopes downward so we always called that direction "down" and the other "up"). As I move downward, I am met by the sound of a thundering motorcycle. It's Gonzalez and his supercharged bike. He is the newly installed "Super" at 455 East 136th Street, our former apartment building. We moved because we needed more space. Actually, we just took our stuff up the block past some six houses and walked up five flights of stairs to our new home. Gonzalez says "Buenas" and roars away. I wonder if I will ever be able to buy such a macho machine. Probably not. Then I fall into step with Billy Carrabine who has a brand new Raleigh bike. He tells me it has four speeds, and proceeds to ride away as fast as he can. Some kind of demo, I guess. Then there's Tootsie Kelly, Dee Dee Braynack, and Bonnie Lou Paulus, all St. Jerome's alums who are part of my burgeoning social life. But being a tough teenage guy, I just nod and pass on by. No need to get into one of those long conversations. Still, I do notice how grown up they are becoming.

So far, I have made it halfway down the block and have met nothing but friends. I cross the street and move down toward the schoolyard where great stickball games can be played. For one thing it has any number of weird walls and angles and that makes you feel as though you were playing in a major league park like Ebbets Field or even Fenway. One has to climb over a fence and then slide under a railing to get into this sacred space. For some strange reason, they always lock it up but everybody uses it anyway and knows many different ways to get in. But this time as I near the playground there are strange noises to be heard. Muffled male shouts and then some high-pitched screams.

I come upon the scene of a major fight. I do not know who the fighters are but one is white and the other black. That adds to the intensity of the scene. They circle each other, bobbing and weaving, looking for a chance to get in a good punch. Then they are rolling on the ground together. The white guy gets on top of the black guy and quickly slams his head on the concrete pavement. He goes out cold. Everybody connected with the white guy runs away. There is blood seeping out from the black guy's head. First time I ever saw so much blood flowing live right in front of me. It is terribly frightening. Then some good samaritan puts his baseball glove under the guy's head. I notice it is a Ducky Medwick model. All at once, the cop sirens sound, some kind of help is on its way, but we know enough to run. In a minute the schoolyard is clear. Everyone has left.

I find myself panting in the front vestibule of the First Baptist Church on the corner of Brown Place and 137th Street. I am hiding from the police. You do not want to get involved in anything like this. Believe me, it is nothing but trouble. As soon as I catch my breath, I slip out the side door. Trying to be as nonchalant as I can, I walk "down" Brown Place and "up" 137th Street toward Willis Avenue. No need now to hang out on Brown Place. It has its own tales to tell. Just the year before, six Puerto Ricans who had tried to assassinate President Truman were arrested inside a "safe house" on this very block. They found a cache of arms hidden in a pidgeon coop on the roof. I am now obviously walking "west" since "up" is west in this neck of the woods. My cool lets me evade the cops who are cruising the streets looking for anyone who appears suspicious. They go right by me and I breathe a great sigh of relief. So I am back on track and still looking for fun. My steps quickly take me to Willis Avenue and with the light in my favor I soon am on the other side.

Now I face a most interesting street. It contains all that is good and all that is threatening. Between here and the corner of Alexander Avenue, I will face the Scylla of guys hanging out under the "El" and the Charybdais of Saint Jerome's School. I gotta run the gauntlet between some heavy remarks and challenges to my manhood and some possibility of running into one of my former teachers. Which would be worst? For me at this time fresh into high school, I can't come up with a decent answer. So I do what I always do when faced with danger in the street. I begin to run. I zip past the shadows lurking in the darkness coming

*from the overhanging "El" and its cold iron spanning the center
of the street. A couple of words are shouted but I go by too fast to
hear. Then I burst into the sunlight and come up parallel to the
Kilpatrick Center of the local Police Athletic League. I know there
are basketball games going on in there but it is too nice a day to
be cooped up inside. And across the street stand the front steps of
the "Brothers" School where for the last three years I have strug-
gled to learn and thereby stay out of "shop." A glance to my right
tells me quickly that there is no one there so I hurtle by and soon
am at the corner of 137th Street and Alexander Avenue.*

*As I head toward the Playground at 136th Street, I feel a real
sadness tighten in my chest. Here it is almost an hour into the afternoon, the sun is getting ready to set and I have yet to get into a
game of any sort. I see them before I heard them—Gypsies—long
flowing clothes on the women, balloon pants on the men, outrageous colors, bandanas, scarves, rings, bracelets, necklaces, droop-
ing earrings, sashes, capes, and hats of all sizes and shapes. There
are children, too, each one holding up his end of this spontaneous
parade. And then the music! Gypsy violins, drums sounding like
they just left the steppes of Asia, tin whistles, flutes, tambourines,
guitars, and whining horns made from animal bones. A sound of
wildness, a lament of loneliness that tears at your soul. They are
announcing their arrival in the South Bronx. They come at this
time of year, every year, to coincide with the arrival of the Ringling
Brothers and Barnum and Bailey circus. I suppose they camp out
down by the freight yards where the circus train waits the return
of the performers and animals from Madison Square Garden. I
never really find out where they live or what they do. For my
mother has sufficiently scared us by telling us she will give us to
these strange beings if we do not behave. (Truth to tell, sometimes
I thought that would not be a bad fate.) I know they read cards
and the girls are the most beautiful I have ever seen. More than
that, I do not know nor do I care to.*

*But what a lift they give to my heart. I am alive again with
the possibilities of life and all its surprises. I do not even mind
that the sun is now setting and the chance for any kind of basketball game is nil. Rounding the corner at 136th Street, I head
home even as I spy out the court and see that there are a few guys
playing a game of O-U-T. It is too dark to play (in those days the
city never thought of illuminating its playgrounds; never even
crossed their minds, I guess). I make it back up to Willis, cross in*

*front of Burke's bar and head back home to 447. Supper is on the
stove and as we get ready to eat I am asked: "Where did you go
today?" I respond, "Out." Then I am asked, "What did you do?"
"Nothing," I reply.*

There is much gained and much lost on the street. A comprehensive urban environmental ethics must be able to account for both dimensions. What is gained is the sense of immediate value. The street is a perfect antidote for the anaesthesia infecting much of contemporary life. Access to intensity of experience as well as a multilayered and polyvalent present temporality are the gifts of the street. In this they echo the metaphysics of firstness represented through the iconography of city life. Freshness, quality, and immediate significance bestow on the street its preeminent place in human culture. Nowhere else is life in all its rich plurality expressed with such clarity. If the city is the place where existence at its height is attained, then no small part of that triumph is due to the energy gathered up in the various forms of street life that have always marked city life at its finest. But this very energy serves to undo the achievements of the street, for the excess of novelty characteristic of rich street life overturns any attempt at consolidating the values expressed within the iconography of the street itself. What is gained in energy is lost in impermanence. This is one reason why Sunday strollers in downtown business districts feel surrounded by an eerie quiet that is quite unreal. They know that the sense of empty stability experienced is only a minor pause in an endless stream of human activity. Lost also is any opportunity to dwell in solid significance. An air of fiction clings to the expressive power of icons of firstness. Such images capture human imagination but they offer little by way of enduring value. True depth and integrity are to be found in the continuity expressed in the symbols characteristic of the realm of thirdness.

In sum, the street is the icon of urban firstness because its spacetime structures enact on a human scale the major characteristics of the category of firstness. Without the original energy provided by firstness the city would never have begun. Furthermore, without the capacity to return to that source of novel value, the city is doomed to a slow and stale decay. An effective iconography of firstness is therefore a necessity for a good city environment. At the same time, firstness has its own perils, first among which is a sense of transiency that can easily promote an effete form of dilettantism. Curiosity replaces solid inquiry and impermanence rearranges all the norms used to measure the valuable and the important. Just how important and treacherous such icons of original freshness can be, forms the conclusion of this chapter.

Original Feelings of Freshness

What is that in our experience that resists naming? Christopher Alexander has called it "the quality without a name."[5] I have elsewhere termed it "The Arrival of Life."[6] It is that singular sense of freshness, vitality, integrity, and importance that overtakes one when in the presence of the uniquely real. In this cosmology I have used various words to identify this elusive quality: inscape, *haeccitas*, and novelty. Value and importance are also suggestive of what I am seeking to clearly and directly express. Uniqueness and spontaneity are also helpful expressions. Here at the end of this discussion of the urban semiotic category of firstness, the term I use to describe it is *freshness*.

Why freshness? As I argued earlier, feelings experienced through habits of aesthetic appreciation are the royal road to understanding the value of urban environments. Now, above all else, freshness must be felt immediately and directly upon being encountered. Freshness is therefore first, a One that awaits its qualitative recognition. Precisely because it is a first, freshness must be experienced exactly as it is. To experience freshness indirectly or through some intervening medium is to distort its presence. Any and every true expression of freshness must entail some kind of direct participation in the experience itself. Secondhand versions of freshness are of no help whatsoever. Another way of saying this is: Every quality of freshness necessarily is an instance of originality. Freshness is therefore the most direct, immediate, and true quality of urban firstness available. In terms of this urban semiotics, to be a first is to be a feeling of freshness.

Feelings of freshness carry the day whenever iconic representation dominates an urban region. Insofar as an icon is a likeness, it ought to be fresh, immediate, and direct. Staleness and repetition are the very opposite of what is required in the iconography of the city. Therefore, urban images that become too familiar provoke the disdain of the aesthetically attuned citizen. One stimulus for the incessant reinvention of urban images in the arts is precisely this well-grounded sense of the importance of originality in iconic representation. Without the freshness that novelty brings to urban life, slow routine sets in and the city slides inexorably toward a too-early end. When a city loses its edge of iconic freshness, it has degenerated into a necropolis, a city of the dead. At that point the very meaning of the city as a source of novel human existence has been lost. Cities too dependent upon one type of commerce or one kind of class or one manner of behavior soon cease to thrive. They become "centers of . . . (fill in the blank)" rather than cities.

A constant source of freshness must be ready to hand if the city is not to stagnate and perish. One such source should be the lives of its citizens whose aesthetic sensibility is such as to draw out of urban experience continuing layers of original meaning. This is why the form of urban goodness includes spontaneous value. In fact, as I argued earlier, its immediacy, especially as spatially expressed, is the first aspect of the goodness of the city. Now, this means that the doctrine of normative measure and its four ideal standards of intensity, integrity, depth, and wholeness must become part of the urban curriculum. In addition, citizens should become adept at spotting the presence of the four levels of aesthetic order—triviality, vagueness, narrowness, and width. Equipped with such normative measures, members of planning boards, environmental policy commissions, and other vitally important urban institutions could serve as an important check on the power of experts. In this age of scientific materialism, authority is too often handed over to those who know only by reason of quantitative analysis.

It is no accident that I begin the construction of an urban semiotics with a chapter on qualitative value. An aura of undeserved prestige clings to the professionals whose sole method is that of quantitative decison making. As long ago as 1925, Whitehead inveighed against types of professional technical education that produced only "minds in grooves."[7] In calling such professionals "a public danger," he foresaw just how much havoc they would wreak through modes of city planning entirely dependent upon the tenets of scientific materialism. The sign of one must hover over all modes of urban politics. Otherwise, a dreary sameness will register itself in those urban institutions devoted to the planning and construction of the city's material and cultural life.[8]

It is helpful to draw on comparative philosophy to deepen our understanding of freshness as the meaning of firstness. In Japanese culture, Zen has inspired an entire discipline dedicated to the discovery, expression, and upholding of freshness as the very sign of the real.[9] I am speaking of the Zen devotion to the immediately presented here and now of experience. Whether it is through one of the seven arts of Zen or the practice of zazen meditation, the goal is always the same: To experience reality exactly as it is here and now. Invariably, the quality that is uncovered in this search for the present moment is the feeling of freshness. And whether it is named spontaneity or original essence, this goal of Zen discipline may be taken as the spiritual equivalent of Peirce's category of firstness.

I have now reached an important moment in this cosmology of urban experience. Through the category of firstness a reconciliation of the spiritual and aesthetic realms can be glimpsed. The value of original freshness resides precisely in its power to make available to humankind an experience of value as the ground initiative of all reality. Reality is the neverending creation of instances of value that are first of all felt as moments of fresh originality. Prior to any further reaction, growth, or development there exists this realm of the One. It is the region where the experience of value is first met. It is so quick and so sudden that, as Peirce noted, often it simply passes by unnoticed. It is felt as a feeling of original freshness and it is available as both an aesthetic and a spiritual experience. In the immediate here and now of urban experience, there lingers largely unremarked the presence of quality as the bedrock meaning of urban human experience.

Such a conclusion runs directly counter to present day scientific materialism and advanced late capitalism. Insofar as a cast of mind devoted entirely to the identification and explanation of facts prevails as the cultural standard, city dwellers will be hard pressed to find anything more than vacuous matter as the bedrock of their experience. Likewise, a similar emptiness settles down upon the city insofar as profit is made the measure of worth. But all the while the human heart knows better, for we continue to marvel at the beauty and value of the cityscape. Thus, the most important result of this analysis of original freshness is that it stands foursquare against the nihilism brought about by this age of scientific materialism. In place of an empty world of matter in motion devoid of value, we are given a vision of living value as the very texture of reality. Icons of firstness are the signs of the presence of value. The human capacity to read such icons must be expanded and made available to all citydwellers if something like an authentic community of ethical discourse is to emerge some time in the future. For now, it is important to note that through this consolidation of Peirce's semiotics and Whitehead's cosmology an intellectual place for the discussion of types of normative measure has been clearly established. The inscape of all urban events is original freshness and its value can be experienced through the creation and development of a powerful urban iconography.

What will make us alert to such iconographic activity is instruction along the lines of aesthetic appreciation of originality and exercises in spiritual experiences of freshness. For it must be kept in mind that the forms of urban goodness are grounded in aesthetic sensibility. This means the creation of an urban curriculum steeped in the science of normative descriptions and the spirituality of the present moment. Resources for such an overhaul of our primary educational activities are available today in many different forms. Through the efforts of comparative philosophy the treasures of Eastern spirituality become increasingly part of our cultural endowment. Likewise, attunement to the aesthetic dimension of experience is increased with the growth of therapeutic communities of all kinds. Twelve-step recovery programs, for example, are grounded in the effort to live life fully one day at a time and even one moment at a time. And the need to cultivate some form of emotional intelligence becomes more recognized as a necessary daily component of wise living. In fact, much of the attention now being paid to possibilities of human growth runs along the lines of creating a deeper sensitivity to the original freshness lying hidden at the bottom of our experience.

The value of original freshness resides in its power to restore to human activity a sense of intention and purpose. To live mindfully in the here and now is the equivalent of becoming sensitive to the presence of an original freshness at the base of reality. This primordial level of value is what makes the city (and nature) important. In isolating it as a synonym for firstness I hope to make available to human experience a dimension of reality entirely different than the dictates of scientific materialism. By stressing the normative dimensions of urban experience, I challenge the reigning orthodoxies of a value-neutral materialism and a greed-driven economics. As the previously discussed pragmatic maxim made clear, all forms of inquiry are value laden. The real question is whether or not human beings are in search of the right values. The first step toward realizing such a project of value inquiry is to be able to appreciate value when it expresses itself. The twin sources of inscape and firstness secure a place for the identification of such values. Until the city is seen as an ever-emergent stream of events of value, there can be little hope of cultivating a normative sensitivity to types and forms of value. The capacity to read the signs of One in urban experience is a first step toward renewing the basic level of civic participation in the good life (see figs. 4 and 5, pp. 74, 75).

The sign of One represents qualitative value. Through icons of its likeness, urban dwellers encounter the real presence of value.

The street is only the most obvious icon of urban firstness. There are many other possible iconographies, including, most importantly, the cosmic city identified by Kevin Lynch as the very first model of good city form. Here we find a historical confirmation of the validity of this urban semiotics, for, above all else, the cosmic city sought to replicate the powers of the heavenly forces of which it was a simulacrum. Thus, the first historic model of the city was through and through an icon of freshness, for it sought to reproduce the world exactly as it came fresh from the creator's hand. Urban firstness is therefore an exercise in the continuing emergence of freshness as a determinate region of value and experience. Icons of firstness engage us in a neverending round of spatiotemporal epochs, each one of which is an instance of intense value.

But great danger lurks in the sign of One, for it can easily trap human consciousness in a scene of immediate presences, no one of which is more important than any other. In other words, firstness stands always on the edge of triviality. At any moment it can degenerate into an excess of incompatibility. This establishes a region where everything is important and therefore nothing is important. Importance implies selectivity and without a method of comparison, no such discrimination is possible.

Comparison involves at least two things. The limits of firstness have now been set. Every one implies a two. That there must be an other is guaranteed by the pluralism of the scheme's cosmology. This means that conflict is inevitable. Competing firsts form the realm of secondness. It is a realm equally important for a full understanding of urban reality. Without secondness, little of solid reality could ever come to be and establish itself. This brings us to the sign of Two and its impact on city life.

Chapter Seven

The Sign of Two/Collision

The move from firstness' qualitative immediacy and unanalyzed wholeness to the state of secondness is marked by the introduction of resistance, effort, force, compulsion, striving, and enforcement into the texture of reality. Both the manner in which secondness is signed as well as its effect on the physical, biological, and cultural levels of the city is an essential dimension of urban experience. This chapter examines secondness under the general meaning of collision. By this aggressive term I wish to suggest the real presence of harsh actuality within the ontological domain. All is not sweetness and light. There is conflict, loss, pain, and peril. A comprehensive examination of the city requires a full expression of this side of the real.

I begin with a discussion of secondness as an essential dimension of the real. I then examine what I term "The Urban Index," which involves the representation of those dimensions of urban life associated with the struggle for existence. The third part uses the urban skyline as the index of all types of "bottom-line," "real life" experience. The physical, biological, and cultural levels of order are deeply implicated in all such forms of evaluating the fundamental meaning of city life. Here the market, the commercial aspect of city life, is met head on. Whether economic discourse must ultimately be determined by a vocabulary of secondness is a question at the heart of this study. The chapter concludes with a final analysis of the domain of the actual when seen through the sign of Two.

Secondness

A philosopher using Peirce's categories has to be able to count to three. To do so, she must also be able to get to two. Here the sign of two represents the teaching hand of experience, for within secondness, humankind is confronted with value choices, opposition, and resistance. Such secondness must precede any reconciliation of opposites and movements toward wider synthesis. Two is not one, because it presumes the presence of another. Furthermore, the status of the relation between that one and the other is entirely uncertain. The best that can be said is that the relation is always a relation of difference. This is the ground of the drag we feel in the conduct of our lives. It is a healthy opposition; without it we would sink into the primary narcissism of the infant. Dealing with secondness is what the child must do in order to become an adult. But before dealing with the realm of two, it is necessary to discover just what it is. Here is Peirce speaking on the meaning of secondness:

> [T]he Second is precisely that which cannot be without the first. It meets us in such facts as Another, Relation, Compulsion, Effect, Dependence, Independence, Negation, Occurrence, Reality, Result. A thing cannot be other, negative, or independent, without a first to or of which it shall be other, negative or independent. . . . The genuine second suffers and yet resists, like dead matter, whose existence consists in its inertia. [W]e find secondness in occurrence, because an occurrence is something whose existence consists in our knocking up against it. A hard fact of some sort; that is to say, it is something which is there, and which I cannot think away, but am forced to acknowledge as an object or second beside myself, the subject or number one, and which forms material for the exercise of my will. [T]he idea of second must be reckoned as an easy one to comprehend. That of first is so tender that you cannot touch it without spoiling it; but that of second is eminently hard and tangible. It is very familiar; too, it is the main lesson of life. In youth, the world is fresh and we seem free; but limitation, conflict, constraint, and secondness generally, make up the teaching of experience.[1]

Secondness is all about what people mean when they speak of "reality," "the school of hard knocks," and "the way things are." Furthermore, secondness emerges wherever relation dominates. Thus, the city as par excellence the ultimate exemplar of plural relations abounds in instances of secondness. Hard, resistant, factual, and objective, secondness is what makes city life so tough. If the city is the place where the experience of meaning is most forcefully encountered by humans, this is in no small part due to the ready presence of secondness. As an exceptional arena for the collision of values, the urban environment provides prime evidence for the accuracy of Peirce's description of secondness.

Secondness expresses itself on the physical, biological, and cultural levels of experience. It exhibits itself in the neverending round of engagements that mark the struggle between the made and the natural within the borders of city life: the park versus the street, the building versus the field, the monument versus the tree. In the realm of physical being, on the level of secondness there is always stark collision. The seemingly irreconcilable quarrels over the natural versus the artificial spring from looking at this opposition solely on the level of secondness. Such a stance provides ready grist for the polemicist's mill, but all such debates continue to miss the point of Peirce's semiotic metaphysics. For it is on the level of thirdness that adjustment and reconciliation of values can take place. In the realm of two there is only room for a fight. The physical indicates this when it reveals itself as the domain of blind force.

Similarly, on the biological level, it is the struggle for life and survival that is the index of secondness. Nature spills over with struggle, competition, and the fierce fight for resources. In the city such struggles largely take the form of economic competition and the inbuilt competitive structures of the modern market. While city life may appear more civilized than the leopard stalking its prey, there remains great truth in the phrase "cut throat" competition. Part Three details the characteristics of this commercial side of city experience. What I wish to stress here is that while competition is real and collision is actual, it is only one phase of a continuing process. As in the case of the physical dimension, biological secondness is but part of the story.

As anyone who has lived in a city knows all too well, the city is also the great realm of cultural collisions. Values smash into each other. Conflicting interpretations of experience scream out for attention. Rivalry rises on every street corner. In the city, cultural collision is incessant and intense, expressing itself everywhere through an index of struggle and strife. Whether it be one immigrant group challenging the ascendency of another or a neighbor raising the hackles of nearby residents, the appropriateness of Peirce's characterization of secondness as the realm of conflict is evident. And again, if a philosophy of urban experience merely leaves citizens at this ontological level, it has shortchanged human possibilities. One of the great ethical tasks still facing the contemporary city is to devise institutions and modes of discourse that can lift human experience beyond the potential cultural fierceness of the sign of Two. For just as existence on the level of firstness can induce a false sense of narcissistic completion, so also existence confined solely to the level of secondness brutalizes the human spirit.

Furthermore, the sign of Two need not always represent the savage fury of conflict. There can also be a gentle index pointing toward the presence of otherness. I recall April 22, 1970, in New York City. To mark this very first Earth Day, one of Manhattan's busiest streets, 14th Street, was closed to traffic along its entire length. So from the East Side to the West Side, a distance of some ten blocks, citizens were able to walk in the middle of the street. Among the many chalk graffiti that sprang up so quickly on the asphalt was the following: "Follow this line to see something very neat." The chalk line traced a path from First Avenue to Eighth Avenue, and there at the crossroads of 14th Street and Eighth Avenue, it terminated in an arrow pointing to a very small blade of grass that was growing through the asphalt. As an indexical sign, the line had brought me (and countless others) on a journey to secondness where the relation of a difference asserted itself in the most fragile yet evocative manner. Understanding how the sign of Two—the index—works its effects in city life is the next subject.

The Urban Index

Like the other ontological phases, secondness has its own characteristic form of representation. Peirce calls the sign of the representation of secondness an index. By this term he aims to stress the fact that in the realm of two what counts most is the direct relation between two events. An index is a sign of relation because it points directly to the presence of another. The most obvious example is that of a physical symptom that points to the presence of a disease. In the realm of two there is always another that must be accounted for. The index as a sign directly accounts for this presence of otherness within the domain of the real. The term itself—*index*—is highly instructive. It means that what is present indicates the presence of something else somewhere else. In the index to this book, for example, the words point to other places where the concepts signified are laid out in full relation. To quote Peirce:

> An index represents an object by virtue of its connection with it. It makes no difference whether the connection is natural, or artificial, or merely mental.[2]

The urban index represents the ways in which both the physical compulsion characteristic of urban life as well as important habits of urban interpretation express themselves. Both dimensions of the index—the physical as well as the cultural—can be best understood through what Peirce calls the "dynamical object." Recall that Peirce's semiotics is always triadic. It consists of an object to be represented by a sign to an interpretant. The object is therefore one important controlling character in the semiotics of city life. It is the object that in the first place determines the meaning of the experience to be interpreted. As was discussed earlier, this is the ground of Peirce's realism. There is an extramental object that grounds our semiotic experience. This is not the dyadic formula so favored by continental postmodernism. Therefore: In speaking of an "urban index" I am referring to real things that make a real difference in the actual lives of people.

I begin with the physical side of the urban index. By this I mean the largely spatiotemporal dimensions of urban environments. I have already developed this theme under the category of place. An index is a designator. Spacetime designations are crucial for urban existence. We speak of "the New York minute" and the urban skyline. Both phrases register some of the ways in which spatiotemporal physicality enters and becomes a part of city life. To be an effective dimension of city experience the urban index must be clearly legible. Thus, indices such as traffic lights and directional signs must be instantly recognizable. For the major function of an index is to convey in a straightforward and clearly legible way certain types and kinds of information. It is this "informational character" that is the most important dimension of an index.

Now, there is a world of difference between information and meaning. The essence of information is factual; the core of meaning is interpretation. The difference between these types of representation is what establishes the difference between secondness and thirdness.

A fact is resistant and compulsive. The semiotic function of an index is exhausted when it designates its information in a direct manner. If an index requires excessive decoding, it ceases to be an index, for it has violated the aim of indexical representation—the speedy transmission of factual information. An index that makes humans hesitate has lost its effectiveness. What the physical side of the indexical form must do is manifest in the most direct way possible its connection to the dynamical object. To repeat Peirce's definition: Its connection must be indisputable. As we shall soon see, it is the blunt force backing up indexical representation that makes "bottom line" thinking seem so undeniably and realistically true.

Similarly, the cultural or interpretive side of the index is established when well-understood conventions transform certain types of representations into indexical signs. It is these habits that make up a culture's way of negotiating its world. A rich set of such agreements is necessary if a culture is to survive in a universe beset by unexpected novelties. It is these traditions that are responsible for the efficient transmission of important cultural cues. When these cues fail to establish a harmony between a citizen and the urban environment, a sense of dislocation grows. And such moods can eventually settle into moods of despair. As the previous chapter argued, successful evolutionary behavior depends upon the adoption of appropriate signs. It is the special role of the cultural index to stimulate these adaptive responses with immediacy and clarity.

Interpretation always concerns itself with meaning. Therefore, no matter how direct the indexical designator, there is always a penumbra of interpretation that lingers around it. For example, on the physical level the red light causes an almost immediate response—Stop! But the church steeple can only function as an index for those familiar with a certain religious understanding of the spatial precincts of the sacred. The recognition of cultural indices requires a long apprenticeship in the fundamentals of a culture's worldview. In fact, as the next chapter will make clear, indices on the cultural level bring the discussion very close to the domain of thirdness and its special powers and characteristics.

An index stands halfway between one and three. To the extent that it slides toward iconic resemblance, it loses specificity; likewise, to the degree that it becomes a symbol of thirdness, its directional force is lessened. The index must stand its ground between one and three. Cultures that confuse the iconic with the indexical are in danger of falling into a cultural narcissism where only the unanalyzed wholeness of the present moment is given recognition. Sybaritic cities are a case in point. On the other hand, cultures that confuse the indexical with the symbolic overstress empirical facts and thereby make material reality the touchstone of all culture. Cities obsessed with their commerce and the economic side of the ledger are examples of a false identification of two with three. Rigid empiricism converts bottom-line thinking into the single most important normative measure for grasping the value of an urban environment. In this way, scientific materialism joins hands with capitalism to define the texture, tone, and significance of city life. The results of such indexical thinking are disastrous, for it prevents the full development of human potential. Frozen in the realm of secondness, urbanites never experience the generous generality of thirdness; consequently, possibilities for beauty and harmony become more and more remote from urban culture.

Empire Skyline

Skyscrapers so dominate the contemporary city that each episode of urban renewal seems to demand a new addition to the skyline.[3] In fact, buildings tend more and more to approximate the status of works of sculpture. Whether it is the Sears Tower or the Empire State, these indexical monuments point the way toward what seems most important in the contemporary city. I am talking about "Downtown," the marketplace, the commercial center—indeed, all those nodes of economic activity toward which urban traffic flows. I call it "Empire Skyline" for three reasons. First, the modern skyline does represent in the most direct indexical manner the empire of business and commerce as practiced in these days of advanced late capitalism. Second, as a skyline, these collections of buildings establish a horizon against which the seemingly most important dimensions of urban life are carried out. With such a background hovering over the spacetime of the city, it is no wonder that "bottom-line thinking" stands out as the most essential foreground activity of urban experience. Third, because they so dominate our urban existence, these monuments to commercial activity establish a symbolic penumbra within which their true nature as indices is camouflaged.

Recall the earlier discussion of symbolic reference, presentational immediacy, and causal efficacy. Symbolic reference is the mixed mode of perceiving the environment within which information from one of the two pure modes (causal efficacy and presentational immediacy) are transferred to an object symbolizing such information.[4] In the present case, what occurs with distressing regularity is the displacement of the indexical form of the skyscraper into a symbolic mode promising depth and a sense of continuity. This confusion of realms distorts the real meaning of secondness in such a way that thirdness, the full development of human culture, comes to be equated with the imperial skyline. In its dominance, it brooks no opposition. It is so obviously present that no arguments against its preeminence seem possible. The dazzling but shallow brilliance of perception in the mode of presentational immediacy overshadows whatever dim but important nuances of value the perceptual mode of causal efficacy might bring to the situation.

What is really only an index of the ontological domain of secondness now overshadows the complexity of urban life, steering it toward the fallacy of simple location. In this fallacy the citizen's mindset is dominated by the sheer vertical mass of the skyline, and our consciousness confuses commerce with the full reality of city life. Precisely because it is so immediately present, the empire skyline blots out any possibility of a thirdness that might be richer in value than the accumulation of wealth. Once again, scientific materialism has triumphed. But this time the victory is made all the more overwhelming by the false identification of index with symbol. Whenever secondness replaces thirdness as the guiding hand of process, there exists the danger that brute force and acts of punishment will rain down on the urban dweller.

What is only part of life comes to swallow up more and more of the energy, feelings, and intelligence of city life. Entrepreneurial imagination replaces real encounters with beauty and provides in its place empty substitutes. Commercialized experience dominates urban culture and all sense of graciousness and subtlety fades before the imperial power of market forces. Theories of urban design conflate economic progress with human progress and result in the tyranny of profit as the sole determining factor in the building of cities. And of course, the higher the buildings go, the more godlike we feel. The tower of Babel peeks through this dense skyline of economic traffic.

Consider what I called earlier the "canyon effect."[5] When the cultural signifier is really an index masquerading as a symbol, depth of meaning and the invitation to explore value is decisively cut off. All sense of nuance and variation is sacrificed to the demands of commercialism. Will it sell? replaces what is its environmental value? The bottom line obscures the many dimensions of contribution to others and the whole that is at the heart of authentic environmental participation. A singular blindness tends to accompany the growth of the empire skyline. What Blake called "single vision" not only affects actual human vision and feeling, it also causes culture to degenerate into a series of commercial additions to the skyline. What could have been a deepening horizon of feelings is now experienced as the sole reason for human existence. In the domain of capitalistic second-ness, there is no space for that which is simply beautiful in itself.

The canyon effect also distorts the human sense of time. In place of a multitextured present filled with varieties of potential experi- ence, there arises a sense of the sameness of the work week. Empire skyline beckons Monday to Friday in a never-changing set of de- mands for productivity. Weekends become temporal oases where re- pairs to the savaged human psyche are attempted. But all these deeply important human activities take place outside the arena bounded by the Empire Skyline. The past is only useful insofar as it can help predict an economically profitable future. The future is only significant insofar as it can turn into a scene of unexpected accumu- lation of wealth. The present is turned into a mere instrument for the furthering of the commercial empire. Time, and its environmen- tal depths, is steadily reduced to a thin occasion for profit. At the deepest level of our being we know this to be true, but we feel pow- erless to do anything about it. In the face of so large an empire, big possibilities of revolt vanish.

By turning itself into a cultural symbol rather than an index of one form of valuable human activity, the Empire Skyline prevents the meaningful growth of thirdness as a real factor in urban experi- ence. More and more, such things as goodness and beauty become subjects for weekend discussion. The Empire Skyline has already in- dicated the brutal reality of commerce as the guiding but invisible hand of city life. Empires are meant to reign and skylines dominate. As such they are precisely in line with the tone and tenor of second- ness as the presence of compulsive force. What is indicated in sec- ondness is the real effectiveness of external force as a controlling factor in the ongoing development of the process of reality. However, when the dynamical object is reduced to the premises of capitalism and the forces of the market place, the richness of what is really pos- sible for human dwelling is shrunk to an almost unrecognizable sliver of experience. It is testimony to the force of indexical second- ness that it can so obscure the other two dimensions of reality.

When secondness dominates an urban environment, a mood of fatalism settles over it. Brute force comes to represent reality itself.

Self-control, habits of restraint, and intelligence fade before the omnipresence of an "obsistent" reality. In one of his more fortunate metaphors, Peirce likened secondness and its indexical sign to that of the sheriff that enforces the law. It is necessary to have such powers available but it is not sufficient for a complete and comprehensive account of the real. Empires without armies are as unthinkable as skyscrapers without dominating height.

The Collisions of the Actual

Why is the actual so filled with harshness? Ought not there be some measure of reason even in the realm of the factual? A response to these questions involves an examination of the difference between the persuasive and the compulsive. The realm of the factual is discovered by observation and not by reason. Further, all this objectivity is exactly what it says itself to be: The expression of that which cannot be denied. Thus, what accounts for the harsh collisions in the realm of two is the peculiar perspective adopted by indexical signs. Every perspective is finite. And so is every expression derived from that perspective. Thus, the importance of two revolves about its own special perspective. This perspective is one of pure relation without any attempt at compromise. It therefore invites an exceedingly intense traffic in values. The category of transmission that is so much a part of this urban cosmology is prevented from fulfilling its categoreal obligations within the realm of secondness. The perspective afforded by the sign of Two is too limited to stretch beyond the obviousness of conflict toward the width of contrast needed to reconcile opposing dimensions. Scientific materialism can only provide facts, for it claims to have no overarching metaphysical framework. But as has been seen, this is not the whole story, for the commercial business of capitalism when allied to the philosophy of scientific materialism does indeed have theoretical underpinnings. The fact of striving and its consequent creation of a field of objective force combine to determine the meaning of reality as unceasing struggle for existence. Ayn Rand was not far off in calling her philosophy "objectivism." The social Darwinism inherent in the realm of two fits exactly the perspective of those who would see reality as confined to the collision of values.

But freedom is as real as determinism within a Peircean framework. What constitutes freedom is the equally important factor of reason as part of the ontological domain. This reason spreads itself beyond the axiological collisions characteristic of the realm of secondness. What is involved in this refusal to settle for secondness as the terminus of process is the difference between force and persuasion and between reason and the compulsive "obsistence" of the dynamical object. I am here reintroducing the theme of Platonic naturalism discussed in my earlier work, *Nature*.[6]

Secondness confines itself to patterns of reaction and therefore establishes the ground of a pluralistic metaphysical vision. It marks out a set of events that establishes relation as a way to be, and it thereby marks experience as, in part, a domain of struggle. Secondness is absolutely dyadic and therefore registers narrowness as a defining phase of the process of reality. It is also energetic in the sense that the dynamical object demands a direct relational pattern between the object signified and the index that denotes its presence. An understanding of secondness demands that action and reaction take a primary place in any attempt to describe the texture of the actual. This is what Peirce means when he compares firstness to youth and secondness to age. It is the harsh lesson of the sign of Two that not everything fits together in some type of saccharine harmony. Loss, displacement, tragedy, failure, and uncertain peril fill the interstices of the real. The next chapter will stress the ways in which the real moves from this sense of contraction to a fuller realm of emergent width. For now, it is all-important to point out the fact that the domain of blind force exerts a significant reactive presence within urban experience.

It is through secondness that collision occurs and thereby demarcates something from something else. In temporal terms, this ontological collision creates a rudimentary sense of "before" and "after" even as in spatial terms secondness determines the effective presence of the spatially contiguous as a mark of the real. Side by side, in stark opposition, or simply in indifference to the value of the other, the two that make up secondness bring into existence the effective reality of the external world. In jostling for a share in existence, the plural events that make up the urban environment express that tough texture of resistance that is part and parcel of the urban scene. The index as an energetic interpretant draws human attention to the automatic responsiveness of the external world when its order is challenged. Patterns that emerge do so by vying for a spatiotemporal niche within which they can express their unique value.

It is this competitive dimension of secondness that makes Platonic naturalism necessary for a right understanding of the domain of urban values. Without some standard for adjudicating the rival claims of urban patterns, no sense of axiological weight can emerge as a standard for judgment. Now, the construction of just such a normative measure is the burden of Part Three, Urban Praxis; still, at this point it is important to note the fact of harshness as a real element in the structure of the real. Any attempt to deny the brutal collisions that make up actual existence is doomed to failure for the simple reason that it is not realistic. In fact, an appropriate understanding of secondness demands the admission of tough reactive forces within the precincts of the real.

One meaning of secondness is that certain effects are inexorably produced. The destiny of these effects is not measured out within the realm of the sign of Two (except for those who would confuse an index with a symbol) but rather awaits the emergence of thirdness as a realm within which habits of generalized activity and meaning can take root. But that is getting ahead of the story. For now, the fragmented and separated character of the actual within one phase of its development needs to be underscored. Even the immediacy of the interpretive index is evidence of the stark divisions operating within secondness. The directness of denotative force residing within the index's interpretive power is the result of the closeness between the sign and its object. As Peirce might say, the symptom "indicates" the presence of the disease precisely because it is one index of its presence. This is what is meant by the quality of inexorability that characterizes an index.

To move toward more concrete matters: When urban environments are judged solely by their indexical qualities, then citizens are cheated of the full richness of city life. All talk of "bottom-line" realities and market forces as ultimate determinants of reality is symptomatic of a refusal to take a step beyond indexical thinking and entertain other, more generous ways of transmitting values within and across a city. Now, I am not denying the presence of market forces or the laws of economics and the theses of supply and demand used to explain commercial traffic in the age of advanced late capitalism. What I am doing is denying the metaphysical ultimacy of such doctrines. There is no reason to be found within the phases of the real sketched out in Peirce's semiotics to grant absolute importance to the production, distribution, and consumption of goods and services as the sole meaning of urban experience.

What makes such an interpretation of the real so inviting is the fact that within the sign of Two, the individual comes to reign supreme. It is the relation separating two entities that defines secondness. This creates an intellectually satisfying ground for those forms of laissez-faire economics that emphasize the struggle of individuals to gain an advantage over another. Taken to its extreme, this way of thinking results in a deadly identification of brute fact with personal and social value. Competition is seen as the inevitable outcome of natural forces that ought to be respected if a sane interpetation of human existence is to be developed. The struggle characteristic of secondness is simplistically (and literally) transferred to the human domain as an unquestionable principle guiding all forms of urban interaction. And in no small measure this manner of thinking brings about the second great historical model of the city—the machine. But a human being is not a machine.

The phallic ultimacy of the empire skyline indexically denotes the kind of forces at work within the urban environment. Struggle and then more struggle is the only actuality allowed room to express itself. All else is a sign of some kind of weakness, either emotional, intellectual, or some combination of both. The sign of growth of character is the ability to survive and thrive within such a brutalizing environment. The ontological toughness of secondness is to be matched by the cultivation of a personal toughness. For the rest, it ought to be as Carlyle suggested: the very public presence of a constable with a club. Force disguised as a law of nature and compulsion dressed up to appear as a law of the marketplace—these are the ways in which the forces residing within the domain of secondness are tamed and civilized. Now, all this has a very familiar ring. Freud endorsed such a vision in *Civilization and Its Discontents* and so did the materialistic philosophers of the Enlightenment.[7] Now, due to the dominance of scientific materialism such a vision of *Homo Economicus* has become a sort of dogma. No thinker hoping to appear orthodox dares challenge its supremacy. This is why a complete reconstruction of our metaphysical presuppositions is required if a real change in human consciousness is to be made possible. To halt before the harsh collisions of secondness is to endorse the truth of laissez-faire thought. It is therefore time to move toward thirdness as an equally real domain of city life.

Before doing so, I return to *Homo Urbanus*, the same young man described in Chapter 6 as experiencing the surprises of firstness. While he was "out," he also encountered rich indices of secondness.

During my great circle route I experienced more than the spontaneous and immediate presence of original and fresh value. Indeed, that was there, but so also were the collisions brought

*about by an environment steeped in secondness and its major
sign, the index. My path was crossed with an unending series of
sounds and smells. Was that $ 00.50 the knifesharpener yelled?
Did the vegetable man say carrots or broccoli? Not very good indices if I can't understand them. I guess one has to be a housewife
listening for many years to decode these indexical sounds? But
there is no mistaking that smell. Its plain old, freshly dropped,
very smelly dog shit. I must avoid that pile. The index was right
on. But what was it that brought the idea of a soda to my mind?
How did I get to Jake's store so quickly? I remember now. It was
the crash of the returnable bottles being loaded on the Pepsi truck
that collided with my thinking and set that desire going.*

*Likewise, it was the smell of the girls' perfume that made me
turn my head as I walked past them. And it was the shouts and
cries from the schoolyard that drew me to it. But not before I
crossed the street and dodged a car whose driver viciously honked
his horn and then gave me the finger. And all those feints and de-
fensive and offensive moves made by the fighters brought me a
clear sense of danger, even the real possibility of death. And the
blood that so scared me. It, too, was an index but so lacking was
my experience that I could not tell whether it was a symptom of a
serious injury or of imminent death. Cultural cues need to be
learned. But I, along with everybody else, certainly knew what
the police sirens were all about. And I was clued in enough to seek
sanctuary in a church. One is never too far from the Middle Ages.*

*Now, here is the real reason why I did not tarry on Brown
Place. I did not know its signs. It was forbidden territory. Neither
I nor my friends knew what happened in that particular part of
the urban scene. It therefore had a kind of semiotic gloom hanging over it. I knew there were prize fights a little bit down the hill
at the Forum. But those guys and their fans just moved quicky in
and out of the neighborhood. Like all tourists, they were ghosts as
far as I was concerned. In the shadows of Brown Place, most of
the language spoken was Spanish, a result of an enormous increase in the Latino population in the early and midfifties. Even
the subway stop was unfamiliar. I always got off at Third Avenue
and rarely went as far as Brook Avenue. The height of the apartment buildings also seemed ominous, as well as the huge blank
brick wall that housed the emergency exit of the Forum. In all my
years I had never seen anyone coming out of that door. I could
neither hear nor see very effectively, and what signs I could, never
were immediately decipherable. All the signs on Brown Place*

*were vague, shadowy, and lacking in the clarity so necessary for
identifying the presence of secondness.*

*So as I said earlier, I quickly turned the corner and made my
way up 137th. I neglected to mention the fact that my effort to be
cool and nonchalant was seriously challenged by the smell of the
sewer rot. It was so strong that I did not cross to the other side of
the street. In a quick glance I saw a foul index (heaped-up
sewage) that the sewer situation was even worse on the other side.
Maybe the cops did not stop me because the smell was so bad.
Maybe my cool was lost on them. Maybe, like me, they just
wanted to get away from the stench. I did and so did they.*

*I negotiated Willis Avenue by reason of clear indices; viz.,
traffic lights turning red and green. There were no cute little
pedestrian signs saying "Walk" back then. Also, the scream of a
siren, the honk of an auto, and the engine roar of a truck shifting
gears showed me the way to go and the way to avoid. It was
through a major investment in secondness that I made it across.
So now I faced the gauntlet lined up and waiting under the "El"
and my former teachers at the Brothers' school. I could not see
under the "El," it's too dark under there. Nor could I see the steps
of the Brothers' school. The "El" blocked my view. In the absence
of any sign of secondness I just took off and ran as fast as I could.
Now, this may be good strategy for a young teenager but it is not a
good thing for older people to do. Maybe that is why we feel so
helpless in the creepy darkness of a street that we do not know.
With the possibility of flight taken away, our most natural way of
avoiding trouble is lost to us. And with no signs, there is no possibility of intelligent action.*

*Then came the Gypsies, an absolutely positive parade of
signs. Here we are! Different from you—exotic, dangerous, our
clothes, our hair, our jewelry, our makeup—all different. But here
are some cultural cues. We play music. We make magic. We tell
fortunes. We read cards. Unlike you, we have a different relation
to the animal world. We even have a different religion (if you
want to use that word). These signs drew me out of my sadness.
On one level, they had the power to signify firstness, but on another level, they were an array of indices pointing the way to a
collison in values. We are happy. You are not. We are together in a
community. You are alone. This double layered quality of signs
whereby one can find firstness and secondness, icon and index together is the result of Peirce's recognition of the tranformative
power of all signs. There is a firstness to secondness and a*

secondness to firstness and, as we shall see, there is a similar polyvalence in thirdness as well.

    But enough philosophy. Back to the street! I am almost home now. Once again, I cross Willis by reason of direct clear indices. It is amazing how helpful true signs can be. They cut down the travel time for one thing. (Yet another indication that secondness and urban time are closely associated in marking out spheres of collision.) But before I reach home I must face one more collision. Remember that woman's face carved in stone and set over the basement entrance of Burke's bar and grill? Well, I told you it had different meanings to me. Sometimes a life-threatening Medusa. Sometimes a provocative Diana. Well, someone had taken a greasy crayon and disfigured this Janus-faced woman. It was no longer even recognizable as a woman. Nor could I guess what this new creature was supposed to be. Before, it never functioned very well as an index. It was too ambiguous. Now it could not function as any kind of sign. It had lost its semiotic power. I felt stunned and even somewhat lost. One can only imagine what happens to immigrants who come to America and are forced to move their own signs to the background and learn an entirely new system that now dominates the foreground. It is either that or the Gypsy way. Cognitive dissonance is much the same no matter where, how, or when it exists. Such a dissonance, I am sure, was at the bottom of my "Out," and "Nothing" responses. Why bother to describe and explain what others (especially parents) would critically receive. Sounds like a normal teenage reaction.

Chapter Eight

The Sign of Three/Continuity

As the real develops through the three primal phases of process, the fragmentation and separation of the realm of secondness yields to the continuity of thirdness. Likewise, the isolation of firstness is replaced by a sense of involvement and participation. When $1 + 2 = 3$, then there emerges a sense of a flowing urban whole that invites deep and profound human participation. This chapter examines that intense involvement under four motifs. I begin with a discussion of involvement itself as a primarily aesthetic mode of being. Then the symbol as the sign of effective thirdness is presented as the ultimate triumph of a fully human and fully urban semiotics. I then present the neighborhood as a concrete example of such thirdness. The chapter concludes with an analysis of the necessity of inclusion as a permanent urban trait. Thirdness as the establishment of rich continuity is the culmination of urban experience.

Involvement

It will be recalled that involvement was the mood that corresponded to the aesthetic order of width. This coherence between an order that calls for full participation and a felt reaction that acknowledges the generosity of such an invitation remains even more vibrant at the level of an urban semiotics. In fact, the ideal normative measures of intensity, integrity, wholeness, and depth are precisely the standards needed to appreciate the urban environment when it is functioning at its highest level. Involvement signifies the effective presence of internal relations as a major determinant of environmental value. It also entails the sustained recognition of matters of importance. Both aspects—internal relations and matters of importance—interlock to form the basis of the feeling of involvement that qualifies all forms of authentic urban thirdness. This is why it maps so congruently onto the form of urban goodness discussed earlier in Chapter Four. Goodness expressed through the experience of place is in fact an expression of ever-growing wholeness. When experienced appropriately, place ties together in a consummatory way the aspects of urban space and time. As a third, place is the most concrete symbol of urban goodness. It expresses wholeness and depth through the symbolic breadth felt within its precincts (see figs. 4 & 5, pp. 74, 75).

Internal relations come into being when the conditional features of an environment are made a major part of the growth of the essential features of that same region of value.[1] This means that the external dimensions of environmental processes are brought into the real internal constitution of the growing features of the environment. There is an exceptional intimacy established between the public nature of objectively achieved values established in the past and the private struggle of each nascent environmental process to express its own special environmental importance. What is objectively outside is transferred with minimal alteration into the subjectively felt inside processes of environmental growth. The result is a significant intensification of feelings of continuity and value. There is a seamless melding of the external world with the internal tegument of the environment that reveals the deep connections between various environmental processes. What was once shattered and in tatters is now felt as a deeply real field of mutual values.

The reciprocity spanning events within an environmental field thickens to such an extent that mutual commitment of resources and values is felt as a natural dimension of urban existence. Participation replaces isolation, because what is at stake involves all participants to a significant degree. This is urban engagement at its height for it lays a demand on all members to participate intensely in the creation and future direction of urban life. To be involved in urban affairs is to recognize the stake one has in the events of city life. Internal relations means the emergence of community as a distinctive normative measure guiding the actions of urban dwellers. Without such involvement community cannot develop the kind of roots needed to sustain a spreading width of mutually shared values. Now, community is the subject of Part Three's argument, but it is important to note right here that community has its natural roots within the semiotics of the urban environment.

Similarly, the creation of authentic involvement calls for the mutual recognition of matters of importance upon the part of those reading the urban code. A matter of importance is a value that is widely recognized as having great import for the continued growth of the environment in question. The phrase "vitally important matters" captures the sense of urgency for life that I wish to identify with thirdness. The reason for this insistence lies in the tendency to take thirdness as the most general and therefore the most abstract of the Peircean rhythms of existence and meaning. Nothing could be further from the truth. Thirdness is the dynamic sense of continuity that grounds all forms of concrete urban involvement. Without thirdness to drive the community forward into useful engagements, there would be no movement beyond either the alienated opposition of secondness or the lotus-eating amnesia often brought about by excessive involvement with firstness.

Intense involvement demands full participation by all actors in the urban scene. Now, secondness has already guaranteed the plural character of urban existence. As has been this study's contention all along, compatibility demands recognition of otherness. Tolerance is therefore essential for the growth of thirdness within the urban environment. This means that participation is not just allowed but also actively encouraged. Within the city the coerced display of agreement is the death knell for any kind of vibrant life. The aesthetic equivalent of tolerance is width. Now, width is the form of aesthetic order resulting from the effective presence of forms of intense contrast whereby what is different is put into a unity with what it is not. Earlier in this study, I argued that this aesthetic form was the very base of human consciousness, for it is grounded in the act of negative judgment. Consciousness is the affirmation of a negation. It recognizes what is not there as the backdrop against which real forms of otherness can appear. Diversity's effective presence is made possible by the contrasts spanning many differing identities. From this set of theses a very precise formula for increasing urban consciousness can be derived: the more contrast, the more awareness.

What is of course required is some vehicle for conveying this width of order and its felt involvement throughout an urban region. This is the function of the symbol, which acts as the vector of thirdness in city life. Effective symbols demand intense involvement. The act of participation that allows for the rich use of symbolic exchange determines both the quality and the meaning of city life. Weak symbols degenerate under the pressure of difference. They also can infect public discourse with an intolerable sameness that reduces all values to a similar form of triviality. The resulting indifference deprives the community of those institutions capable of generating novel forms of internal relations based on shared matters of importance. Effective urban symbolism supplies the oxygen city dwellers require to express the intensity, width, depth, and integrity of their social relations.

The Urban Symbol

Symbols make possible intelligence in action. They provide a rich spatiotemporal bed within which the union of feeling, thinking, and willing can flower. Here is Peirce's definition of a symbol:

> A Symbol is a sign which refers to an Object that it denotes by virtue of a law, usually an association of general ideas, which operates to cause the Symbol to be interpreted as referring to that Object. It is thus a general type or law, that is a legisign. As such it acts through a Replica.[2]

Three important aspects of this definition require underlining if the full import of thirdness as that which brings together the separated realms of firstness and secondness is to be understood. First, the symbol mediates between one and two by invoking the power of the dynamical object that is the final referent of Peirce's semiotic system. Second, this rise to generality is brought about by community agreement. This is to say, that convention is the only way in which symbols can come to be. As Peirce puts it:

> I do not think that the signification I attach to it, that of a conventional sign, or one depending upon habit (acquired or inborn), is so much a new meaning as a return to the original meaning. Etymologically, it should mean a thing thrown together, just as *embolon* . . . is a thing thrown into something. . . .

But the Greeks used "throw together" (*symballein*) very frequently to signify the making of a contract or convention.[3]

Finally, there is what Peirce means by using the term *replica* in his definition. Now he certainly does not mean likeness, as in the case of an icon, nor can he possibly mean indicative denotative force, as in the case of an index. Rather, he uses replica to underscore the communal force of agreement lying behind the authentic use of symbols:

> [A] conventional sign is neither a mass of ink on a piece of paper or any other individual existence, nor is it an image present to consciousness, but is a special habit or rule of interpretation and consists precisely in the fact that certain sorts of inkspots— which I call *replicas*—will have certain effects on the conduct, mental or bodily, of the interpreter.[4]

These three aspects—the dynamical force of the object, the conventional origin of the symbol, and the symbol's power to elicit communal involvement through embodied habits of interpretation—are among the special ways in which symbols function to create urban environments possessing great semiotic richness.

As Part One was at pains to demonstrate, the city is a real place with spatiotemporal regions existing independent of the mental landscape of its inhabitants. It is the dynamical power of the object to be symbolized brought into contact with appropriately effective interpretants that brings together these different sides of reality. As shall become clear, it is part of the import of Peirce's semiotics to heal the gap between the supposedly unbridgeable dimensions of the physical and the mental. What this means in the realm of urban experience is that effective symbols are capable of drawing ever-more significant meaning from the objects that are represented. There clings to such objects a quality of depth such that a certain ineffable dimension remains even after an understanding of the symbol has been gained. Again, this is the reason I added "symbolic breadth" to the semiotic domains functioning within urban goodness (see fig. 6).

In Part One of this book I argued that this was the effect of the presence of truthful beauty which, when experienced, brought about a truth of discovery that was beyond the dictionary meaning of words. Here I wish to stress the fact that this symbolic truth arises when felt intelligence touches upon the deepest strata of urban experience. There are times and places that form a kind of continuous totality immediately felt as important for the life and growth of the urban order. When maintained by a culture, such a symbolic register forms a range of potential meanings appropriate to the power of the dynamical objects present in the urban scene. When this occurs, dualisms of mind and body, mental and physical fade before the intense unification of experience made possible by the marriage of object and symbol. Such experiences are rare but they are the bedrock out of which a lasting sense of community arises. It is because of the special relation between the dynamical object and the symbol that intelligence-in-action as well as habits of effective response can inform the framework of urban discourse.

This special relationship represents the establishment of law as a generalized norm for interpretation and behavior. In turn, the law receives embodiment through the practice of habits that spread through the community and thereby witness to the regularized acceptance of such interpretive modes of symbolic reference. Since thirdness is by nature triadic, there is an immediate and undeniable tie to the "objective reality" existing within the urban semiotic situation. It is the function of the dynamism of the object yoked to the evocative power of the symbol to enforce all such habits of interpretation. Sign-object-interpretant form a seamless unity healing the gap between body and mind and theory and practice. Meaning continues to live in the city by reason of the effective presence of symbols evoking the dynamic power of the object represented. Actively directed intelligence demands the effective presence of symbolized thirdness.

The second aspect of the symbol is its "conventional" nature. It is the agreed-upon interpretation of the symbol that makes possible the initiation of a rule that future generations will follow. Now, the achievement of such community agreement is not solely an intellectual event. There must be more than mere cognitive assent behind a community's constancy. I would suggest that what really serves to bind the community together is the emotional weight involved in the effect that the sign has on the community of interpreters. This weight results in what I term "symbolic breadth," the power of symbol to evoke both wholeness, depth, and width at the same time. Thus, when Peirce defines the interpretant "as the effect produced in the interpreter by a sign," he surely means that the symbol is intimately bound up with what is of ultimate importance in the life of the community.[5] It is exactly at this point in the triad of semiotic forces that habit, survival skills, regularity, and belief mix together to form the deep structure of interpretation that must pervade any successful community.[6]

This brings us to the third aspect of urban symbols: the binding force that unites community members within the act of symbol recog-

nition. This is brought about in two ways. First, as George Herbert
Mead tells us (in a way to be discussed more fully in Part Three), the
act of communication is sealed when I am able simultaneously to recognize the sign of the other and to take it over into my own internal
constitution and then repeat it back to that other. What arises in this
semiotic act is the "replica" that Peirce identifies as the sign of thirdness. The second way in which the semiotic communal bond is fostered
is through the succesful habits of survival continually enacted by reason of these same signs. This is what is behind Peirce's insistence
upon the role of results in determining the meaning of concepts. If the
community cannot "feel" the successful results of its symbolic code, it
will not long survive as a unified entity. To call mind "intelligence-in-
action" is but to acknowledge the binding force of emotion that sweeps
over a community when something truly important has been
achieved. The conventional origin of the symbol is grounded in the felt
successes of a group that has moved from the precarious to the stable
over an extended period of time. The pragmatic maxim is a rule of
thumb for gauging the symbolized survival habits of the community.

But a human community is much more than a survival machine.
This is why the importance of aesthetics as the ground discipline of the
normative sciences is such a key to estimating the quality of life in an
urban area. It is also why what I have termed "the truth of discovery"
emerges as a significant philosophical issue as soon as urban thirdness
asserts itself. It is the union of habit, value achieved, and regular success that stabilizes a community's symbolic code. Felt intelligence
bears with it its own warrant of emotional security and satisfaction.
What was once a threat because unknown is now part of the community's endowment. Of course, what ultimately grounds the sense of
achieved worth is the capacity of the symbol to uncover more and more
layers of meaning within the dynamism of the object. In place of the
stupefaction often associated with firstness and the unintelligent collisions of secondness, there emerge the regularity, law, and smooth
sense of expected continuity that allow a community to grow and develop in further directions. With these aspects of the urban symbol in
mind, I turn to the most concrete instance of thirdness in city life.

The Neighborhood

Let us make a double return to Saint Jerome Church in the
South Bronx. I will begin with a description carved, like the others
in this part, from my memories of what it was like to live in this

neighborhood in the early and mid-fifties. Then I will actually revisit this same neighborhood in 1998. There will be differences but there will also be striking similarities. Thereby adding one more demonstration of how useful the vagueness associated with cosmology and metaphysics can be in siting what is important for authentic urban experience.

Homo Urbanus is still a teenager. Today, he is confining his walk to 138th street and its immediate environs. I begin at the corner of Alexander Avenue and 138th Street. There sits the church with its famous outdoor statue of Saint Jerome, the Lion, and the Lamb. How many times have I passed that particular sign of thirdness. Violence yoked to innocence by reason of the Word. Diagonally across the street is the 40th Precinct, home of New York's Finest. Only they were not so fine when they broke up our stickball games and confiscated (I would now say "stole") our gloves, bats and balls and whatever sums of money had been bet on the game. But there was no swarm of patrol cars in front of it nor was the precinct house ever blockaded by angry demonstrators. One could easily gain access by simply walking in the front door. But I start "up" 138th because I am heading East. I look ahead and see how the "El" tracks darken the middle of the street for right here they pass straight through the neighborhood on their way to Harlem. This is the last stop in the Bronx. As we so often said, we live down here where the Bronx begins. Next stop, Manhattan! The "El" neatly divides the block in two. Below lies the church grounds, above lie the stores and shops that made my neighborhood so familiar and such a place to call "home." Same thing on the other (north) side of 138th. Only there it was all apartment buildings and stores and shops. There was no break in urban space such as that brought about by the nuns' convent and garden or the Brothers' school. The street was a major artery for cars and trucks negotiating the twisting streets of the Bronx. In fact, 138th was anchored at one end by the Triboro Bridge and at the other by the Third Avenue Bridge. It was the connection between Queens on the one hand and Manhattan on the other.

I move underneath and then beyond the "El." I note Vaccaro's, where the most delicious Italian sandwiches could be bought, along with an Italian ice. The store had sawdust on its floor and on the open shelves were every variety of exotic product. Egg tomatoes, linguine (nos. 1–9), biscotti, olive oil in brilliantly shining gold cans that had handles! And the garlic, cheeses, meats, and sauces. But I only wanted an Italian small, no peppers. Back on the street, I spy the corner of Willis and 138th.

Now, here is a corner sufficient to tie the needs of the neighborhood together. On the other side of Willis is Beck's bakery. Hot cross buns in Lent. Across the street is Greenburgh's Hardware. My father would take me with him when scouting for tools and material to repair things at home. Greenburgh's was always worth the visit—locks, keys, chisels, brooms, paint brushes, trash cans, ladders, nuts, bolts, pliers, turpentine, paint, work gloves, light bulbs, plumbing fixtures always made of copper or brass, oil cans, shovels, nails in every size imaginable, vises, hammers, screwdrivers, saws, drills, bits, toilet plungers, hooks and eyes— everything a guy would ever need and all of it industrial size and industrial strength!

I forgot to mention that down the block was Klee's, a classic soda fountain with marble counters, real ice cream made right there, booths in back for boyfriends and girlfriends as well as for guys to do their thing and girls to do theirs. A juke box, candy jars with round open oval necks offering licorice, chocolate kisses, mary janes, Sultana taffy (once again, I could go on and on). But this was a place you could hang out. Great hordes of us did so. All day and all night.

But back to the corner of Willis and 138th. There, right across the street stood The Casino. Home of the movies, double features that would change weekly. Also, home of "The Chapter," which was really a continuing series chopped up into weekly episodes featuring Flash Gordon, Tom Mix, Hopalong Cassidy, and various detectives, good guys, and bad guys. It was the entertainment center of the neighborhood. Children at noon, teenagers in the afternoon, and adults at night. It had a balcony and an extraordinary chandelier. A marble floor in the lobby and huge posters in brass window frames announcing the coming attractions. There was a marquee hanging out front to keep you informed of what was playing. Everybody met at the Casino. As youngsters, you met your friends so that you could see the "Chapter" each week. Also so you could drive "the matrons" nuts by running across the stage and diving under the seats just when you were about to be caught. Goofy stuff, but enough to make "a world" within the dark confines of that movie house. I still remember the shock of coming out into the afternoon sunlight when you were used to the perpetual nighttime darkness of the Casino. Or the shock of coming out when it was cold, raining, or even snowing and you had

just seen a technicolor version of Uncle Remus, Br'er Rabbit,
Br'er Fox, and Br'er Bear gambolling in the warm southland.
    So within the confines of a single block, there were available
the major dimensions of a neighborhood. Places to meet, eat, see
each other, be entertained, encounter new values. Places whose
presence lent continuity to my life. Places where 1 + 2 did equal 3.
Community was anchored by these places as well as the neigh-
borhood schools, churches, and synagogues. And I have already
singled out the playgrounds as significant places where experi-
ences of firstness, secondness and thirdness could be had. Thus
did Homo Urbanus "have an experience" (in John Dewey's sense
of undergoing and doing) in the mid-fifties.

    And what is it like today? A monster surrounds the church on
three sides. It is called "The Mitchell-Patterson Housing Project." It
is a faceless brick wall with windows barred by iron cages. It reaches
some twenty stories and obliterates the sky as well as potential
views of all sorts. It also drives sunlight away from the street. A vast
number of families live in this "project." The stairwells are the hang-
outs of junkies and the elevators potential crime scenes. Only the
word "hopeless" comes to mind when it is viewed from the perspective of the church. It is all at once a prison, a corral, and a social
blight. The fourth side of the church opens onto 138th Street, which
has its own miseries and pain. It is bare of trees. There are many
closed shops and businesses with their doors boarded up or simply
burned away. A terrible roar of traffic rushes down the street, for it
continues to be a main artery for those seeking to move quickly
through the South Bronx and away from its supposed terrors. And
when the traffic slows down, the boom boxes pick up the urban beat
and give forth a constant reverberation of hiphop and salsa.
    And yet there is great hope on 138th Street. The houses are pre-
war "dumb bell apartments" whose windows and roofs are graced by
corbels, intricate carvings, and whose stoops still retain their neoclassical structure. In contrast to the Patterson Monster, there are
interesting places within this vernacular architecture—open spaces
within which human awareness can dwell if for but a moment. The
eye is not merely repulsed by a smooth, glacial wall of anonymous
brick. In fact, there are even patches of joyous colors to be glimpsed
on the outside of these damaged buildings, placed there by the Mex-
icans who are the street's latest immigrants. Now, at one level these
are sorry reminders of a once-vibrant neighborhood. But on the level
of this urban cosmology they are strong evidence that the neighbor-

hood still lives despite the drugs, crime, and poverty. Space and time have not been frozen out on this fourth side of the public square. Unlike the Project, not all resemblance of human being and dwelling have been cancelled out for the sake of an efficient, "bottom-line" way of housing the urban poor.

Spatially, there remains a vague backdrop of interesting and detailed achievement against which forms of life can take on new meaning. Temporally, the past still exists as a lure for future development. In the place of the modern faceless project with its bland walls and terrifying sameness and boredom, there lie the remains of a streetplace alive with intricate detail and potential meaning. This is something that can be worked on. For at this level, 138th Street is only the icon of urban firstness—"the Street" is a quality seeking full regeneration through the habits and symbols of its inhabitants. What remains to be done is to move 138th Street toward urban thirdness, the symbolic region where continuity, habit, and meaning grow into patterns of wholeness. Indeed, it is already happening. There is the Bodega Oajaquena, La Merced Mexicana, and the Delicatessen now named Mar del Caribe. Even Greenburgh's is still there side by side with May Hwong Lee's Chinese takeout parlor. But on inquiry I find that Greenburgh sold his place long ago. The new owner simply kept the sign. Still, right there is a symbol of the beginning of continuity.

Above all else, what is needed here is an interpretant that can tie together the neighborhood objects and the symbols employed to represent their values. By interpretant I mean precisely what Peirce meant:

> The first proper significate effect of a sign is a feeling produced by it. . . . This "emotional interpretant," as I call it, may amount to much more than that feeling of recognition; and in some cases, it is the only proper significate effect that the sign produces. . . . . If the sign produces any further proper significate effect, it will do so through the mediation of an emotional interpretant, and such further effect will always involve an effort. I call it the energetic interpretant. The effort may be a muscular one, as it is in the case of the command to ground arms; but it is much more usually an exertion upon the Inner World, a mental effort. It can never be the meaning of an intellectual concept, since it is a single act, [and] such a concept is of a general nature.[7]

The interpretant required for the resurrection of a neighborhood must have two characteristics. First, there must be a strong emotional tone

act of interpreting the symbol. Second, this felt recog-
ccompanied by some form of dynamic action.[8]
ue my walk on present-day 138th Street, I realize
nt in its history this street is on the verge of taking
on, once again, important and strong emotional power. The immediate cause of this resurgence is complex but certainly among the leading factors are the programs of the South Bronx Churches, the
neighborhood's community action organization. In the first instance,
this organization insists on creating an intensely felt quality to its
presence within the neighborhood's activities. It does this through
rituals ringing with emotional vigor. Parades, marches, demonstra-
tions, fiestas, prayer vigils, and other types of symbolic activities
serve to engender a sense of neighborhood responsibility, solidarity,
and belonging. At some level the members of a neighborhood must
"feel" that what is going on is "ours." The function of liturgy and political action is to provide precisely the kind of felt interpretant that
can bring forth a fresh sense of belonging at the neighborhood level.
And this becomes all the more difficult to pull off, since two thirds of
the area binding the church and the neighborhood has been de-
stroyed. The building of Mitchell-Patterson demanded that the
Brothers' school go and in turn this meant that more than 90 percent
of 137th Street, from the Church garden to the corner of Alexander
Avenue, was demolished. Effectively, there is no more 137th Street.
There is just a fake cul-de-sac pretending to some sort of suburban
elegance. Garbage gets piled up there and drivers wage war over
parking spaces. So much for good city place.

By calling such neighborhood activities "Actions," the South
Bronx Churches also provide the necessary dynamic component to
these newly felt instances of neighborhood belonging. Emotion is
wed to action. Effort comes after intense feelings of solidarity. What
is going on in the rebirth of Saint Jerome Church and neighborhood
is the creation of a community that can emotionally recognize its
own symbols and act on them with decisive intelligence. This is neither nostalgia for a long gone past nor overheated rhetoric concerning a future not yet born. It is, rather, the creation of an urban
semiotic appropriate for the South Bronx.

What is actually happening in this radically situated South
Bronx neighborhood in the making? At one level it is the dignified
simplicity of human beings trying to reclaim their lives in the midst
of the most terrible conditions. This is its political dimension. But
without the addition of a felt domain of meaning, such activity would
not last very long. It would disband after the first series of defeats.

What is required is an interpretant that can, *on recognition*, summon up new reserves of feelings of mutuality and necessary effort. This is what turns a neighborhood around in a lasting way. For it provides a rich semiotic network of meaning within which participants can live and find themselves. Mere political sloganeering will not suffice nor will well-intentioned interventions by various government agencies. What the South Bronx Churches have managed to create—against all odds—is a symbol of urban rebirth concretely tied to the lives of its community members. In many ways they have achieved what the radicals of the '60s meant by a truly participatory democracy. They have welded the spiritual to the political.

In offering this concrete example of a neighborhood in the making, I have been trying to make visible and real the true value of thirdness as a dimension of reality. The importance of symbolic action should now be evident. Through the effective presence of feelings of belonging, it makes possible the kind of human solidarity required to bring about effective action. It brings the affective and the energetic domains together so that authentic human participation can take place in the South Bronx. What I have been at pains to demonstrate in this discussion of an urban semiotics is the absolute importance of communication as a means to human growth and betterment. Until it is recognized that we are fundamentally communicating beings, there will not be any urban form of living that can effectively and consistently mold human behavior into modes of excellence in action. This means that other human beings are as important to me as I am to myself. Now this directly contradicts the central tenets of advanced late capitalism and contemporary liberalism. It gives priority to social life over individual existence and it subordinates such beloved concepts as privacy, personal freedom, and individual choice. In the last section of this chapter, I will argue for the appropriateness of this point of view, not from the perspective of any political ideology but from the rational demands of a fully human semiotic.

Inclusion

An essential part of the domain of the logical and the reasonable lies in its capacity to make inclusion the primary category of urban existence.[9] As Peirce (and along with him James and Dewey) maintained, reason grows in spots and patches. It starts in one corner of experience and when its value stabilizes, it can then be transported to another. I have already discussed the emotional and dynamic interpretant in the previous discussion of the neighborhood as the symbol of thirdness. In this section, I wish, as it were, to get under the skin of the community and see what constitutes both the force and the bond of its directed intelligence. This is best done by examining the relationship between reason and what Peirce termed the ultimate logical interpretant.

What then is reason for Peirce? It is certainly associated with some form of finality, since it resides in the region of thirdness. Also, it is intimately connected with the community for, as we shall see, it is the community that gives the logical interpretant its ultimate warrant. Other characteristics of reason include factors of habit, regularity, law, and generality of application within a range of assured results. Reason also has to do with the creation and support of intelligence-in-action. Likewise, growth as well as stability require the active presence of reason. But in all these aspects of reason, one factor stands out as supreme in Peirce's understanding of the achievement of reason: habit as experienced by members of the community. For habit unites reason, gesture and action. It is what Sandra Rosenthal has called the all-important "living idea" of Peirce.[10] For "it is habit that binds together into a systematic unity the various possibilities, thus making the logical interpretant possible."[11] One cannot talk about reason without speaking of habit, just as one cannot talk about pragmatic consequences without talking about meaning. Consequences that are for the most part predictable are really successful responses to the existential collision that qualifies secondness. Thirdness smooths out the interruptions in human experience by establishing patches of reasonableness that can then spread to unite other dimensions of human life. To look for consequences is not merely to identify effects. It is, rather, much more a matter of finding the lines of continuity existing within nature and culture.

Peirce summarizes his understanding of the relation between interpretant, logic, reason, and habit in the following way:

> [T]he real and living logical conclusion *is* that habit, verbal formulation merely expresses it. I do not deny that a concept, proposition, or argument may be a logical interpretant. I only insist that it cannot be the final logical interpretant. . . . The habit alone . . . [t]he deliberately formed, self-analyzing habit—self-analyzing because formed by the aid of analysis of the exercises that nourished it—is the living definition, the veritable and final logical interpretant. . . . But how otherwise can a habit be de-

scribed than by a description of the kind of action to which it gives rise, with the specification of the conditions and of the motive.[12]

Thirdness expresses itself through the habits of interpretation that are established within regions of experience. It is the continuity spanning meaning, action, and interpretation that establishes the reasonableness of thirdness. In sum, if one be the sighting of value and two be the recognition of opposition, then reasonableness is the experience of finding a way between the exclusions marked out by one and two. To count to three is to exercise the fundamentally reasonable act of inclusion. This conjunction of reason and inclusion is at the heart of what makes a great city. And as Part Three shall show, it is also at the heart of the unification of truth, beauty, and goodness that takes place whenever an enlarged harmony of habits is experienced.

Felt intelligence is the mode of knowing required to experience the reasonableness of thirdness. Peirce calls it abduction, and it signifies the act of reason that unites emotion, effort, and understanding in a concrete instance of interpretation. When fully coordinated with a rich communal life, felt intelligence breaks in on us "like a flash" . . . for "[I]ts end is, through subjection to the test of experiment, to lead to avoidance of all surprise and to the establishment of a habit of positive expectation that shall not be disappointed. . . . This is approximately the doctrine of pragmatism."[13] It is important to underline the factors needed to establish thirdness as a real presence. There are at least four such factors: firstness, secondness, thirdness, and a habit-creating community. It is the contention of this study that the city—ancient, classical, medieval, modern, and postmodern—is humankind's concrete attempt to establish such a place of meaning. And, it is here in the symbols replicating a community's sense of achieved semiotic inclusion that Lynch's final model for the historical development of a theory of good city form— the organism—finds its true resonance. But an organism bent on learning through shared meaning needs a praxis to ground and stabilize its habits of interpretation.

This presentation of an urban semiotic can be enhanced by a return to the cosmological scheme developed in Part One of this volume. It will be recalled that "Pattern" was the category used to identify the structures existing in the mesocosmic world. Now, I argue that a habit is essentially a pattern of meaning that can be consistently enacted with the reassurance that its effects will remain relatively stable throughout a particular urban environment. This means that a habit is a real part of the environment and therefore has important existential consequences. It is neither a mere mental event nor simply a routinized reaction to certain conditions. What a habit does is establish a locus of meaning within an unsettled region of experience. It serves to anchor reasonableness and at the same time provides an opportunity to foster continuity and growth as the exigencies of the particular situation unfold. Good and true consequences are therefore meanings that fit the needs of the situation. Furthermore, consequences that are beautiful enlarge the patterns of existing meaning in order to include more and more difference. Thus, the fittingness of a particular habit is in direct proportion to the way in which it enhances a situation so as to bring about more and more inclusion. Reason and beauty remain close partners within the experience of thirdness understood as the act of interpreting symbols through the skills of felt intelligence. Finally, the habits needed to thrive in city life are decidedly different from other ways of human dwelling. This entire Part Three is a massive argument for distinguishing between the city and the village while at the same time maintaining an essential connection between them.

If felt intelligence and habit unite in the act of abduction, it is only because the neighborhood establishes a locus of meaning where the fitting consequences of good habits can be directly experienced. This can be seen in the difference between the index understood as the representation of secondness and the symbol as the sign of thirdness. What prevents the index of the Empire Skyline from being a symbol of concrete reasonableness is precisely its lack of inclusion when it comes to identifying all the values ranging through a situation. "Bottom-line thinking" is too abrupt an act to qualify as concrete reasonableness. True enough, adherents of this doctrine are always promising that it will affect all lives for the good, but the history of advanced late capitalism remains that of an agency built on the backs of the many for the sake of the few.

The theme of this chapter is continuity rising out of the capacity of reason to actively transform conflicts into contrasted levels of concrete reasoning. This active intelligence is felt through the habits secured by generations of humans working together in community, first in order to survive, then in order to thrive, and finally in order to enhance their experience in the deepest ways possible. Reason as the way to continuity is also therefore the way to growth, for what felt intelligence does, is feel the lines of continuity bridging occasions of experience. In this way it weaves a place for meaning through the inclusion of difference into the fabric of city life. Now, sometimes reason has to force its way in. We have the sorry history of urban riots as testimony to this act of secondness hoping to become thirdness. There are always gaps and surprises on the road to concrete reasonableness, but eventually it is the hope of every community that inclusion can mark its historical development. Social organizations that refuse such an obligation to grow are really enclaves, not communities. The recent history of the Balkans proves the gruesome effects of habits that produce exclusionary consequences. In weaving an open place for thirdness, a community expresses the ideal values of intensity, integrity, depth, and wholeness. Thus, the categories of Part One join hands with the semiotics of Part Two to suggest the following provisional conclusion. The city stands as that special human institution that throughout evolutionary history has always been the source of reasonable answers to individual and social crises. It does so by uniting intelligence, feeling, and action. Felt intelligence is activated by habits that enlarge the place of meaning. So, to pick up the argument of my earlier work on nature: Aesthetics as the root of reason and ethics as the directed habits of action come together to form the flesh and blood of city life. Jurgen Habermas expresses what this means in terms of understanding the demands of a worthwhile urban praxis:

> [I] see the great achievement of Peircean semiotic in its consistent expansion of a world of symbolic forms beyond the limits of linguistic forms of expression. . . . He thereby opened new realms to semiotic analysis: for example, the extra-verbal sign world, in the context of which our linguistic communication is embedded; the aesthetic forms of representation, especially the formal repertoire of nonpropositional arts; finally, the abductive decoding of a symbolically constructed social world upon which thrive . . . our everyday communicative practices. . . . Our lifeworld, which is semiotically constructed from the bottom up, forms a network of implicit meaning structures that are sedimented in signs which, though non-linguistic, are nonetheless accessible to interpretation. The situations in which participants to an interaction orient themselves are overflowing with cues, signals, and telltale traces; at the same time, they are marked by stylistic features and expressive characteristics which can be intuitively grasped and reflect the "spirit" of a society, the "tincture" of an age, the "physiognomy" of a city or of a social class.[14]

Thus, the ultimate act of city intelligence is carried out through habits of abduction, which are creative acts of beauty functioning through the power of reasonable inclusion. It remains to employ these tools in the search for an adequate urban praxis for the contemporary city.

PART THREE

URBAN PRAXIS

If Peirce is correct about the progression from firstness to thirdness, then every human activity must be marked by some form of continuity. This doctrine is best understood in light of the pragmatic contention that all forms of learning are equally forms of doing. It is also evident in the close relation established between art and science as qualitatively similar forms of intelligence-in-action. Finally, it is the doctrine of thirdness that ensures an affective as well as a logical dimension to every act of human learning. Part Three seeks to take advantage of this nondualistic vision of intelligence-in-action by offering a praxis for urban dwelling that will include the intellectual, the practical, the voluntary, and the affective dimensions of human praxis. In effect, I am offering an urban curriculum that examines the major problems confronting contemporary cities as they seek to become places of wholeness within which human learning and growth can take root and flourish. Part Three, Urban Praxis, is continuous with Parts One and Two with this difference. Where Part One stressed the significance of the spatiotemporal texture of the city and Part Two focused on the symbolic meanings arising from urban existence, this concluding part concentrates on the transformative dimension of human action when it allies itself with intelligence.

The problems to be examined include the role of intelligence within city existence, the importance and possibility of community, the meaning of justice, and the reconstruction of the theory of a good city. In considering these matters the subject matter will be informed by the cosmology and semiotics worked out in Parts One and Two. What I hope to do is reap the rewards of the systematic speculative philosophy articulated up to this point. My major resources will be the great social pragmatists, George Herbert Mead and John Dewey. Both these American philosophers provide important insights and suggestions for a reworking of the city and its major institutions at the end of this century. Whether the city will actually have a future in the twenty-first century depends largely upon how much room for growth is left within this important evolutionary form. The comprehensive vision afforded by systematic speculative philosophy provides a thoroughly applicable answer to this question.

In moving from speculative cosmological philosophy to a semiotic framework for urban meaning and finally to this concluding analysis of urban praxis, I am following John Dewey's advice that the separation and divisions we use to divide up our disciplines often produce negative results. They split experience into unrelated wholes and thereby give a false picture of the real world. Similarly, I have been at pains to find ways to connect and distinguish the city from other forms of social dwelling. The difference between the city and other ways of being together in a human way lies in the critical mass achieved by the quantitative increase in population in the city. This creates a demand for qualitatively different modes of communication. On the other hand, the continuity that connects the city to alternative forms of social dwelling is grounded in the fact that all forms of being together share a similar character: To be together in a human way always demands a real but seldom consciously acknowledged backdrop of spacetime. It is against this backdrop that forms of urban goodness as well as the phenomenon of city place can find special expression. The same need for a stable spacetime structure as well as important (usually sacred) places can be seen in all the forms of human dwelling about which we have reliable knowledge. For example, the city connects with the village by reason of the essential need for humans to communicate. It differs by reason of a quantitative shift in critical mass that in its turn produces a qualitative difference between these forms of dwelling. John Dewey expresses clearly what is at stake:

[T]he chief obstacle to a more effective criticism of current values lies in the traditional separation of nature and experience, which it is the purpose of this volume to replace by the idea of continuity.[1]

Thus, the difference between the city and smaller units of human dwelling (for example, the village, the town, the campsite) is one of species to genera and not genera to genera. But I am uncomfortable with such Aristotelian distinctions. To paraphrase both Aristotle and what I have argued throughout this work; "I am a friend of Aristotle but a greater friend of Plato," who sought the truth in the weavings and not simply the threads of reality. Separation must always yield to continuity; otherwise, we are condemned to live in an unlivable world. There is a reason why I have italicized my concrete examples throughout this volume. I ask the reader to go back over them and see if any of the experiences I describe could have happened in exactly the same way in other forms of social dwelling. Finally, I repeat my central thesis: The city is the site of current evolutionary change in knowing, feeling, and doing. It is the cultural form of the good as so far experienced in the history of this planet. What it needs is an effective urban praxis that can eliminate what is wrong in the city and develop what is good.

■ Chapter Nine

Intelligence-in-Action

A major thesis of this study is that human beings are primarily learners and that the city is the special place for such learning. There is more, however, for as Christopher Alexander argued, the city is at its normative best when it learns to pursue wholeness as its guiding measure for excellence. In this chapter I develop the thesis of urban praxis as the process of learning forms of wholeness through the themes of symbolism, communication, meaning, and action. Understood together, these aspects of learning fill out the doctrine that intelligence-in-action is always a form of doing and ought never be equated with a disembodied intellect standing apart from its concrete circumstances. Learning is a unified process of thinking, feeling, willing, and doing that takes place within social existence and not outside it. It is such a concept of intelligence that is at the heart of this American version of urban praxis.

Symbolism

The forging of symbols is primarily an act of transformation, for it is through symbolism that the environment is remade into intelligible patterns of meaning.[2] These meanings in turn serve to mark

159

out the regions of importance that humans will concentrate on in order to survive, thrive, and grow. There are four major dimensions to this critical activity of symbolization. First, a symbol always has a double character for it mutually transforms both the knower and the environment. What ties together the knower and the environment is the felt intelligence granted by the aesthetic reenactment of appropriately effective symbols. Second, the medium through which this dual transformation is carried out is the community's endorsement of these particular patterns of aesthetic and emotional identification. Third, the meaning of a symbol in community life is achieved by repeating in our own individual actions the significant gestures of others. Fourth, this symbolic action enables intelligible form (universality) to sink into concrete instances (particularity) by reason of the community's consistent acknowledgment of the appropriateness of such gestures. Thus, symbolism is the instrument the community employs to establish those "patches of reason" that it hopes to cultivate so that a consistent spread of rationality can be felt throughout its confines.

In terms of the cosmological scheme developed in the first part of this book, symbols are to be located within the category of transmission in general and as propositional presences in particular. A symbol is therefore the transformation of reality into a mode of being that can be handled intelligently by humans. It is a marked instance of the power of abstraction, for it represents the powerful presence of an absence. Its proper use involves the entertainment of its meaning rather than the assertion of its correctness. In this act of imagination, what is tested, prodded, and ultimately pushed forward is the power of the symbol to deliver into human hands a way of approaching reality that is effective, useful, and compelling. Symbolism allows us to work fruitfully with the domain of the possible. It enlarges our felt reaction to environmental pressures beyond the level of the merely physical. Through symbolism, the material dimension is transformed into the field of felt intelligibility. From there, steps toward the creation of intelligence-in-action become feasible and practical.

Likewise, in terms of the urban semiotics sketched in the second part of this study, symbolism is the act whereby thirdness is identified and made ready for use. A symbol is more than an icon and more than an index. It represents the integration and internalization of successful habits of interpretation. As such, a symbol is the most direct route to feeling the real presence of intelligibility within urban regions. As Sandra Rosenthal has put it: "The general idea is the mark of the habit."[3] When symbols become deeply rooted in sensory cues and actions, they result in the types of structures that communities can employ in order to negotiate effectively their respective domains. Thus, the appearance of a symbol is the royal road to urban intelligence-in-action. Such symbolism must be learned by doing. For whether it be the act of learning how to spell or read or communicate directly with another human, it is the symbol that carries the weight of intelligence into action. Symbolism is the means whereby learning through feeling, willing, and doing is shaped into a practical unitary structure. When it occurs in an established pattern of communication, then the great transition has been made from felt intelligence to intelligence-in-action. No urban praxis can be successful without such a development.

This is also the reason why perception in the mixed mode of symbolic reference marks the height of active intelligence. When humans perceive their environment, symbolism is already at work. The significance of the four levels of aesthetic order should now be immediately evident. For without a certain narrowness woven onto a backdrop of vagueness, the possibility of wide symbolic resonance being intensely felt throughout a community's life is decidedly diminished. In a similar manner, the importance of using the four ideal norms of intensity, integrity, wholeness, and depth to measure the effective presence of symbolism in a city should also be clear. The more intense, integrated, whole, and deep the symbol, the more actively intelligent will be the praxis in a given urban environment.

In sum, symbolism is the way in which human beings feel the value of the real by transforming it into manageable proportions. It is the essential modality of intelligence-in-action for it embodies the category of transmission whereby values are transferred around environmental and cultural systems. In its propositional modality, symbolism is also the chief way in which the persuasive agency of thirdness makes its presence directly felt. And finally, in the vibrancy of perceptual experience, the world of urban experience can on occasion take on the symbolic richness required to do justice to the beauty of human dwelling. This miracle of transformation is matched by another astonishing human achievement—the act of communication.

Communication

It is the great contribution of George Herbert Mead to have laid out the basic forms and activities involved in the human act of communication.[4] In following Mead's account of this deeply human activity, I wish to stress the importance of the following dimensions: "Gesture," "continuity," "participation," and "habits and institutions." Taken together, these themes comprise the most significant aspects of the act of urban communication. They are therefore vital for the healthy functioning of any city.

A gesture is a propositional form embodied in human flesh. It has the character of rationality deeply embedded in its composition. It beckons us to entertain its meanings. A gesture is a plan of action structured around a certain pattern of meaning. But it is also a very specific pattern of meaning. For to understand a gesture I must have in some way or other already performed the gesture myself. This is to say that in understanding a gesture I take the form of the other into myself and repeat it back. In this way, I "know" what the other says because I stand in for the other. By sharing in the roles announced by the gesture I come to understand the intentions of the other. Thus, purpose is the key to both understanding and enacting gestures. And whenever purpose is present, then intelligence is also there. The gesture is therefore the preeminent symbol whereby I take part in intelligence-in-action. Without symbolic interplay there could be no response to the action of others. Neither could there be any divination of the aims and plans of others. Without gestural articulation, the world would be unintelligible and devoid of purposes.

Continuity is the essential feature required for the shaping of an effective urban community. Without the transitional smoothness offered by continuity, intelligence-in-action would be even more sporadic and fitful than it already is. I have offered an analysis of the concept of continuity in the previous chapter under the rubric of semiotic thirdness.[5] In what follows, I wish to explore what I call the "social body" as the real ground of continuously felt active intelligence in city life. By this term, I intend to underscore the fact that communication takes place first of all on a prereflective level that is the outcome of the lived body in its intelligent dwelling in the world.[6] A spontaneous "grasp" of situations in their environmental import is carried out by the human body long before anything resembling discursive thought appears on the scene. Furthermore, this act of prehending the environment in terms of its relative importances is dependent for its growth and development on the emergence of an actively intelligent community alive to the various values in its environment. John Donne's poetic insistence on the connections between humans is lived out concretely in the act of communication: Indeed, "no man is an island." And further, this act of sharing is never merely a matter of learning a code of abstractions. Such an understanding of human communication (favored by structuralists like Saussure and Jakobson) impoverishes the social life of the mind by reducing it to mere acts of puzzle solving. Rather, the way in which humans learn to communicate is through robust, full-blooded participation in the social body of the community.

This act of incorporation is carried out through the inheritance of well-integrated threads of somatic behavior, by which I mean gestural propositions capable of almost immediate recognition. Thus, I wave my hand and the other says, "Hello." A substantial part of the social education of each individual is given over to mastering these regularized reactions to environmental forces. The social body is incorporated into each individual's personal body as a kind of "shadow soma"—a mode of somatic alignment that begins with various types of nervous disturbances and ends in a continuous sense of appropriate habitual reactions to a variety of situations. The distance between the gesture and the word is as narrow as the distance between feeling and thought. Effective communities take advantage of this uncommon human capacity to establish firm and effective networks of communication.

It is this sense of thick webs of relations grown by communities that is behind Mead's characterization of social life as "the conversation of gestures." The phrase is a fortunate one for it captures both the fluidity of community life and its stable mooring in recognizable symbolic forms. What weaves this matrix of signs into effective webs of meaning is the fact that each member of the community repeats back to the other what the other has shown him or her. In so taking on the role and symbols of others, I live through the effective presence of "the generalized other." In its turn, this act of establishing a corporeally shared field of meaning grounds the concreteness of all the various types of "internal relations" possible within community life. There is no ultimate separation between the form of the gesture and the fact of its interpretation.

It is through the act of communication that I occupy the standpoint of others and invite their reality to wash over my being. Thus, "participation" in the act of communication is never merely an intellectual enterprise. Any process of authentic communication must entail the felt reenactment of the experience of others. This is the ground of solidarity and identification. To the extent that such sharing is missing or in any way compromised, the community's life is threatened. Finally, this is why habits and institutions are the essential life forms of every community worthy of such a name. Habits make readily available the generalized responses of the community to its environment. Upon their effectiveness depends the very survival of communal life. As we have already seen, "the habit is the sign of the generalized idea." Similarly, institutions ought to be understood as public expressions of the established ways in which sustaining and novel communal responses to environmental challenges are successfully met. They are vitally important forms of life and not necessary evils to be put up with by impatient individuals. Just how important such institutions are will be seen when the question of capitalism as a form of community life is taken up later in this study. Here again, I wish to stress the fact that levels of cultural participation are similar as well as different when seen across the spectrum of types of social dwelling. The city is the same as the village in terms of the presence of communication but different in terms of how the act of transmitting symbols is carried out. No phone ever rang in the village of Madawska, Maine, prior to its invention. They communicated then and they communicate now, but there is a very real difference in quantity and quality.

The act of communication begins in the primal act of somatic gestural experience and ends in the fashioning of deeply symbolic experience. The difference between the beginning and the end is marked out by the degree of continuity, participation, and institutional growth achieved by the communities employing the symbols to transform their universe of concerns into a living thriving environment. Thus, the reconstruction of urban experience must involve an appropriate understanding of the interplay between symbol and communication in city life. For the city is the place of signs, and citizens are those who live in communication with each other. They are not and never should be atomic selves isolated from each other.

Meaning

In the course of this study, urban activities have variously been called events, patterns, *haeccitas*, and symbols. To understand what is involved in the rise and creation of meaning it is necessary to concentrate on one aspect of these "final real things" which in their complex relations make up the texture of every urban environment. This study and its companion volume, *Nature*, have developed an intricate theory of harmony.[7] In every urban experience what is at play are entwined sets of harmonic unities. In this section I wish to employ that theory to define just exactly what is involved in the act of meaning.

Every harmony exhibits a pattern of relations. Sometimes, what stands out is the pattern and what is submerged are the relations.

Other times see the exact opposite. As when particular relations dominate the pattern. The term *meaning* designates the relative weight given to the pattern and its component elements. By reason of the values assigned to either the pattern or its constituent relations an emotional tone collects around such harmonies and it is this resonance of felt value that is at the heart of all acts of meaning. I therefore argue that at the bottom of every act of meaning there resides a purpose or an aim that calls out for recognition. Thus, the pattern as a bare "It" collects around itself the values aimed at by its arrangement of relations. This allows for the identification of meaning with purpose, for within the harmony there resides a unity of emotional tone and felt intelligence. Thus, the meaning of every object is the pattern of action defining that object. The purpose underlying the constructed harmony is the key to understanding the meaning of the event. An effective "city mind" therefore involves the capacity to point out meanings (plans of action) to oneself and others.

In Chapter Three of *Philosophy in a New Key*, Susanne Langer points out the importance of understanding meaning as the outcome of a purposive arrangement of parts within a whole:

> Meaning is not a quality but a *function* of a term. A function is a pattern viewed with reference to one special term around which it centers; this pattern emerges when we look at the given term *in its total relation to the other terms about it.*[8]

Now such a theory of meaning is usually classified as a functionalist one. To a degree, such a designation is true, but it is not true if it implies that the meaning of an object is exhausted by its effects. Such a view is precisely the crass misunderstanding of pragmatism that Peirce, Mead, and Dewey fought against. For if meaning is not a property of terms but rather a function of the relations of parts to wholes, then any attempt to reduce significance to isolated effects or simple consequences is itself a falsification of meaning. Furthermore, this theory of meaning implies that meanings do not change but rather are replaced by other meanings. And this act of replacement is carried out by shifting the relations and patterns constituting the whole/part configurations of the social body. Thus, effective social change is a matter of evolving more appropriate meanings. The act of intelligence-in-action concerns precisely this art of reconfiguring the relations making up city life. Whenever charges of scientism are brought against the pragmatic tradition, it is usually a misunderstanding of meaning that is at work. The pragmatic tradition is not concerned with the crass manipulation of material consequences for the sake of some cheap form of success. Neither does it see effects in isolation from each other. It is always the patterns and relations between events that matter. Thus, as was the case with the natural environment, aesthetics understood in the sense of feelings arising out of the relations between parts and wholes becomes the prime discipline for any normative understanding of city life.

Meaning is therefore closely allied with feeling and requires for its articulation and analysis deft sensitivity to the interplay between competing patterns of relations. This is what I take to be at the heart of Alexander's *New Theory of Urban Design*. It is never a matter of one cause in isolation from all others. It is always a case of many causes arranged in a constellation of relations and that is exactly the primary meaning of a harmony. I repeat this at the risk of boring the reader because it is much too easy (given our cultural assumptions) to equate harmony with matters of taste, or even the pretty, or, what is worst of all, the nice. Harmony is not sweetness. Rather it is the way in which things come together into patterns of relations that are more or less meaningful in terms of the feelings generated by these modes of togetherness. Think of the feelings aroused by Mozart's Piano Concerto no. 21. Then think of the feelings aroused by Bob Dylan's "Like A Rolling Stone." Different arrangements of relations create different feeling tones, which in turn make possible different reactions. Both are harmonies but decidedly different in scope, purpose, and cultural effect.

To be meaningful is therefore always to be in relation to something else. The wholeness, depth, intensity, and integrity of the meaning depends upon the specific arrangement of parts and wholes inscribed in the pattern of relations constituting the semiotic situation. Therefore, Plato's fundamental insight into the importance of forms remains true: It is with the emergence of forms that meaning develops and accrues in cultural situations. These forms, symbols, and harmonies (at this point the terms are nearly synonymous) are the vectors that carry meaning within, through, and about cultures. They are the semiotic equivalents of the physical forces of the natural world. Therefore, whether the symbols are nondiscursive and directly presentational, as in the gestural conversations making up much of city life, or discursive, as in the use of language to structure experience, the essential import of meaning as an exisential fact resides in its power to convey relations of value across an urban environment. Meaning is what is delivered through the category of transmission.

It is also important to insist upon the continuity spanning the many widely differing regions of meanings that can extend from direct acts of feeling to sophisticated forms of understanding. There is no understanding without some form of feeling and there is no feeling that does not involve some form of understanding. As Langer puts it: "Feelings have forms, which become progressively articulated."[9] Furthermore, the ground for this continuity is to be found in the ever-present need for a relation to a greater whole. For whether what is being felt is a direct presentational symbol (for example, a red light) or an elaborate linguistic structure (as in a complex verbal statement), the need for a reference to a whole is always required. Thus, in the case of the traffic light, the meaning of this nondiscursive symbolism "depends upon the common total reference of the symbol."[10] Or in the matter of discursive symbolism, "the meanings given through language are successively understood, and gathered into a whole by the process called discourse; the meanings of all other symbolic elements that compose a larger articulate symbol are understood only through the meanings of the whole, through their relations within a total structure."[11]

In conclusion, it must also be remembered that all references to wholes and parts as well as feelings aroused by patterns of relations imply something equally important. There is at work in all acts of meaningful symbolic communication a search for purpose. This is what I mean by the phrase "intelligence-in-action." But this intelligence-in-action is neither the classical intelligence of Greek culture nor the teleological sensibility of the Middle Ages nor even the hard-nosed empirical drive of Enlightenment science. It is through and through the great discovery of the American pragmatic tradition. This is to say, intelligence-in-action is the effort to find meaning through the results of interactions grounded in the aesthetic appreciation of the relations of parts and wholes. To understand the nuances of this revolutionary epistemology is, at the same time, to set the stage for a genuinely effective urban praxis. For even as aesthetics was the way to an appropriate theory of the worth of the natural environment, so also it remains the most effective guide for understanding the relation between intelligence and action.

Intelligence-in-Action

The founders of classical American philosophy sought to make time a real option in the lives of human beings. They did this by stressing the place of the future as an integral part of the present.

This meant providing a space for future time that was located neither in an already guaranteed future (as in some kinds of Aristotelian metaphysics) nor in a timeless afterlife transcendentally isolated from all temporal travail. It is likewise this insight into the ultimate significance of time that brought about pragmatism's reliance on experimentalism as a central component in cultural experience. By so radicalizing the future, American philosophy stood in need of a method that could both protect past achievements and at the same time encourage novel experience. The reason for my earlier insistence on the importance of propositional experience for the effective conduct of urban life should now be evident. For it is in entertaining possibilities in an intelligent way that the road to inquiry is cleared for action.

Three important questions are involved in the problem of intelligence-in-action. How does one turn issues and situations into problems to be solved? What is the role of the public in finding solutions to such problems? And, finally, how does one lure the public into intense participation in such problem solving? Each question involves a necessary reference to the foregoing issues of symbolism, communication, and meaning. Answers to these questions provide a summary conclusion to this discussion of how to develop an actively intelligent city mind.

In response to the first question, mind is to be seen as a form of symbolic behavior that acts to construct problems that can then be solved by the cooperative intelligence of the community. It is to be remembered that all matters of meaning and communication revolve about the identification and satisfaction of purpose. In this respect, effective thinking is always a matter of marking out indications of meanings to oneself and others. As the previous analyses indicated, these indications are always along the lines of plans of action or purposes to be achieved. For to establish meaning is to establish appropriate relations between parts and wholes so as to achieve some sort of satisfactory harmony. Therefore, thinking is stimulated when the relations between patterns of meaning become uncertain or destabilized. What the search for meaning is really all about is the reinstitution of satisfactory harmonies between the events that make up the human environment. The form of Platonic naturalism guiding this study sees thinking as both a natural reaction to the experience of unsatisfactory situations and a search for more appropriate (or fitting) normative measures whereby the unsettled can be reharmonized to take advantage of new conditions and circumstances.[12]

This, of course, means that the future is both immanent and imminent within the present. It is therefore imperative to reconstruct existentially troubling situations into problems that can be solved. For if such practical steps are not taken, then our only choice is to wallow in the anxiety of the moment. Existential philosophy has already shown the inadequacy of such a response. A direct answer to the first question, how does one turn situations into problems? should now be evident. The most effective way to turn situations into problems is by living life directly, forcefully, and honestly. Once the cultural veneer of denial, pretense, and distraction is scraped away, then the problematic nature of existence becomes evident. If that occurs, one is faced with a further choice. Shall I live in the solution or shall I live in the problem? It is evident that a methodology of problem solving is an immediate cultural imperative.

Understanding the art of turning situations into problems is the singular achievement of American pragmatism in general and John Dewey in particular. Dewey's chief contribution lies once again in his refusal to accept dualistic answers as adequate responses. In fact, much of Dewey's greatness resides in his creation and articulation of what he called the act of "social inquiry." More specifically, this achievement involves the reconstruction of the means/ends dichotomy that so often has bedevilled the question of effective social reform. In its place Dewey substitutes what he astutely called "ends-in-view." I would call attention to the temporal structure of this method for it is to be noted how intimately Dewey yokes together the present and the future (and, by implication, the past) in this powerful phrase. This is because in a process environment all forms of a priori reasoning are already condemned to failure. Therefore, what is required are hypotheses apt for testing in direct experience. Another term for such methodological instruments is of course *proposition.*

Therefore, the first step toward living life directly and thereby creating problems fit for solutions is really a double step. Fixed ends must be stripped away and a commitment to a radically contingent universe made part of public policy. More than sixty years ago, John Dewey gave us four significant pointers on how to turn situations into problems ready for directed intelligence. They are as follows:

- All inquiry proceeds within a cultural matrix which is ultimately determined by the nature of social relations.
- Just as the validity of a proposition in discourse . . . cannot be determined short of the consequences to which its functional

use gives rise, so the sufficient warrant of a judgment as a claimant to knowledge cannot be determined apart from connection with a widening circle of consequences.

• The conclusion that agreement of activities and their consequences is a test and a moving force in scientific advance is in harmony with the position that the ultimate end and test of all inquiry is the transformation of a problematic situation (which involves confusion and conflict) into a unified one.

• Until . . . ideas formed and used are . . . employed as *hypotheses*, and are . . . of a form to direct and prescribe operations of analytic-synthetic determination of facts, social inquiry has no chance of satisfying the logical conditions for attainment of scientific status.[13]

Within these four points there resides the heart of pragmatism's revolutionary transformation of the idea of intelligence. In the first place, what Dewey is really asking us to do is to abandon the classical Greek distinction between *poiesis* and *praxis* so as to use both in order to set up and solve deeply human problems. In the words of Hans Joas, "The guiding metaphor is neither poetic expression nor material production nor revolutionary transformation of society, but instead the creative solution of problems by an experimenting intelligence."[14] Thus, the transformation of situations into problems proceeds by way of an intelligence willing to be directed by the results of its actions. This "city mind" must give up the idea of ends set beforehand. For solutions come as interactions within the process of social inquiry.

Now, all this calls for a considerable amount of trust. It is no easy thing to let go of anchors and moorings that have had a past usefulness. It is precisely here that the second question, what is the role of the public in finding solutions to such problems? becomes important. What the "good" public allows intelligence-in-action to do is to go forward with support and confidence that its findings will be taken seriously. Now, a "good" public is one that takes seriously the circumstances and conditions of its birth. For as Dewey has argued, there is not just one public; rather there is a plurality of publics.[15] In fact, a public arises each and every time my actions spill over and affect another citizen. There is no way out of this communal situation. For the pragmatist, human beings are condemned to be their brothers' and sisters' keepers. At its heart, the public is both the source and the recipient of creative intelligence. So Joas is correct when he maintains that "collective creativity is the goal of intelligence."[16] The public good of the good public is the establishment of places where intelligence-in-action can grow and be of service to the community. Now, all this has significant bearing on the quality of urban experience. For lacking a ground in the real interests of the community, intelligence-in-action is impossible. There is no recognition of the importance of abductive praxis by individuals who must lean on the community for support. Here is where the third question, how does one lure the public into intense participation in such problem solving? comes into play. Surely, the hedonism lying behind many forms of contemporary bourgeois liberalism cannot promote such interest. Its notion of the rationally self-interested self is much too thin to sustain anything more than a cursory interest in social problems. The rise and fall of the popularity of the "L" word is evidence enough of the poverty of such a conception of self-interest. Once "my" problems go away, I tend to forget about the difficulties facing others. Such is the inevitable result of the concept of the atomic individual crafted by the praxis of advanced late capitalism.

The task of inviting others to the process of solving problems calls for more radical measures than the mere declaration of the need for a more "enlightened" definition of self-interest. It is at this point that the four aesthetically founded orders of triviality, vagueness, narrowness, and width can be of considerable help in providing a more realistic understanding of the social roots and conditions of every human self. Furthermore, without the aesthetic pull made possible by a reconstruction of the social domain along lines of feelings, intense participation in significant acts of directed intelligence is unlikely.

Consider the following integrated review of important aspects of this essay in speculative urban cosmology. There stands forth the category of transmission as the vital vector force carrying values around the urban environment. It does so through the creation of intense propositional experiences that are most important for the way in which they evoke interest. Furthermore, there are the four aesthetic orders of triviality, vagueness, narrowness, and width within which such propositions have their predictable emotional correlates. Finally, there are the three dimensions of urban semiotics: firstness with its iconic expressions, secondness with its indexical references, and thirdness with its propositional symbolic transformations. How do these philosophical abstractions serve to reconstruct the all-important instrument of intelligence-in-action?

First, it is absolutely necessary to stress the feeling dimension that underlies all urban intelligence. Without the concreteness supplied by this felt sense of importance, any urban analysis is as likely as not going to fall into Whitehead's fallacy of misplaced concreteness. (In fact, Joas is not far from this truth when he criticizes the deeply flawed character of scientistic sociology.)[17] What the concept of felt intelligence provides is a constant reminder that our feelings are the roots of our thinking and any form of thinking that strays too far from this source is bound to occasion misleading interpretations of the urban environment. Therefore: Analysis that trivializes the background of social order required to create an effective urban region necessarily brings about a feeling of indifference that so often characterizes the public's reaction to deracinated social inquiry. On the other hand, an emphasis on the order of vagueness can push the inquiry toward feelings of expectation that can at times serve to further citizen participation. However, it is when narrowness (unfortunately, in this case most often the outcome of types of atomistic liberal thinking) arrives that self-interest emerges with intense forms of expressions. But it is only when this narrowness and its felt reaction of intensity is woven onto appropriate forms of vagueness that width of involvement can arise.[18]

Now, what can sharpen and deepen this way of setting reason on a course toward the concrete is the urban semiotics developed in Part Two of this study. Thus, the iconic presences dominating certain modes of urban analysis can be appreciated for what they achieve: a felt experience of firstness or qualitative value. But this is not enough to push the study of urban environments forward in a thoroughly concrete fashion. At its best, it can remind us of the potential beauty lurking in the streets of city life. At its worst, it merely celebrates a kind of urban aesthetics that is content to observe rather than participate in urban experience. It settles into a vagueness that is always threatening to slip back into an aestheticism that trivializes the very forms of value it seeks to celebrate. Types of postmodern thinking insisting on the importance of *différance* and the putative weakness of "logocentric" thought to capture the value of human experience are examples of the genre.

When urban secondness dominates felt intelligence, then there is a stress on the collision of facts as they indexically express themselves throughout the city. In its emphasis on the hard reality that is a genuine dimension of the urban scene, this kind of felt intelligence raises to a high art form the realm of self-interest. In fact, the narrowness attendant upon this type of thinking together with its fierce proclamation of the ineluctable struggle for survival is precisely what advanced late capitalism relies upon to keep the empire skyline clearly in the forefront of human consciousness. No amount of reasoning about wider social concerns or even types of more "enlightened" self-interest can drive this violent indexical presence from the marketplace of goods and ideas. If the aestheticism of types of iconic thinking leads to a world redolent with hints and suggestions but devoid of plans for intelligence-in-action, then the indexical realm of secondness is always in danger of elevating self-interest into the only form of rational action. At its best, it provides a useful reminder that the city is not a child's playground where all is for free and without cost. At its worst, the empire skyline blots all the other important dimensions of human life and thereby points toward a scene of bloody competitive strife. What is most dangerous about an urban environment dominated by secondness is the way in which it narrows down the field of felt intelligence to the most selfish of human drives: types of self-interest closely allied with greed.

It is only when the third level of symbolic expression is encountered that a full integration of Whitehead's types of aesthetic order and Peirce's forms of concretely felt reasonableness is possible. Symbols weave narrowness (in the form of their material structure) onto vagueness (in the form of their semiotic power) so as to provide a mode of thinking that is characterized by both intensity of meaning and width of applicability. And as my argument has demonstrated, it offers in terms of emotional reactions based on the four aesthetic orders the greatest likelihood of eliciting intense involvement upon the part of community members. In terms of urban reality, it is the neighborhood in its concrete reasonableness that is the spacetime locus of felt intelligence operating at its peak. This is why neighborhoods die without effective participation. As troublesome as service on neighborhood committees may be, they are the concrete instruments whereby intelligence-in-action can gain a foothold against various types of disruption that demand the creation of new habits of response. Furthermore, it is precisely the directed intelligence of urban thirdness in alliance with the ideal norms of intensity, integrity, wholeness, and depth that brings about the spread of the patches of reasonableness that form the plural centers of effective city life.

Intelligence-in-action is not the simpleminded application of the advice of "experts" to various urban trouble spots. Neither is it the raw venting of pent-up emotions displayed at times of community anxiety. Intelligence-in-action is learning what forms of wholeness are possible in various types of situations. It means replacing discordant conditions with harmonic ones. If and when this actually occurs, then a situation has been turned into a problem and a possible solution tentatively offered by the community's concrete directed intelligence. Wholeness means thirdness. Thirdness means continuity. Continuity in the city means the establishment of vibrant community. All acts that strive to create a genuine place involve the kind of intelligence-in-action sketched in this chapter. That such intelligence is absolutely dependent upon a vibrant community is the theme of the next chapter.

Chapter Ten

Community

What makes intelligence-in-action possible on a widely regularized basis is the persistent presence of community as an integral part of the individual city dweller's life. Of course, by intelligence I mean much more than the capacity to be drawn by the iconic power of firstness or to follow efficiently the indexical pointers of secondness. All such modes of behavior, while intelligent in their own right, fail to promote the continuity, full meaning, and lived participation that are the marks of effective thirdness. To speak then of community is to raise once again the question of the possibility of intelligence-in-action in city life. But such a theme is made more difficult by the absence of real community as a widespread contemporary human experience, as well as by the tendency to invoke the term as a cure for any social problem. It is only recently that philosophers have begun to reach back to the beginnings of the American Republic for examples of living "civic community."[1] It appears that we know little of the philosophical history of the term and even less about how to bring it about.

This chapter begins by recalling the origins of the idea of community in the works of Plato. Next, it singles out the process that lies at the heart of any effective community—the making of connections.

This activity finds its most concrete expression in "the desire of recognition by the other," which plays so profound a role in Hegel's systematic thought on the origins of human consciousness and social existence. This experience of desiring and desirability is then reinterpreted through the experience of sharing symbols. Finally, this fundamental act of urban cooperation is seen for what it really is: an invitation to make sharing in all its dimensions the ground of a concrete and equitable participatory democracy. In sum, the philosophical history of the idea of community is traced from its imagistic origins in the *Symposium* through its dialectical presence in Hegel's *Phenomenology* to its place as the very pivot of intelligence, freedom, and responsibility in the tradition of American naturalism and pragmatism. Urban praxis therefore follows Peirce by first painting an iconic likeness of community. Second, it opens up the workings of city life by identifying the activity lying at the base of urban community. Third, it argues for the central importance of democracy as the political form best suited for inculcating consistently good habits of sharing intelligently felt meanings and values. It concludes by presenting democracy as the epitome of the good community.

Something in between

The experience of community has played a decisive role in both the survival and successful evolution of the human race. Without it, knowledge understood as habits of successful reaction to all sorts of environmental stress would not have been possible. What to do when the lion strikes or where to go when the water holes dry up would never have become part of the intelligent traditions of human groups. Somehow or other humans became acutely aware of the need to double their chances of survival by sharing information, habits of response, and intelligence-in-action. What community fundamentally means is caught in this picture of human beings at their most desperate. Community is the recognition of "something in between" that bonds them into a whole greater than the sum of their individual existences.

It is precisely this understanding of community as something in between that characterizes Plato's discussion of eros in the *Symposium*. The theme, as is well known, is the nature of love: "Is Love a god or a mortal?" And while this particular form of the question appears, disappears, and then reappears as the various participants express their understanding of love, it is Socrates at the end of the dialogue who resurrects the question in its original form by recalling the words of Diotima concerning the nature of love. And it is from her iconic presentation of love as neither a god nor a mortal that the picture of *Koinonia* takes on such an engaging character:

> In that case, Diotima, who *are* the people who love
> wisdom, if they are neither wise nor ignorant?
> That's obvious, she said. A child could tell you. Those
> who love wisdom fall in between those two extremes. And
> Love is one of them, because he is in love with what is
> beautiful, and wisdom is extremely beautiful. It follows
> that Love *must* be a lover of wisdom and, as such, is in
> between being wise and being ignorant.[2]

Now, earlier in this dialogue Plato defines what it means to be in between:

> [N]ow do you see? You don't believe Love is a god either!
> Certainly not.
> Then what is he?
> He's like we mentioned before, she said. He is in between
> mortal and immortal.
> What do you mean, Diotima?
> He's a great spirit, Socrates. Everything spiritual, you see,
> is in between god and mortal.
> What is their function, I asked.
> They are messengers who shuttle back and forth between
> the two, conveying prayer and sacrifice from men to gods,
> while to men they bring commands from the gods and gifts
> in return for sacrifices. Being in the middle of the two, they
> round out the whole and bind fast the all to all.
>   . . .
> He who is wise in any of these ways is a man of spirit but
> he who is wise in any other way in a profession or any
> manual work, is merely a mechanic.[3]

What is being translated here as that which is in the middle and that which conveys meanings back and forth and as that which is between extremes is the experience of community, or as the Greek puts it, *Koinonia*. Three important dimensions are involved in this experience of *Koinonia*: philosophy, sharing meanings, and spiritual meeting. Each is an indispensable component of community as a human experience.

What makes possible each of these three aspects of community is the effective presence of "internal relations." (By this very abstract term I mean the very concrete experience of encountering within one's own being the lived values and real feelings of another human being.) I use this abstract term for now because I wish to raise in as general a way as possible the question of just how we get to know the feelings and values of other humans. Furthermore, an adequate answer to this question lies in forging a relation between the abstract disciplines of speculative philosophy and semiotics. Parts One and Two of this work dealt respectively with speculative philosophy and semiotics. In the final analysis, their ultimate reconciliation is made possible through the active presence of internal relations as a real factor in human experience. And that is the heart and soul of an intelligently effective urban praxis.

It is through internal relations that one feeler feels the feelings of another so as to make those feelings part of her own internal constitution. I insist on the abstractness of this formulation so as to avoid the smarmy smugness of such expressions as "I feel your pain." (Despite the power of the American presidency, the capacity to feel another's pain is not as easy as such a glib phrase might suggest.) Internal relations come about through the very hard work of bringing into one's sphere of experience the feelings and values of another. This can only be done by repeating back to another what they have expressed to you. This is what grounds Mead's "conversation of gestures." Unless I can reproduce in myself a simulacrum of what another has experienced, I cannot enter the conversation of gestures that makes up the domain of the socialized self. This simulacrum is the icon by which the other knows that I know what is going on in a particular situation. As instances of firstness, all such internal relations are about quality or value. The community begins with a gesture toward the value of others. That gesture is first of all a gesture of welcome. It take seriously the experiences of others:

> [T]he self to which we have been referring arises when the conversation of gestures is taken over into the individual form. When this conversation of gestures can be taken over into the individual's conduct so that the attitude of other forms can affect the organism, and the organism can reply with its corresponding gesture and thus arouse the attitude of the other in its own process, then a self arises. . . . . Each individual has to take also the attitude of the community, the generalized attitude.[4]

From this perspective it can be seen just why the experience of community necessarily entails the active presence of philosophy, shared meanings, and spiritual meeting. Philosophy is the love of wisdom where that love is expressed through the effort to achieve the right balance between fact and value. This balance is brought about by reason of the adoption of an appropriate normative measure for balancing the roles of facts and values within particular concrete situations. To be a lover of wisdom is to know how factual expressions (the gestures of the human body) display the real presence of values (the meaning of the gestures). Thus, the love that is an essential part of philosophy is a knowing grounded in the capacity to feel the real presence of another as a formative part of myself. Likewise, the sharing of meaning is essential for community since without it, no measure for balancing facts and values can be had. And lastly, spiritual meeting occurs when I encounter the other through his or her own experienced values. As Plato puts it: "Love shuttles back and forth" and "round[s] out the whole and binds fast all to all," for this is what happens in all communal "being in the middle."

All genuine spiritual meeting takes place within some sort of community, because a community is founded on the love of wisdom (which is the traditional goal of speculative philosophy) and shared meaning (whose achievement is the goal of semiotics). The something in between that is the very essence of community is a fusion of the love of wisdom and the sharing of meaning. This iconic presentation of community must now encounter the realm of secondness where the collision of values is worked out to the advantage of an enlarged sense of just what that "something in between" is really all about.

Making Connections

Just what is it that drives humans to such exertions on behalf of wisdom, love, and spiritual experience? What could possibly account for the expenditure of such energy and effort? Only some fierce and primal form of desire could explain such a prodigious drive for community. It is Hegel who provides the most compelling account of this desire and its place in human culture and self-understanding. In *Phenomenology of Spirit*, he tells us of the life and death struggle of the master and the slave as each seeks to win the recognition of the other as the way to their own self-awareness of who they are.[5] Recognition by the other of the worth of one's own being is the indispensable causal factor in the rise to concrete self-awareness on the part of individual human beings.

Now, in telling the story of the master and the slave and their dynamic failure to acknowledge each other in a free manner, Hegel points the way toward a true understanding of the connections that make or break community life. Without a free and full recognition of my being by another, I cease to be. (Just ask Captain Boycott what happened when the Irish refused to acknowledge his existence.) In the story of the master and the slave, the irony of course rests most heavily on the master since he must ask the slave to do what no slave can do: Grant full and free recognition to him as master. It is the very power of the master that thwarts the growth of his self-awareness. On the other hand, the irony deepens because it is the slave who can work (no master can work and still be a master) and thereby establish a realm of potential recognition within which his consciousness can in the future be recognized by another.

Thus, in terms of this study the primary work of the city is the establishment of modes of recognition that can stimulate full and free self-awareness. Those who decide to remain in the castle and/or any other privileged locus of isolation can create no history. They make no contribution to the manifold ways in which human self-consciousness gains recognition of its effective and real presence in culture. It is eros dialectically transformed (*aufhebung*) into the desire for recognition by another that sets free the human self toward its polymorphic modes of self-realization. When Mead speaks of the conversation of gestures wherein I repeat back to the other the form of his desire, he is reconstituting within the tradition of American pragmatism the essentials of the master/slave dialectic sketched in Hegel's *Phenomenology*. And insofar as the city remains the preeminent place for the establishment of human community, instituting, tending, and repairing connections generative of recognition become the paramount human activity.

But this is not the end of the story, for Hegel also reminds us of the potential for terror and willful blindness lurking in every corner of this drive for mutual recognition. For it is not beyond humankind to enslave the very persons whose freedom it needs so as to ensure for itself a false and empty form of self-consciousness. All forms of imperialism from Asia to the Middle East to the British Empire to American colonialism vitiate the conditions of full human growth in self-awareness. It really does not matter whether the deed of enforced recognition is carried out by the Bengal lancers or loan officers of the World Bank. The result is the same: A vicious form of secondness freezes the possibilities of life into a bloody collision of forces bent on recognition through destruction.

When the need for recognition is stifled by futile collisions of cultural forms, then no matter who gains the upper hand, the ultimate victor is always some manifestation of the fallacy of simple location. As I argued in *Nature*, such a fallacy is bad enough when it infects our view of the value of the environment. Its viciousness is exponentially increased when it is used to found and structure false forms of community. Healthy and vibrant internal relations cannot survive the threat of rampant, violent acts of self-assertion. The very possibility of community as the love of wisdom, the sharing of values, and the sharing of spiritual experience is negated. What is demanded is capitulation, not dialogue. In and for and of themselves, genuine human connections are branded as contraband. Simply located human relations rest upon the logic of domination. Every attempt to seek another way is dismissed as foolish and irrational.

When forms of domination are the only permissible paths for social relations, the art of making connections is seriously compromised for then, forms of violence are the only media allowed entrance "into the middle of things." And if the middle is permeated by violence (however well disguised), then what hope for rationality exists? It is therefore no wonder that in the time of advanced late capitalism celebrations of the irrational and wholesale adoptions of *outré* lifestyles tend to proliferate among those who would rebel. But we ought not endorse rebellious postures as the only possible reaction to the tyranny of secondness disguising itself as thirdness. There is also the experience of work as the way out of the condition of bondage.

The work required to bring about the condition of free and full self-consciousness is the work of building a community. For it is within this realm that acts of social recognition can take place and thereby ground human awareness in the kinds of structures needed for its growth. Urban work involves making the kinds of connections that allow for the creation of meaning through shared experiences. It is here that eros joins hands with desire so as to form a base of rationality suffused with symbolic import. When philosophy is actively practiced as the love of wisdom, then the relation between facts and values assumes paramount importance. The love of wisdom demands the experience of shared meanings. This in turn requires the real presence of spiritual meeting on a widespread communal basis. And such spiritual meeting, Plato tells us, always involves the establishment of something in between as the ground and source of an ever-evolving rationality. Making connections in the city involves active participation in the symbolic realms that convey meaning throughout the various domains of city life. And such participation is rightfully called work because it demands philosophic effort, the communication of values, and the recognition of the deeply spiritual dimensions of human life.

Connections that embody reason are the most difficult to create for they must be grounded in intelligence-in-action. It is relatively easy to force connections (one can always get a bigger hammer). The true art of reason consists in locating those forms of praxis that persuade "by reason" of their effectiveness in providing solutions for seemingly intractable problems. And even if such a truly difficult feat is pulled off, there remains the task of persuading others to accept and practice the solution. This can only be done by invitation. Forced participation violates the intent of communal forms of reason. The connections that count as constitutive of community must be the outcome of a freely engaged praxis. This means that the community's internal relations must be forged through a variety of ritualized symbolic interactions. To the degree that such connections express depth and width, to that same degree they also propose powerful lures for community participation. In brief, ritual makes a real difference in the life of a community.

Connections are the concrete manifestation of the reality of internal relations. All such relations are signs of eros at work for they manifest the real presence of something in between. What is between is the desire for recognition that promotes healthy forms of self-consciousness. It is the task of philosophy to create such realms of community understanding. For the love of wisdom promotes the sharing of meanings through spiritual encounters. These encounters are occasioned by the effective presence of richly evocative symbols in the life of the community. Working at the establishment of such symbols is what creates patches of intelligence in an otherwise brutal world. Working through such symbols is what transforms those patches into a widespread and effective range of intelligence-in-action. It is here that the symbol reveals itself most clearly as the royal road to shared experience.

Sharing Symbols

Speculative philosophy and semiotics are indispensable disciplines for understanding just how vital symbols are for the proper functioning of community life. I have already discussed the significance of symbolic reference for human perception. Also, the category of transmission was seen to function best when it was transferring symbols around the various domains of urban experience. Here, I wish to bring all these dimensions under a single theoretical umbrella whereby the symbol will be seen as the media of meaning itself. In so doing I am putting to work the theory of transformative symbolization elaborated by Susanne Langer and discussed in the previous chapter. Human beings survive and prosper by reason of successful efforts to transform the environment into a stable place for their growth and development. The prime mover of such transformations is the symbol.

The act of symbolic transformation takes place whenever a sign, object, and interpretant are brought together in order to render effective a particular approach to a particular environmental problem. All symbolic acts from puberty rites to learning traffic signals to funeral processions are similar in this sense: They attempt to transform situations into problems and thereby render them open to the beneficial presence of intelligence-in-action. But more is demanded, since finding ways to creatively embed these symbolic activities in the lived social body of the community is also necessary. This is what I mean by the somewhat awkward term *sharing symbols*. By it, I wish to suggest the supreme value of wedding reason to action through concretely felt aesthetic responses to environmental pressures. It also involves recognizing the power resident in the dynamical object to bring about qualitatively different symbolic responses to semiotic stimuli. The communal act of sharing symbols must have some "give" built into its structure of learning so that the community's responses to problems are simultaneously general and specific. If this does not occur, then habit will quickly degenerate into instinctual response and the force of what Peirce called "the living idea" of all "mental phenomena" will dissipate and be replaced by blind instinct and frozen custom. The power of an effective urban semiotics depends entirely on its ability to develop a praxis that will consistently generate the abductive creativity demanded by the problems of existence.[6]

Put in metaphysical language, sharing symbols means learning how to carry out the symbolic transformation of reality in such a way as to keep alive the ultimate ontological fact that the world is always one and always many at the same time. Thus, when Sandra Rosenthal quotes Peirce to the effect that "the general idea is the mark of the habit,"[7] she is noting the fact that Peirce is saying many things at the same time. First, he is insisting on the importance of readily recognizable sensory cues that, secondly, can stimulate intelligent activities that, thirdly, bind themselves into some kind of effective structural whole that is appropriately normative for that time, that place, and that situation. Thus, habit is a process capable of adjusting itself to the special respects of special circumstances. And this is precisely what Robert Neville means when he suggests that Peirce could have added a fourthness to his triadic scheme—where this fourth would be the deftness of intuition to pick out just that "respect" with which the event in question expresses its own special *haeccitas*.[8] It is the objectively vague character of symbols that promotes the kind of flexibility needed to do justice to the uniqueness of each and every urban situation. And it is the specific application of the symbolic act that tests its adequacy.

Now, all this is to say that the place of aesthetics as the lead discipline for creating successful forms of urban praxis remains in force. For without a sense for the feel of a situation, there can be little hope for a sympathetic reading of the "respects of interpretation" that can fill out the form of the good that is normative for this special situation. As a practical matter, it therefore makes great pragmatic sense to make available to the community lessons in aesthetic training. For institutions fail when they do not enlist the felt participation of the people affected. Recall my earlier analysis of the communities of Saint Jerome Church and the South Bronx Churches. It is precisely the exclusionary practices of the political culture that rendered them powerless. And by way of redress, these institutions must respond deftly and sensitively through forms of community praxis in order to regain political power and authority. Liturgy and ritual are not simply pretty "add-ons" to political action. They are precisely the ground and the source of the something in between that demands recognition by the political powers of City Hall as well as the power brokers in the Chancery Office of the Archdiocese of New York. What animates these urban experiences is eros transformed into the desire for recognition and a willingness to work for such moments of recognition.[9]

Also imperative for a fruitful communal sharing of symbols is the opportunity to allow for an active critique of a community's symbolic code. Another word for this community responsibility is participation—a concept that has a long and distinguished philosophical history. To participate in a good way entails the possession of appropriate normative measures for such acts of sharing. This brings the discussion back to the theme of thirdness, where reason grows by reason of its capacity to generate fitting responses to changing life situations. Thirdness is the realm of habit, rule, and order but it also involves a kind of reasoning that is at the same time a kind of feeling. In the course of this study it has been called various names. Sometimes it has been termed normative thinking, sometimes it has been called abduction, and sometimes it has simply been called felt intelligence. Whatever it is called and however it is identified, it always concerns the aim at experiencing the difference that "the truth of discovery" makes when it is at work in a particular situation.[10]

The transformative power of this truth of discovery is grounded in what Professor Ralph Sleeper fortuitously called "the experienceable difference."[11] If the sharing of symbols does not make a difference in the lives of the community, then all such symbols fail the pragmatic test. For it is through the supremely practical act of participating in the symbolic life of the community that levels of value spread their influence through types of urban environments. What unites sharing and participation is the felt recognition of particular values within particular factual contexts. Now, this act of normative understanding demands standards that the community can use to ultimately identify such relations between facts and values. I say "ultimately" because it is here that Peirce's insistence on the "long-run"community of inquirers dedicated to the discovery of truth is most relevant. For such a requirement is both a sign of the possibility of normative truth and an admission of the steady presence of fallibilism in all our attempts to share symbols within communities of inquiry. It is precisely here that logic and ethics depend upon the active presence of an aesthetically sensitized community of inquirers who can feel the rightness or wrongness of a particular response to a situation. Thus, Peirce's insistence upon the importance of the convergence of interpretations in an idealized long run as the ultimate guarantor of truth is basically the same as the pragmatic maxim's assertion that the meaning of an idea is proportionate to its possible consequences.

Now, both the doctrine of the experienceable difference and that of the community of inquirers, as well as the pragmatic maxim itself, receive speculative and systematic enhancement in Robert Neville's hypotheses concerning network and content meaning. For what is felt intelligently in the long run is both the content meaning and the network meaning of a sign, its object, and its interpretants. In terms of intentional human activity, content meaning names the significance derived from the triadic use of object, sign, and interpretant as directed toward existent external objects. My categoreal scheme sees content meaning as the inscape of each event expressing its special value within an evolving urban environment. On the other hand, network meaning names the level of significance achieved when all the relevant semiotic connections are taken into consideration. In terms of my categoreal scheme, network meaning is akin to the category of transmission when that environmental function is working in "the respects" of a certain tradition of interpretation. Network meaning is therefore the functional equivalent of the postmodern emphasis on the importance of textuality, but with this difference: Genuinely pragmatic networks point toward really existent values and are not to be understood as merely self-referential structural skeins of words, images, and indices. Whether the case be that of content meaning or network meaning, the interest of the community always lies along the lines of the truth value of the semiotic experience. And since truth here means the "carryover of value" brought about by "true" representations, the next section of this chapter constitutes a final cumulative argument demonstrating the pragmatic effectiveness of this coordination of speculative philosophy, urban semiotics, and urban praxis.[12]

Community Is Democracy

Urban praxis finds its most direct expression in the ways in which symbolic codes enable participation in the wealth of experience generated through the ontological creativity and sign activity of a community. Therefore, this urban cosmology ought to be applicable to the value experience of city dwellers and also speak directly to their major experiential concerns. That experience has three dimensions: physical, biological, and cultural.[13] By physical I mean the important spacetime qualities of urban life developed in Part One. Most especially, I mean access to the richness of place as an indispensable physical element for the growth and development of human beings. For without place the possibility of communty disappears as a real option. The placelessness infecting so much of contemporary urban environments (both rich and poor) is among the cruelest punishments visited on human beings in this age of advanced late capitalism. It does to city dwellers what the British did to the Irish when they forbade them the use of their language and religion. It deprives human community of the very physical foundations needed to help them grow even as it sets them adrift in a spaceless, timeless vacuum.

The biological level of urban participation is marked by the need for sound housing, healthy air and water, and the kind of food humans need for their growth and development. Foul air wastes human lungs, a filthy water supply poisons their bodies, and lack of nourishing food stifles all growth. All these facts of good urban biological participation are commonplaces. The real wonder is that arguments have to be continually put forward in order to win them again and again for the urban populace. But when the city is seen mostly as a place to earn a living through participation in "an increasingly competitive global marketplace," these self-evident biological levels of participation require continual justification.

But it is the cultural level of participation that witnesses the worst crimes against city dwellers. How cruel that even as they preen themselves on their cultural resources, the great cities deprive the mass of their citizens of the means to enjoy such wealth of experience. If the previous arguments on the importance of sharing symbols mean anything at all, then the viciousness of such inequality should be self-evident. What condemns the poor to their poverty is not simply the absence of money. In and of itself that could be remedied; rather, it is when the experiences that make life valuable are sealed off from human beings that the most awful kind of deprivation sets in. Depression, loss of insight and foresight, the urge for the quick fix—all these symptoms of urban sickness are for the most part directly related to the loss of significant participation on the cultural level.

What cultural participation is really all about is learning the symbolic code whereby the wealth of human experience can be transferred among the people of a city. Take away these vectors of meaning and you have killed the soul of the people. Deprive them of these vectors of truth and you have rubbed out the real and effective presence of value in their lives. Erase these vectors of felt intelligence and you have eliminated what is most distinctive about human beings—their capacity to feel the good and communicate it to others.

I quote again from John Sherrif's brief but powerful essay on Peirce's philosophy, for he spells out quite clearly what is at stake when the cultural level of participation is blocked: "Aesthetic experience is the awareness of the possibility of meaning; that is, the awareness of recognizable feelings."[14] If this study of the city has attempted anything bold, it is its effort to dispel forever the notion that culture is some kind of "nicety" humans can do without when other matters are more pressing. Culture is not about pretty things or even "beautiful" things. It is about those things that make life human: meaning, value, and importances. Recalling Peirce's triadic ontology: What would happen if the field of quality experienced in firstness were forever sealed off from large segments of the city population? Would not a kind of numbness that dulls the eyes even as it threatens the soul steal over all those who lurk in our streets? Consider the clash of values characteristic of urban secondness: Would it not resemble Hobbes's "state of nature"—a war of all against all that takes place in full view of the Empire Skyline? And when we left that battlefield of secondness and returned to the neighborhood to seek out the gift of community which is thirdness, would not Eliot's words echo in our minds: "I did not think that death had undone so many"?[15] In sum, cultural deprivation constitutes the most permanent and damaging offense possible against the city dweller. It makes interaction impossible because it destroys the social bonds needed to forge a living connection between abductive intelligence and collective ideals.[16] It prevents confirmation of our values through concerted community action and thereby doubles the sense of helplessness felt at this level of urban cultural poverty.

In my earlier study of nature I used the philosophy of Spinoza to articulate certain important attitudes that should inform our character.[17] Here also, I wish to enlist Spinoza's wisdom but in connection with what he understands to be the great advantages of social life (and by extension, city experience). For Spinoza the decision on how we shall live with our fellow citizens comes down to a stark choice: Shall we love or shall we hate?[18]

To begin, it should be recalled that for Spinoza the most powerful form of knowing is not a knowing that knows a thing or object. Rather, Spinoza judges knowledge by the degree to which it enhances or diminishes our experience of union with what is to be known. Therefore, when Spinoza speaks of knowing God or Nature, he is indicating the degree of unity felt between the knower and the known rather than an abstract knowledge of something external to us. In other words, Spinoza's alleged rationalism is through and through imbued with felt intelligence-in-action. Thus, community is also to be judged by the standards it upholds concerning the importance of our relations with each other. In the *Ethics* Part IV, propositions 35–45, there is a stark contrast drawn between a society founded on hate and one that stresses the ultimate significance of internal relations. With characteristic directness and with the power brought about by a vast systematically normative deduction (*viz.*, the rest of the *Ethics*), Spinoza simply says: "Hatred can never be good. (Q.E.D)"

If hatred is never good, then it is one of the very few things in Spinoza's universe that does not take on its character from the context in which it is experienced. The reason for this absolute negative judgment of hatred is because it destroys all community and is therefore proof of the most supreme form of ignorance possible in the universe. This ultimate foolishness, this sickness of the mind that above all else requires healing[19] cancels out the something-in-between that is the very "substance" of Spinoza's universe of unity.

The result of hatred is a feeling of fear that destroys the possibility of the healthy presence of reason in our dealings with one another. A destructive mood invades our natural desire for recognition and overcomes any sense of sharing with our fellow humans. Hatred, of whatever sort, is the worst habit that can take over a human person or a social order. Until its invasive presence is expelled, there is no genuine possibility for community.

John Dewey's conception of democracy as the process best suited for gaining each individual what they require in terms of freedom, power, and respect mirrors this Spinozistic judgment:

> All deliberate action of mind is in a way an experiment with the world to see what it will stand for, what it will promote and frustrate. The world is tolerant and fairly hospitable. It permits and even encourages all sorts of experiments. But in the long run some are more welcomed than others. Here there can be no difference save one of depth and scope between the question of the relation of the world to a scheme of conduct in the form of church government or a form of art and that of its relation to democracy. If there be a difference, it is only because democracy is a form of desire and endeavor which reaches further and condenses itself into more uses.[20]

Besides noting the fact that these words (with their use of "desire" and "endeavor") could have been written by Spinoza himself, I wish to stress Dewey's insistence on the significance of "depth and scope" as the normative standards by which excellence in democractic community is to be judged. Now scope and depth are aesthetic terms with far-reaching implications. I have used them to express the importance, on the one hand, of perspective and on the other the ideal measure by which the value of an event's *haeccitas* and transmissive urban power can be estimated. Now, both the scope of an urban event as well as its depth is also directly related to its functional excellence as a symbolic form. Symbols, it will be recalled, do two things at the same time. First, they transform reality so that humans can handle it. This is a symbol's scope and it registers the "respects" with which any interpretation can or will proceed. Second, a symbol's success in terms of scope also touches upon the "dynamical power" resident in its object. This is its "depth." Both together, scope and depth, mark the boundaries of excellence within a democracy's attempt to create a healthy community. Such is the power of symbolic breadth (see figs. 4 & 5, pp. 74, 75).

The disastrous effects of failed institutions should now be evident. Due to a loss of contrast that springs from a failure to permit real otherness into its presence, institutions can suffer an absence of width, balance, depth, and integrity. Needless to say, as any one who has had to deal with a bureaucracy knows all too well, these institutions also suffer from a deadening absence of intensity. Taken together, these aesthetic failures account for precisely that loss of aesthetic sensibility that Peirce saw as the vital heart of his guess at the riddle of existence. Institutions that do not register feelings cannot possibly communicate fitting forms of the good to their clients. This loss of the ideal measures of depth, integrity, and wholeness is made far worse by the substitution of a bad form of intensity: competition. For when advanced late capitalism is granted free rein, the only standard of achievement it can offer is "more." What vanishes in this competiton for more is the common good, for it is not within the proprietary interests of the great multinational corporation to pay attention to that which is outside the standard of profit. Any possibility of a "great community" is dashed on the rocks of secondness taken as the ultimate form of life. And likewise, any possibility of concrete egalitarian existence vanishes under the pressure of greed as a form of public and private virtue.

My reference to Dewey is deliberate, for more than any other American philosopher it is he who identifies community with democracy. It is democracy with its insistence on the interaction of individuals within a social setting that points the way toward a resolution of the conflict between individuals and the social order. From the perspective of building community there is for Dewey no irreconcilable struggle between these two levels of existence. The normative measure to be used in judging the rights and duties of both dimensions is how well they assist each other, not simply the degree of conflict they engender. Once again, it is the category of contrast that comes into play to push social situations toward moments of achieved thirdness. The community is built up out of the relations of individuals. It therefore requires strong individuality for its wellbeing. So also the individual requires a nurturing set of relations to foster growth. Thus, the questions are: "How numerous and varied are the interests which are consciously shared?" and "How full and free is the interplay with other forms of association."[21] Mutual support and mutual interest is the definition of community. It is also what marks democracy as the form of government best suited for realizing community in everyday life:

> [R]egarded as an ideal, democracy is not an alternative to other principles of associated life. It is the idea of community itself.
> [W]herever there is conjoint activity whose consequences are appreciated as good by all singular persons who take part in it, and where the realization of the good is such as to effect an energetic desire and effort to sustain it in being just because it is a good shared by all, there is in so far a community. The clear consciousness of a communal life, in all its implications, constitutes the idea of democracy.[22]

Now, this conjunction of democracy and community lays certain demands on the idea of the city. It says that the city must be a place where meaning is shared. Also, it demands that urban knowledge take on the form of an intelligence-in-action that can be felt by each member of the community. As Peter Manicas puts it: "such knowledge is *shared*, . . . (it) funds experience with *common* meanings, transforms needs and wants into *mutually understood* goals and . . . thereby *consciously* directs *conjoint* activity."[23] These demands, understood in the context of the urban praxis developed here, are best met through the unification of urban cosmology and semiotics proposed by this study. The cosmology supplies the broad categoreal dimensions needed in order to maintain a good understanding of the city, while the semiotics offers a sign system keyed to the sharing of meanings and the solicitation of fitting acts of felt intelligence. Once again, it is the underlying aesthetic achievement of intense contrast felt and transmitted throughout the community that makes democracy the ideal form of city life. Speculative philosophy provides the necessary enlargement of awareness needed to welcome difference, and urban semiotics prepares for the task of providing appropriate symbolic inclusion of that increase of difference. Such is the heart of the democratic ideal.

This is not the end of the story. Dewey also insisted on the importance of keeping community localized within neighborhood settings. In fact, he saw local community as essential for the realization of the good life:

In its deepest and richest sense a community must always
remain a matter of face-to-face intercourse. . . . The Great Community, in the sense of free and full communication is conceiv-
able. But it can never possess all the qualities which mark a
local community. It will do its work in ordering the relations and
enriching the experience of local associations.
 . . . Whatever the future may have in store, one thing is certain. Unless local community life can be restored the public cannot adequately resolve its most urgent problem: to find and
identify itself.[24]

The tension between the local and the regional, the national and
the global intensifies on a daily basis as civic values are driven more
and more by market forces. So much so that, as the next chapter will
show, the question of city justice can no longer be separated from
economic policy. This final section could have been called: "Sharing
the Wealth of Experience." The choice of the term *wealth* is deliberate, for experience as understood within this cosmology and semiotics is a form of value that brings wealth to community members.
But this wealth is not in the form of monetary gain. Rather, it is, as
should always be the case when talking about human beings, in the
form of participating in the lived values of a social order bonded by
internal relations and educated through dynamic symbols of thirdness. Furthermore, when the urban public is brought into the discussion, this wealth is always also communal, for community is the
human meaning of thirdness. And when forms of political order are
introduced into the discussion, then the question of democracy is
also raised. But democracy also raises the question of justice, which
in turn brings economics into the forefront of the analysis. For the
great community is unthinkable without an examination of the relationship between community, democracy, and economics in the contemporary city.

Chapter Eleven

City Justice

When I originally planned this chapter I saw it as a rather straight-forward defense of communitarian ideas of justice as opposed to varieties of contemporary liberalism. Such a position would be the inevitable and logical conclusion stemming from the argument developed in the previous chapters. But I soon became increasingly aware of just how simpleminded such an approach really was. It neglected entirely what I had been at pains to articulate throughout this study: the thesis that the city was evolution's answer to the question of human survival, growth, and development. Therefore, any discussion of justice would have to stress such a point of view. But it also became painfully obvious that many, many human beings were not thriving in the city; in fact, they were barely surviving. And the heart of their difficulty was to be found in the economic theory and machinery that was driving the creation and distribution of wealth within urban regions. Put most bluntly, it was obvious that advanced late capitalism was eating its own children in order to satisfy the unquestioned demands of a market economy made manic by global greed.

What was missing was the normative dimension of urban economics. Where I was about to argue for justice as a form of third-ness, market economics had already defined the field of play solely in terms of secondness, wherein the collision of market forces pretended to be the road to concrete reasonableness (understood as the accumulation of capital in the hands of successful enterpreneurs). What blocked the road to inquiry was an unreflective commitment to a very raw and primitive form of capitalism. This unquestioning allegiance to a very questionable set of economic assumptions produced a cultural blindness similar to what scientific materialism had inflicted on our understanding of nature and its workings.[1] The single vision of market economics blinds us to the real value of the city.

My aim in this chapter is to question these economic assumptions at their root. This is done in the first two sections, where the limitations of the capitalist ideology are set forth. But the question of liberal and communitarian theories of justice still remains a vital issue for the question of city justice. The third section argues that the key to understanding the normative measures appropriate for city justice is the concept of self-rule. The chapter then concludes with a defense of the proposition that the true form of city justice must always be some form of community life.

Market Place or City Place?

Part One of this study provided a vigorous defense of the supreme importance of place as an indispensable dimension in city life.[2] Place is that region of experience that gathers together into a unity spatial and temporal values such that an importantly evocative horizon for human experience is established. This environment is the ultimate structural achievement of city process because it enables the four ideal measures of intensity, integrity, wholeness, and depth to gain full expression. This openness to ideal expressions of value is grounded in the power of place to establish contrastive qualities of space and time. For place expresses volumes of space and time intertwined so as to articulate a region of experience and meaning unmatched by other forms of urban expression. Place is where urban goodness most richly occurs.

In the most general sense, place is the locus that gathers the one and the many into a creative moment of exceptional value. In framing this analysis of place I deliberately avoided mention of such distinctions as public and private place. My reason is simple: Place as an experience is prior to any division into collective or individual modes of expression. The importance of understanding this concept of place is seen most clearly in the discussion of signs, which was the subject matter of Part Two. Signs are forms of third-ness. What is third is the result of the consolidation of one and two. Only place has the "room" (both logical and existential) to accommodate the continuous growth of concrete reasonableness marking authentic human growth and development. Icons are necessary but they engage us only at the level of possible values. Indices are necessary but they represent only the collision of values. Symbols as signs of thirdness demand full participation as well as inclusion. Therefore, the fundamental role of place in urban semiotics is to provide a sphere of meaning within which human beings can grow through the "full speech"of the urban conversation.[3] It is inside place that city dwellers express the full measure of their humanity. Place is where the urban environment discloses most directly its urbanity. I use the term "urbanity" in its best sense as the expressively intense harmony that integrates individuals into a community of wholeness and depth. City place locates the gestures of meaning that foster "elegance" understood as the proper combination of simplicity and complexity.[4]

Cosmologically, place is created by all determinate harmonies for these ultimate *haeccities* take up their place by sculpting their own unique setting in space and time. Semiotically, place is where signs gather together their objects and interpretants so that meaning emerges within communities. Urban praxis demands the conservation of place, for the work of the city primarily concerns the creation and sharing of the wealth of experience.

By comparison, the marketplace is a dull affair. It involves the exchange of goods and services through a single medium of exchange—money. It brings to place a single vision that derives from a single perspective: profit making. Now, what exactly is profit? Given the structure of the market, profit is the increase in the amount of money one possesses after the exchange of goods and services. It is entirely a matter of quantity. Profit or loss is therefore the precise difference in the quantity of money one has at the end of the market day. I stress precision because it invokes the norm of narrowness so often used in this study. Narrowness is the means whereby intensity is raised in various environmental situations. It is altogether necessary if some measure of value is to emerge in the process we call reality. But by itself, it is inevitably self-destructive for it cuts off the range of possibility available for creative action. As this cosmology has maintained, it is narrowness wedded to vagueness that brings about the width necessary for excellent human experience. By itself, narrowness is self-defeating, for it triumphs by reason of exclusion.

Now, advanced late capitalism has a solution to this predicament. The width necessary for the proper growth of value is provided
by the individual players in the market. Each acting out of her own
self-interest will provide the necessary expansion of interests required to widen the market's span of attention. Given this expansion, narrowness is necessarily wedded to width through the free
choices of the players themselves. In the words of Adam Smith: "it is
not from the benevolence of the butcher, the brewer, or the baker,
that we expect our dinner, but from their regard to their own interest. We address ourselves, not to their humanity but to their self
love. . . ."[5] Freedom understood as the right to pursue one's own self-
interest within a vaguely identical society of economic agents ensures a proper width for the continued growth of the market. Since
we do not know beforehand the decisions of the market players, this
many is loosely (that is, vaguely) grouped as a one whose identity
can be calculated through the utility-maximization model of neoclassical economics.[6] The axiomatic character of this attempt to weld
narrowness to vagueness so as to provide economic width is well expressed by Donald Frey:

> [A]n economic agent who possesses a set of tastes for certain
> goods and services must spend a given income to buy goods and
> services in a mixture that maximizes personal "utility" or satis-
> faction. The agent is constrained by limited income and the
> prices that are charged for the goods. Thus, if relative prices or
> income change, the agent recalibrates the mixture of goods pur-
> chased. All behavior is described as the search for maximum
> utility amid changing constraints. This model is almost infi-
> nitely expandable into other realms; for example, one of the
> "goods" may be defined as leisure, and one's "income" may be de-
> fined as time, while the "price" of leisure becomes an hour's wage
> foregone. . . . The self-interest orientation is evident in that the
> economic agent's sole concern is maximizing its own "utility." [7]

It is therefore "utility-maximization" that is at the heart of advanced
late capitalism's understanding of place. That is why the marketplace is so empty of defining features. Its sole function is to provide
a place where utility-maximization can take place. The marketplace
takes on the character of an extreme abstraction such that its physical location can be anywhere and is therefore really nowhere. It is
without location except insofar as it is driven into existence by the
demands of the utility-maximizers. Failing to have a rootedness out-

side the interests of its participants, it can spring up anywhere, any-time. Thus, place understood as the spacetime horizon fit for the emergence of meaning loses all character except that which it can draw from the products and services exchanged within its domain. The placelessness definitive of so many parts of the contemporary city is precisely what a good capitalist entrepreneur requires to start up a business. What is most important about this analysis of city place and marketplace is the kind of activities that take place within their respective precincts. What occurs in city place has already been presented in Part One of this study. Briefly put, city place is marked by participation in shared meanings. These meanings are trans-ferred about city place by the icons, indices, and symbols that trans-form objects into experiences useful for human beings. So far this sounds very much like the purpose of the marketplace, but here is the crucial difference: City place has a multiform structure to convey both its content and its network meanings. The marketplace, on the other hand, is blind to meanings not associated with profit and its singular sign, money. When the marketplace determines the mean-ing of city place, then the fallacy of simple location has been commit-ted. Furthermore, the fallacy of misplaced concreteness is also brought into play, for money is the determining interpretant of the objects exchanged. As Simmel puts it: "since money itself is an om-nipresent means, the various elements of our existence are thus placed in an all-embracing teleological nexus in which no element is neither first nor last."[8] Time involves beginnings and ends. As the transformative symbolic power of the marketplace, money dissolves this time and along with it space as the circumambient horizon for the creation of meaning. When city place becomes marketplace, the city as a structure well placed to fund the participation of citizens in shared meanings collapses by reason of the severe dislocation of its important places.

All this is to be understood against the backdrop of the cosmo-logical vision offered in this study. The city is that place where human feelings are encouraged to rise to new levels of wholeness, which in turn foster new depths of experience. When this is for-gotten, then the words of Karl Polanyi ring all too true: "instead of economy being embedded in social relations, social relations are em-bedded in the economic system."[9] What happens when the market-place takes over is a severe loss of contrast in the feeling lives of city dwellers. No possibility of quality arises because no feelings can gain public access beyond the collision of values characteristic of second-ness taken up as a form of life. Is the right to utility-maximization the form of the good? Or is the good some richer form of meaning shared with one's fellow citizens? The dogmas of market economics side with the identification of the right with the good. But is this a belief claim posing as an iron rule of economic behavior? Are we dealing with theology or with science when it comes to devotion to market economics?

The Theology of the Invisible Hand

Modernism and postmodernism pride themselves on their liberation from the slavish thinking of the medieval past—a thinking they regard as riddled with irrational and unexamined assumptions. Among these superstitions was the conviction that there was a power greater than human beings that ruled them by reason of codes of correct behavior and threats of punishment. The science given over to the study of this invisible force was theology. In mocking tones, Enlightenment thinkers dismissed this pursuit of an invisible and transcendent God; yet, there is a similar transcendental entity alive and well in the corridors of the dismal science of economics. It is called "the invisible hand."

One of its chief modern interpreters, F. A. Hayak describes its power this way:

> The chief cause of [its] wealth-creating power . . . is that the returns of the efforts of each player act as the signs which enable him to contribute to the satisfaction of needs which he does not know, and to do so by taking advantage of conditions of which he also learns only directly through their being reflected in the prices of the factors of production which they use.[10]

Now, this sounds very much like magic. We get to have exactly what we want by following the signs that our own market-based behavior produces. Now, every sign, as Peirce has told us, brings together an object and an interpretant so as to function as a mediating force for meaning within a community setting. What is the object so signified? And what is the interpretant so hard at work here? The object is utility-maximization and the interpretant is the self-interest of the consumer. When markets function properly, they bring together sets of individuals who, acting out of their own self-interest, set up a balance of forces such that each "player" gets exactly what she desires. But it is possible to be even more specific, since the utility-maximization process is really the consumption of commodities and the exchange value of these objects are symbolized by money. Thus, the real magic of the market is that each person gets the chance to satisfy his own needs without upsetting the balance of supply and demand within the market structure itself. But there is a further good involved. Because human desire (understood here as self-interest) must act within a scheme of self-regulative pressures (understood here as the market equilibrium established by the mechanisms of supply and demand, which foster growth and efficiency), this desire itself contributes to the expansion of markets. And it is this "invisible hand" that is the "wealth-creating power" worshipped by capitalism.

I am being deliberately acerbic in this recasting of the capitalist ethos along the lines of a theology of the invisible hand. There are important features to market economics that warrant attention.[11] Nevertheless, my sarcasm has a point: Too often and especially in recent times, the market is invoked to justify policy decisions affecting everything from health care to education. Just as in the Middle Ages the sign "god" was used as an enchanter's wand to explain away the worst excesses of the political order, so also today the market's "invisible hand" serves to camouflage the pain inflicted on human beings for the sake of advanced late capitalism.[12] From the point of view of the process cosmology undergirding this study of urban praxis, it is axiomatic that all forms of absolutism are also forms of dogmatic foolishness destined to destroy important values.

There are three ways in which the theology of the invisible hand threatens important dimensions of city life. First, it absolutely forbids the discussion of any concept of the common good. Second, it denies the something in between which is the ground of community. Third, it replaces the shared concrete meaning that is the heartbeat of city life with an intolerable abstraction—money. For all these vital aspects of urban experience it substitutes the freedom of the individual to choose her own values as long as they are expressed through the market mechanisms of capitalism. Once again, F. A. Hayak expresses the point with admirable clarity:

> A Great Society has nothing to do with, and is in fact irreconcilable with 'solidarity' in the true sense of unitedness in the pursuit of known common goals.
>   . . .
> Many people regard it as revolting that the Great Society has no common concrete purposes or . . . that it is merely means-connected and not ends-connected. It is indeed true that the

chief common purpose of all its members is the purely instrumental one of securing the formation of an abstract order which
has no specific purposes but will enhance for all the prospects of
achieving their respective purposes.[13]

Community has nothing to do with economics. Justice has nothing to
do with community. There are no internal relations bonding humans
together in organizations that are both essential to their growth and
superior to their economic interests. The semiotics of economics begins
and ends with the $ sign. What emerges from the use of this sign is en-
tirely a matter of private choice carried out under the wise pressure of
the invisible hand. Secondness triumphs over thirdness for the sake of
individual liberty. If individual liberty and the exercise of the rights it
entails is taken to be the measure of justice, then the marketplace is
indeed the place where justice is to be found. But it is not right to pass
over in silence the absence of depth in such an understanding of city
existence. Nor should the way in which secondness and its collision of
forces replaces thirdness and community go unnoticed. Even granting
the power of the invisible hand to smooth over the aggression con-
cealed in the doings of the marketplace, its velvet glove does not soften
the sting of its slap across the face of the poor. A social numbness
blocking out " the awareness of recognizable feelings" infects the city.[14]
And despite Hayak's dismissal, this does remain "revolting," for it
shows how the worship of the "almighty buck" is the true liturgy of the
theology of the invisible hand. Within the confines of the marketplace,
the invisible hand may well be logical and even necessary. When extended beyond those borders, it is at least as irrational as any of the
older forms of theological superstition.

Self-Rule

Underlying the disputes between the partisans and the opponents
of capitalism is a deeper philosophical problem—human freedom and
its role in securing human happiness. How is the political body to deal
with the great question of liberty? Contemporary answers usually revolve about liberal or communitarian approaches to the question of
justice.[15] Stripped to its essentials, the debate revolves about the relation between the Right and the Good. True to its empiricist assumptions, liberalism is loath to assign any definite meaning to the Good. It
therefore proposes a procedural and contractual form of political rule
that seeks above all else to create, maintain, and preserve an open

space for the fullest exercise of human liberty. The communitarian response stresses the fact that freedom is always shared with others and
as a goal-oriented experience, it must be directed toward goods useful
for all members of the community. It therefore proposes for government a "formative project" that fosters dispositions, habits, and
virtues that contribute to the greater communal good.[16] William Sullivan elegantly expresses this civic republicanism:

> [F]reedom is virtue's ambiguous child. For the republican tradi-
> tion, civic virtue is the excellence of character proper to the citizen.
> It is freedom in the substantive sense, freedom understood as the
> capacity to attain one's good, where goodness describes full enjoy-
> ment of those capacities which characterize a flourishing life.
> Since humans are by nature social beings, living well requires a
> shared life, and a shared life is possible only when the members of
> a community trust and respect one another. To participate in such
> a shared life is to show concern for and reciprocity to one's fellows,
> and to do so is simultaneously fulfilling for the individual. Thus
> the individual's true good must consist not in attaining a sum of
> satisfactions but in showing in himself, and sharing as a partici-
> pant, an admirable and worthwhile form of life.[17]

One can almost hear the liberal's teeth grind at the sound of
these words. The communitarian vision is filled with prescriptions
for the use of freedom and vague ones at that. The footfalls of the
tyrant echo in the hall. The difference separating the liberal and
communitarian visions seem insurmountable.

But I offer the cosmology developed in this study as a way around
these difficulties. The real issue is not providing a prescription for
good living (which in the eyes of the liberal is the offense of the communitarian). Nor is it an invitation to a mindless use of freedom by
selfish individuals (which in the eyes of the communitarian is the
crime of the liberal). Both positions jump right over the more important question: How shall I rule myself ? This essay on the city has
been an intensive effort to practice what was earlier termed "normative thinking." In essence it is a return to Plato's understanding of
philosophy's purpose: To help human beings rule themselves and others well.[18] Now, to rule well demands the use of standards. Therefore,
it is never a question of having no standards but always a matter of
having the best standards for ruling. Every human being, liberal or
communitarian, uses standards in the conduct of their life. Logically
speaking, it is impossible to exercise one's freedom without the use of

standards. Even the decision to choose without standards is a standard. And it is the selection of appropriate standards that determines both the use of freedom and the question of one's responsibility. Put succinctly, responsibility precedes freedom.

What is therefore needed in this analysis of city justice is public discussion of the standards selected for the exercise of freedom. And it is precisely here at this critical moment in the life of the urban individual and the city community that advanced late capitalism fails us. All it can offer by way of a standard is "more"—more money, more goods, more services. Think of the intricacies of city life described in the last few chapters: Eros as that something in between grounding community in the desire for recognition by another; the dance of gestures culminating in the sharing of meaning; the intense acts of felt intelligence arising out of the habits cultivated by generations of citizens. The "more" of capitalism is not an adequate measure for the evaluation of good action, conduct, and habit. It offers no principle for self-rule beyond that of satisfying a lack; yet, it reigns supreme in city life.[19] Its entirely quantitative measure for self-rule leads to all the excesses of consumption and waste that bedevil city life. It holds out no responsibility for the consequences of one's choices beyond that of the discipline imposed by the marketplace. It is in sum the very antithesis of a useful normative measure for good city life.

Now, the liberal can reply that such measures and standards are best worked out in the actual process of governing. I agree as long as market theology is not used as the normative measure for the working out of the relevant issues. The reason for this ban should be obvious: The invisible hand locates responsibility elsewhere in the neutral workings of the market itself. The issue is self-rule, not rule by another. In its understandable zeal for liberty, liberalism confuses the power of the market to discipline with a free and open discussion of community standards. It grants too much valuational power to an instrument that is solely interested in a quantitative measuring of the good.

On the other hand, the communitarian is not without sin. Too often, appeals to the common good are really attempts by interest groups to retain power and influence. Community is no more of a magic word than the market. There is a tendency in communitarian thinking to justify all policy by reason of some nebulous theory of the Public Good.[20] A genuine community does not spring up overnight. It must earn its rightful place in the lives of individuals. As has been shown, its existence depends upon an artful and sensitive amalgam of customs, habits, gestures, and signs. Slogans do not further community. Furthermore, there is always the danger of covering up and displacing individual responsibility. Just as the liberal too quickly invokes the dubious wisdom of the market, so also the communitarian too often "lets George do it." The results of this form of irresponsibility are predictable. An opening yawns for power brokers to take over the community for their own narrow purposes. And what is worse, a sense of apathy and powerlessness infects the community's everyday life. Recall the "Iron Rule" practiced on the streets of the St. Jerome Community in the South Bronx.

To conclude: Self-rule is an issue to be faced by both liberals and communitarians. There is no way around the question of discussing the uses of freedom. Nor is it possible to avoid responsibility for one's choices. The act of ruling demands rules. It is the thesis of this chapter on city justice that the question of self-rule is prior to either liberal or communitarian positions. The liberal insofar as she asserts individual freedom as the form of the good must concern herself with the question of self-rule. In the same way, the communitarian insofar as he insists on the "formative project" required for good human living must also take up the issue of self-rule. What is at stake is therefore not the question of reducing human freedom or neglecting the rights of the community. These issues are part of a much more primary question: What are the best rules for human living? And the answer to that question will always be the outcome of intense, sustained, and public normative thinking. Liberalism maintains that one's first interest is to oneself. Market economics maintain that self-interest is best served by the operations of the invisible hand. In formulating the question of city justice I am proposing a seemingly slight but in the long run very significant change in the terms of the debate. Self-rule is a more intense, more integrated, wider and deeper concept than self-interest. It suggests that the standards we ought to use to shape ourselves are wider than self-interest defined economically. In ruling ourselves we are affected by much more than market conditions. These other influences demand that we shift from the paradigm of *homo economicus* to that of "person-in-community."[21]

City Justice Is Democratic Community

Nothing could be less concrete than the bare concept of community. This is doubly true in an age dominated by market economics. Late advanced capitalism fosters *gesellschaft* but it does not tolerate *gemeinschaft*. The purpose of this concluding section is to put some meat on the bare bones of the concept of community so far sketched. This will involve providing an understanding of community that takes account of the need for self-rule among its members. Also, community in the concrete must provide for an equitable sharing of wealth. How else can full participation take place? Finally, if it is to be taken seriously, the community must find a way to embed moral understanding within its political structures. An adequate definition of community requires an exercise in speculative philosophy. Sharing wealth demands a reconstruction of market economics. And the welding of ethics to politics calls for a renewed understanding of the place of community in the search for truth.

Speculative philosophy seeks to establish categories that grant a richer and deeper access to the realities under discussion. Here, we are talking about community. The four categories of Part One— inscape, contrast, pattern, and transmission—express the major dimensions of urban community. Inscape names the importantly unique ways in which communities achieve their indigenous values. Contrast enters community life through the concept of "person-in-community"as well as the primary human act of work. Pattern identifies the ways in which the central aspects of a community's life hang together. The category of transmission concerns itself with the transfer of values within a given set of urban events. It marks the ways in which physical, conceptual, and propositional feelings move about the community, and it also locates those community places where feelings of stillness express themselves most forcefully.

Each member of the community expresses self-rule through the inscape that inscribes her way of life. Thus, inscape and character are synonymous. It is through labor "as the act of making a living" that the category of contrast takes on flesh and blood. For what the worker does is bind the actual and the possible together into new forms of urban expression. Insofar as members of a community acknowledge each other's worth, they do so through the pattern recognition sustained by the entwined symbolic systems constituting their semiotic environment. In a similar way, truth in the life of a community is felt as the carryover of value. The category of transmission is vital for the truth process since the degree to which the values of the past and the potential values of the future inform the community's present experience is the measure of the community's commitment to truth. Inscape, contrast, pattern, and transmission are therefore the basic ways in which city justice spreads through an urban environment.

As the master/slave dialectic made clear, the ability to work grounds the experience of achieved self-identity. A concrete grasp of the value of human labor can be had by employing the four categories of Part One. The inscape of work is the unique creative transformation of events into values important for the community's growth in concrete reasonableness. To understand the process of work is to understand the human power to bring into a unity an actual set of events (goods and services) with its potential usefulness. It is this concept of work that gives the lie to the commodification of labor by market forces. Work is never merely worth its market price. Work is the means for human liberation and self-recognition. It is simultaneously the source of human identity and the power to transform the world of matter into things habitually useful for the human community. Work blends semiosis and praxis.

How are we to judge the health of a human community? When the production of commodities, the consumption of goods and services, or freedom made manifest through individualized modes of expression are selected as ultimate norms, then the depth and width of human creativity is fatally compromised. No matter how special the available commodities or how much of them are consumed or how radical the individual modes of self-expression, the value of human work goes unremarked. What is lost in this market interpretation of a community's pattern is the fact that it is human work that holds it together. Furthermore, these workers support families that make up the actual population of the community. Only a culture stunned by the rhetoric of advanced late capitalism could possibly ignore labor's central place in the patterning of human community. Labor is never a mere "commodity" to be priced according to the formulas of market economics. It is what human beings "do" in order to create community and by this act of creation they also establish the conditions that allow for the acts of recognition vital to their own self-identity.[22] The health of a community is to be measured by the various ways in which work is recognized, rewarded, and made available for its members. When this pattern is whole and inclusive, the community hangs together in a way that generates persons committed to self-rule by reason of the recognition of their fellow city dwellers.

It is precisely here in the reality of labor as the cornerstone of a community's pattern that the concept of truth as the carryover of value plays its most important role. The category of transmission deals with the ways in which physical, conceptual, and propositional feelings are transferred around various environments. Physical feelings make up the material components of a community's region of experience. They allow for the vital flow of energy necessary for the biological survival of the members of the community. Without the appropriate distribution of food, shelter, and clothing human community perishes. Conceptual feelings provide the community with the sense of definiteness and possibility necessary for a generalized understanding of its present state, past achievements, and future prospects. Propositional feelings are the ground of the symbolic structure of the community as it faces its need to grow and develop. The truth of a community therefore resides in the material stability, conceptual clarity, and semiotic richness transmitted through and among its members. A community that does not provide its members with a solid material base is not true to its mission. A community that provides only a weak form of self-understanding and future objectives carries a false identity. A community unable to generate strong propositional lures for future growth is already in a state of decline. In sum, the truth of a community is to be measured by its ability to feel and express the full weight of value—material, conceptual, and propositional—coursing through its members' being. And what creates these feelings of worth and sends them around the urban environment is human labor. This is the real reason behind Peirce's insistence that what the community in the long run regards as true is the ultimate pragmatic test of truth. Work, value, truth, and the community are inextricably combined in the context of contemporary city life. Their gradual merger over time and consequent impact on the community's history testifies to the continuing relevance of Peirce's "guess at the riddle."

Granted all this, it is clear why "person-in-community" is the new paradigm for fulfilled urban existence. Without persons capable of generating through their work intense values, no transmission of feelings will take place within community life. Without a community to bind together the efforts of persons, there will be no field within which particular felt values can take hold and spread their influence. Each needs the other for its full expression. This is the doctrine of coherence writ large within the interstices of human society. It is also the reason for the formula, city justice is democratic community. No other understanding of urban existence includes all the complexities needed to bring justice to the contemporary city.

The city in all its features—conditional and essential—should always be in the process of establishing levels of democratic community. To the degree that it is not, it is in the process of collapsing as an institution important for the growth and development of human beings. This is why Alexander's measure of emergent places of wholeness is so apt a sign of urban health.[23] For when the normative measure of wholeness is actively guiding an urban region, then work as intelligence-in-action, community as the ground of emergent truth, and justice as the active presence of forms of effective recognition are living factors in urban experience. Thus, thirdness is the only appropriate form of urban transmission. When indices dominate the semiotic being of the city, then advanced late capitalism has triumphed. Secondness is insufficient nourishment for the growth of the human person. It stunts the community and blocks inclusive participation. Similarly, even as the marketplaces of conspicuous consumption dazzle us, such icons are the "Wonderbread" of a social order lacking in genuine community nourishment. Firstness by itself eventually starves the soul.

I have been self-consciously trying to develop the resources for rebuilding community that are to be found within the tradition of American naturalism. In many ways, this study warrants being called an "American" urban cosmology. I would not quarrel with such a designation, for the heritage of American philosophy still retains profound connections within the daily life of citizens. It is only in the last twenty years that philosophy in America has been distracted by the narrowness of analytic schools of thought and seduced by the perfumes of Continental exoticism. The possibility of restoring to the philosopher an effective and important place in community life has been one goal of this study and its predecessor *Nature*. My concluding chapter suggests some ways in which that can become a public fact.

Chapter Twelve

The Philosopher and the City

In the East and the West the philosopher has traditionally played an important role in the life of the city. Socrates in Athens and Confucius in the city states of China practiced normative thinking in the most public way. The price they paid for this is also well known. The people of the city are not always happy to get the news that there are other, more desirable ways to conduct business. Nowadays, the philosopher's obligation to speak publicly has been exchanged for a much reduced role. No doubt it is safer to be but one more member of a university faculty, but the loss to the city is incalculable. What the philosopher can offer the city is threefold: a vision of the whole, measured public deliberation on values, and the capacity to speak truth to power for the sake of the poor and the vulnerable. Thus, the philosopher ought to offer the city a cosmology that outlines the contours of a fair and fitting city. The philosopher should also provide a public forum for the articulation of values within the city's continuing drama of emergent novelty. Lastly, the philosopher's heartmind ought to embrace the city's powerless and give voice to their concerns, for without them no community is complete. The city deserves a cosmology befitting its grandeur, a semiotics worthy of its values, and a praxis effective for all its citizens. The creation of such a vision

would be a worthy way to put American philosophy back to work on
important matters.

A Fair and Fitting City

All through the study of Part One, I used four classical metaphysical themes to weave together my account of urban space, time,
place, and goodness. It is therefore most appropriate that I conclude
this study of the city by returning to these cardinal concepts. Before
the advent of modern philosophy, being or reality was classically
characterized as "one, true, good and beautiful."[1] Nowadays these
"medieval transcendentals" have a quaint, archaic ring. They also
sound intolerably abstract. Unity? Truth? Goodness? Beauty? Who
uses such terms these days? But reconstructed in the light of the cosmology and semiotics of this study, they take on an elegant concreteness that expresses with great force the major findings of this urban
environmental ethical vision.

Unity names the way in which each urban event, situation, and
place expresses its own unique *haeccitas* and thereby contributes to
the growth of value in the city. It is therefore the ground of the determinateness characterizing every event, urban or natural. It also
makes clear why place is so important a value in the city. Was it not
Gertrude Stein who said about Oakland, "There is no 'there' there"?
Unity is the reason why any "there" actually exists. In separating itself off creatively and uniquely from any other event, each expression of importance in this urban cosmology establishes its own
oneness as the sign of its insistent particularity. Without unity no
expression of truth, goodness, or beauty could ever come to be.

Similarly, in terms of this urban semiotics, the world of signs depends upon the singular unity achieved by each icon, index, and sign
as it establishes the meanings bonding object, sign, and interpretant. The progression spanning one, two, three depends entirely on
the capacity of each "one" to maintain its real unity and not slide
into an undifferentiated sameness with its partners in the semiotic
rhythm of urban life. Hegel's warning about the cave into which all
footprints lead and out of which none ever emerge is a powerful reminder of just how dangerous to truth, goodness, and beauty a doctrine of unanalyzed vagueness can ultimately be. The quality
expressed in the icon of one is just as important as the force expressed in the index of two and the continuity embedded in the sign
of three. The vagueness employed throughout this study is an "ob-

jective" vagueness whose unity is tested by the stresses of actual application in the real world.

Ultimately, it is the world of city praxis that measures the unity achieved by all events in their process of coming to be. This is why the themes discussed in the last part of this study include intelligence-in-action, community, and justice. Each of these "signs," their objects, and their interpretants make possible the actualization of the cosmological categories developed in the first part of this study. Without unity no category of inscape could be communicated by the other categories of contrast, pattern, and transmission. There would be no concrete determinateness energizing regions of urban experience and value. I have already argued how this lack of identity through difference is at the heart of the intellectual confusion infecting advanced late capitalism. It is also the direct cause of the heartbreak felt by all those who fail to please the theologians of the invisible hand. Even though it becomes increasingly difficult to detect it, there is much more to city life than the "almighty dollar."

The truth of this analysis of the power of unity is found in the doctrine of "truth as the carryover of value" that was elaborated earlier in this study. For truth is the way in which the past achievements of urban experience are carried forward into the present and made a ground for future expression. Thus, the meaning of truth is not exhausted by a doctrine of correspondence à la types of empirical epistemology. Nor is its full significance felt in various coherence theories of truth. The meaning of truth is best found in the articulation of the values signified throughout the spatiotemporal domains affected by the various truth claims. Another way of saying this is that the pragmatic maxim remains solidly in place, for it is the ultimate importance of the truth claims in the life of the community that establishes the carryover of value signified by these claims.

Significations of urban importance are the business of a city semiotics. Here again, the connection between the cosmological categories of Part One and the urban semiotics of Part Two becomes clear. A sign must carry the value of an object fully into the world of the community, and its interpretant must render it useful by reason of settled acts of intelligence. Only then can the "truth" of any claim, assertion, or practice be adequately judged. The qualitative value of iconic unity must be tested against the collision of values indexically expressed in secondness. Passing this pragmatic test allows for the continuous emergence of importance that is characteristic of the sign of three. Value understood as importance, truth defined as the real consequences of intelligence-in-action, make clear the cosmological usefulness of the categoreal scheme. It allows us to identify the workings of the various generic traits of reality as they are expressed in city experience.

Central to an understanding of truth as the carryover of value are the categories of inscape and transmission. If determinate inscape is lacking, then no possibility for concrete verification through urban consequences really exists. We are left adrift in a dangerous fog of vagueness, an ambiguity deliciously tempting to all those who would identify truth with power. Likewise, the transferral of values around environmental systems becomes in urban environments an expression of competing truth claims. When various types of transmission occur, then what is at stake are real values and not merely consumer preferences. Be it physical, conceptual, or propositional feelings, what is being moved about the city are public options of real importance. The very way in which they are organized and moved about becomes critical. The transmission of values through force always involves some kind of threat. Force reduces the conceptual room needed for feeling alternative possibilities. Most important, the intensity of the lures for feeling characteristic of propositional transmission fades before the fear induced by appeals to force. This is shown most dramatically whenever a community stands up for its right to have places of stillness as part of its urban environment. Invariably, the collision of forces involved in the fight for a good use of public place is marked by threats of loss of income, jobs, and the flight of business in the face of the usurpation of commercially useful property. The deliberateness necessary for the right assessment of truth claims is fatally compromised whenever the public sphere is narrowed by reason of types of secondness masquerading as reasonable forms of thirdness. The continuity upon which truth depends for the expressive emergence of values is choked off and replaced by an extreme insistence on individual rights. Goodness is denied a place in the public debate on the carryover of value into the life of the community.

Throughout the history of philosophy there has been general agreement on the chief characteristic of the good. Taoist, Confucian, Platonic, Aristotleian, Thomist, Kantian, and Utilitarian positions assume that goodness gives of itself.[2] This act of self-diffusion may also be understood as its noncontentiousness.[3] It is also at the heart of Peirce's metaphysics of the dynamical object and its semiotic consequence; viz., the need for an ideal community whose wisdom and experience can appreciate normatively the novel forms of goodness emerging from the womb of process. This concept of the generosity ultimately marking goodness underlies the present reconstruction of the idea of goodness in the light of an urban cosmology.

Goodness is the value achieved by the harmony used to create the degrees of values expressed by events within the environment. (This definition applies equally to natural and urban environments.)[4] Now, what a harmony actually accomplishes is a very intricate transformation of conflict into contrast. And the way it does this must not be overlooked. It brings about the reconciliation of different values through the act of finding a space—logical, existential, social, natural, and urban—within which opposing types of individuality can find places of expression. What is most important is to understand just how a harmony pulls off this seemingly miraculous feat. As was seen earlier in this study, its creative power resides entirely in its capacity to be nothing in itself but its relations. A harmony provides room for difference by reason of its generosity. In being nothing but its relations, a harmony, as it were, steps aside and allows the full power of what is there to come to expression. The noncontentious quality of a harmony does not consist in its being a pushover for whatever forces are seeking their own way. Rather, a harmony's superior power resides precisely in its capacity to find room for what is essentially different in what is essentially together. This is the constructive power of the good. Its generosity finds a welcoming place for difference.

This is also the connection between goodness and reason. Wisdom is precisely the power to find places for differences in the growing concrete reasonableness of the real. This is Peirce's insight when he places the ultimate power of judgment within the future community of inquirers. It is likewise Mead's contribution when he shows how gestures heal the gap between isolated individuals. This is also Dewey's ideal when he speaks of the formative power of intelligence-in-action to bring about the conjoint reality binding together community, democracy, and justice. And finally, this is the form of the good that this cosmology of the city seeks to put into practice: That the intellectual generosity characterizing speculative philosophy at its best should find practical expression in acts of urban goodness. This is done most powerfully when harmony is at play within the streets, skylines, and neighborhoods of the city.

To speak of harmony is to speak also of beauty, the last of the "transcendentals." Beauty is an activity that culminates in the establishment of a special kind of place. Beauty's achievement consists in the construction of a fair and fitting place for the recognition and transmission of that value. When achieved, beauty infuses into the urban environment the feel of a fair and fitting city. Urban beauty is achieved when there is nothing but the expression of value within the city. Of course, it is rare—perhaps even impossible to achieve in any consistent way—but it remains the ultimate normative measure for urban excellence. It can serve in this capacity because of its power to sum up in a massively effective manner the major themes of this urban cosmology. Both in terms of the categoreal scheme and the urban semiotics developed in the course of this study, beauty acts as a final interpretant for the study of the contemporary city and its future possibilities.

The category most closely associated with beauty is that of contrast, and the semiotic rhythm within which beauty finds its full expression is thirdness. Taken together, contrast and thirdness articulate the culminating importance of beauty within city life. What contrast achieves is the right fit between the actual and the possible such that new forms of value receive novel expression. This major form of beauty summons up from the depths of reality new resources for turning conflict into contrast. In a similar way, Peirce describes thirdness as the conciliation of conflicted forms of opposition found within the rhythms of secondness. Thus, beauty is to thirdness as contrast is to reason. Width, persuasion, reconciliation, and continuity are the results of trusting beauty's power to bring about more intense forms of experience.

In terms of an urban praxis aiming at excellence, the experience of beauty evokes a sense of future efficacy by reason of the depth of present experience. It brings together into richly contrasted unity the achievements of the past and the promise of the future. And it does this by reason of opening a deep and wide space for novelty to enter the cityscape. It is at once the enlargement of experience through imagination and its reconstruction through deft modes of harmonic creation. This is why Dewey insisted on beauty's pragmatic power to provide both consummatory experience in the present and a thick sense of continuity with the past and the future. Beauty achieved is felt thought's tribute to the gifts of novelty. The new demands a reexamination of modes of normative thinking. It challenges past assumptions even as it seeks a status equal to them.

Beauty is therefore as intimately involved with self-government as it is with the sheer intensity of experience. It is no mere invitation to exceptional forms of illusory entertainment. Neither is it indulgence in the pretty or the "exquisite." Beauty's strength resides in the fact that it demands responsibility both from those who would create it and those who would experience it. What ties ethics and aesthetics together is both the unity achieved within the boundaries of any harmonic complex and the truth expressed within those limits. The carryover of value marks the degree of warranted truth recognized within urban semiotic networks. The unity felt in these experiences is in direct proportion to the integrity achieved by good appropriation of complexity by simplicity. It is entirely wrongheaded to wall off beauty from the good. They belong together because the intrinsic generosity of the beautiful fits together the many dimensions of the good. If the city is one, true, good, and beautiful in any important way, then that is the sign that thought and feeling have given up their opposition and entered into the dance of the one and the many.

One Thought/Many Feelings/Three Signs

All cosmological thinking involves an insistence on the importance of order. The construction of the categoreal scheme underlying this urban cosmology is prompted by the need to identify and correlate the varying types of order to be found in urban environments. Now, underlying all forms of order is the experience of unity. The presence of unity is felt in different ways according to the degree of unity experienced in various city regions and activities. Thus, the one thought of this cosmology is the presence of unity experienced through the ever-changing presences of order found within an urban environment.

Order is grounded in unity because all forms of order—tightly knit or loosely woven, closed or openended—arise from the quality of the relations established by and among the members of the order in question. All these relations share a common goal: to bring into a unity that which was previously dispersed. What was once disconnected is now brought into some kind of relation. Unity therefore means the establishment of connections. It is the first gesture of creativity whereby "the many become one and are increased by one."[5] Unity can assume many forms. It can be as simple as the mere display of spatial patterns exhibiting the boundaries of external relations. A circle stands beside a triangle which rests next to a square. Some form of unity has emerged. Or it can be as complex as the internal relations established within the human brain by the actions of its various cells. And of course an indefinite number of unified states stand between these and other possible extremes.

Unity is therefore not uniformity. Any attempt to equate the two betrays a serious lack of thought. There is much talk these days about the Western mind and its hegemonic effort to eliminate all forms of diversity. But when it is said that thought itself is at the heart of this logocentric drive to dominate and oppress, then post-modernism itself has lost its ability to think well. It has badly con-fused uniformity with unity and in so doing set up a philosophic bogeyman that never existed in the minds of great Western thinkers such as Plato, Aristotle, Aquinas, Spinoza, and Hegel. Unity names a rich array of potential relations that have one purpose in com-mon—the creation of connections.

This study of the forms of unity to be found within an urban en-vironment suggests a reformulation of the famous *cogito* that began modern philosophy. Where Descartes said, "I think therefore I am," the contemporary city dweller should say, "I connect therefore I am." Connection demands that one move out of one's selfishness and ac-knowledge the real presence of otherness. Such acts of communica-tion need to be grounded in modes of participation that genuinely demand the full commitment of real persons. It is precisely here that philosophy, especially as developed within the tradition of American naturalism and pragmatism, can offer much to the development of urban experience. What is required above all else is judgment. As I have argued throughout this essay in urban cosmology, to judge well means to be in possession of normative measures that are both ade-quate and applicable. Applicable means that they can be experienced and adequate means that they express not only what is but also what should be. Measures suitable for contemporary urban life must realistically harmonize the actual and the ideal. While it is always important to know one's context, it also equally important to rise above it when such action is called for.

Now, the best way to achieve this difficult conjunction of the ac-tual and the ideal and make it effective within the precincts of urban reality is through an astute sense of the types of order at play within the city. In other words, good urban praxis demands the kind of prac-tical wisdom that comes from daily experience *had*[6] within "the street," "the empire skyline," and "the neighborhood." Participation in the many forms of unity connecting the various domains of city life requires the development of a "city sense." This sensibility in-volves a deftness that can touch the surface of the city and at the same time feel the pulse of values throbbing within it. What I am talking about is what was earlier called "felt intelligence." At its best, normative thinking involves both the feel of a situation as well as an intelligent grasp of the essential and conditional features making up that situation. To paraphrase Kant, feeling without intelligence is empty, intelligence without feeling is blind.

It is time to bring together the various elements of my argument. I have argued that this urban cosmology has pursued a single thought throughout its development. That thought is the idea of unity and its expression through various types of order. More specifically, I have argued that unity is expressed through the effective presence of four levels of order. I have also offered the hypothesis that these levels of order are accompanied by identifiable feelings. Finally, I have developed an urban semiotics that ties the communication of certain urban experiences to the recognition of three types of signs, the icon, the index, and the symbol. Weaving these strands together provides an opportunity to envision the outlines of a concretely effective urban praxis.

Even as cosmology thinks the one thought of unity and its expression through various levels of order, it must at the same time analyze the many feelings arising from the experience of those levels of order. This cosmology has been an extensive inquiry into the many forms of value expressed throughout city environments. A word that sums up all these forms of value is *intensity*. Now, the only way to know intensity is to feel it, and this brings us to the heart of my argument about the city. I maintain that there is a direct connection between the four levels of order and their accompanying feeling tones and the three types of signs deployed within urban environments to express those feelings.

Recall the four levels of order and the feelings that they evoke when they are experienced. Trivial orders express nothing of importance and therefore generate moods of indifference when they are encountered in city life. Vague orders, with their suggestion of emerging types of importance, cause an air of expectation to spread throughout an urban region. When narrowness is expressed throughout a city environment, then feelings register their presence with great intensity. Finally, orders characterized by width wrap the city in interconnected layers of involvement. Thus, the kinds and conditions of unity experienced within the city register their presences in ways that bring to the forefront identifiable forms of feelings.

In their turn, these feelings provide precisely the kind of emotional tone needed to support the urban semiotics discussed in Part Two of this study. Thus, icons are supposed to generate a sense of expectation when they represent modes of urban firstness. Similarly, an index requires a certain sustained level of intensity in order to

function effectively as a sign of secondness. Lastly, symbols by definition must stir up feelings of involvement in order to express the real
presence of thirdness within urban environments. Thus, if we take
triviality in its most literal sense, then there is nothing of importance to be expressed. This leaves the analysis with three types of
order, three corresponding types of feelings, and three kinds of signs.
It is by identifying the complex patterns spanning the cosmological
and semiotic parts of this study that the normative dimensions of
an effective urban praxis begin to emerge. Expressing these ethical
signs to fellow city dwellers is (and historically has always been) the
philosopher's primary intellectual obligation (see fig. 7, p. 97).

Now, all normative thinking concerns itself with the constructive
and destructive use of standards and measures of goodness. In what
follows, I offer a speculative and systematic account of the ways in
which orders of vagueness, narrowness, and width, and feelings of
expectation, intensity, and involvement interact with icons, indices,
and symbols in order to give birth to important forms of urban goodness. Conversely, failure to use these modes of connection in appropriate ways leads to forms of urban alienation. While I deal with
each order, feeling, and sign separately, it must be recalled that all
these types of unity are constantly crisscrossing throughout urban
regions. Thus, the city is a continually shifting crossroads of intelligence, feeling, and expression. It is to the task of sensing these meeting points of the human soul and measuring their respective
axiological weight that the philosopher must bend his efforts.

I begin by returning to the theme of urban firstness and its iconic
presence within the streets of the city. What is the type of order and
the emotional mood needed for the good functioning of iconic representation? Remember that firstness is all about quality and possibility; therefore, a certain level of vagueness must accompany its iconic
representation so that a mood of expectation can assert itself within
the realm of public discourse. Urban icons that do not compel some
measure of anticipation cancel out the very sense of possibility they
are supposed to express. The constructive use of icons is achieved
whenever a vague sense of quality is felt throughout a particular
urban situation. The good parent does this naturally when she joins
with her child in the recognition of some form of beauty potentially
expressing itself within an urban domain. By acknowledging the
vague presence of some quality, the parent leads the child forward
into a world of potential wonder and interest. It is through such moments of interest and appreciation that vague intimations of the potential quality of the world begin to flood the child's soul.

But when such moments become too narrowly intense, specific, or heavy handed, then the whole sense of delightful surprise is lost and the child's natural wonder is frozen in place. Instead of an ever-growing sense of expectation that encourages further exploration, the child is offered some exact version of value and all sense of exploration immediately ceases. What could have been an invitation to an ever-deepening engagement with value in all its many forms has now become fixated on a single object. This is why Peirce warned against the attempt to specify a precise value within the realm of firstness.[7] Of course, he is really warning against confusing icons with indices and symbols.

This is a special danger in this age of overhyped media presentations that employ celebrities to "show us" the way to excellence, power, beauty, and happiness. When an instantly recognizable icon such as Michael Jordan becomes identifed with success, dedication, and all that is good in life, then a singularly destructive semiotic error has been perpetrated on the public mind. The vagueness of the icon has been confounded with the existential width of the symbol. And what was only a vague form of quality and value is now made to stand in for the genuine experience. Proof of the accuracy of this interpretation is found in Jordan's complete inability to recognize his moral obligation to speak out against Nike's exploitation of Third World labor. But that is what happens when an icon masquerades as a symbol. There is nothing particularly excellent or noble about a person who accepts millions of dollars to sell a product made on the backs of the poor. And yet there is probably no more universally recognized "symbol" of excellence than Michael Jordan. Such is the fate of a society that has lost the power to measure the difference between an icon and a symbol.

It is precisely its capacity to unite vagueness, expectation, and quality that makes an icon such an important part of the urban conversation. Icons invite us to the feast of life but they do not specify the menu. As a result, our appetite for value is whetted but no specific object specified. We are encouraged by the strong presence of icons to explore our world and directly experience its many potential forms of value. That is the constructive use of icons. When icons serve to lock human consciousness into a specific modality, then the growth of that mind is seriously threatened. Our capacity to grow in discernment and axiological sensibility is fatally injured when we get stuck in highly predictable forms of urban behavior. Market economics may be delighted by such unquestioning forms of consumption, but the urban person does not live by such buying and selling alone.

When city life loses its feel for firstness, then an obsessive concern with particular forms of gratification emerges and the road to further creativity is blocked by the heaped-up material objects that "stand in" for a genuine life filled with expectation, intensity, and involvement. And all of this becomes even more inevitable and more threatening when it takes place within the confines of a consciousness radically narrowed by an exaggerated consumerism. Stuffed with goods and services, we become blinded to the sheer beauty of the urban world. As this cosmology has consistently argued, the realm of possibility is marked by continuity. Possibilties shade off into each other as they move along a line of continually ramifying forms. Actuality, on the other hand, is specific, determinate, and concrete. What is actual is right here, now, and in this place. When icons lose their power to lure us into an exploration of different forms of values, the realm of firstness is shut down and the rich possibilities of "the street" no longer call out to the city dweller.

Urban secondness is the realm of narrowness and intensity. Its sign is the index, which directly "indicates" to us what is going on in a particular environment. As the sign of a direct relation spanning two objects, it signals the reality of the external world and the important ways in which the objects of that world affect our plans and actions. Insofar as the index points toward those things that just "happen to be" whether we like it or not, it is an invaluable corrective to any lingering forms of narcissism that would urge us to take ourselves as the standard of all that is good, true, and beautiful. Within the spatiotemporal span connecting the two dimensions indicated by the index, there exists the urban quality of secondness that is indispensable for leading a realistic life. For it is secondness that registers the collision of forces that wake us to the fact that there is a really existing extramental world not of our own making.

An index must exhibit narrowness and the intensity of feeling associated with such a level of order if it is to effectively represent the collision of forces it is designed to represent. A weak, ambiguous index is no index at all. When it functions in a constructive manner, an index puts the interpreter in direct contact with what is vital for her well-being. It enforces direct contact with what is of immediate importance. Signs that say, "Safety is here; danger is there," bring to the forefront of urban consciousness the intense power, clarity, and force associated with the realm of secondness. No urban dweller could survive without a sufficient reserve of such indexical signs. Secondness erases all traces of narcissistic self-involvement left over from too indulgent an exposure to firstness. It is the real world as it is currently constructed and as it is presently affecting our actions that is represented through the semiotic power of the index.

But that "real world" is also at the same time a world in the process of transformation, for its destiny is to grow beyond secondness into a wider, deeper, more integrated display of creativity. Therefore, there always lurks within the realm of secondness a great danger. When the index is mistaken for the symbol, then its capacity to alert us to the need for further growth is fatally compromised. Insofar as the index points to an oncoming collision of forces, it serves to locate a place of energetic stress emerging in the world of urban experience. But it does not tell us what to do with that strife or how the struggle between values represented by the index is to be resolved. In short, the index remains forever embedded in the realm of secondness. This is as it should be, for the index is the sign of two and therefore merely represents different experiences in relation. It has nothing further to say about the possibility of growing beyond that impasse.

Now, just as the icon is subject to exploitation due to the inappropriate power granted to the media in the contemporary city, so also the index can be used to confuse urban citizens about the values caught up in the struggle represented by the index. As was discussed in the previous chapter, this is especially true in an age where market economics has come to be seen as the ultimate arbiter of values. That this is the case in the present day should be obvious to even the most casual observer. Over and over again, the so-called "bottom line" becomes the standard by which values are to be selected. Now, market economics is a precisely calibrated (or at least it presents itself as such) measuring tool for deciding the monetary value of various items to be bought and sold, but it indicates nothing directly about the intrinsic value of these items. Their worth is their price as determined by the invisible hand of the market. But this tells us only about the way in which the forces of supply and demand have come to a certain equilibrium concerning certain material objects. To use this index as the sole measure whereby personal choices and social policy will be set is to confuse the realm of thirdness with the realm of secondness. It says in effect that there is no way to some wider vision whereby we can attain greater clarity and conviction about what really matters in human life.

The index becomes destructive when it is used to fix a certain way of looking at the city and its problems. As an important moment along the continuum that marks out growth of concrete reasonableness, the index no longer points beyond itself to a greater reality.

Instead, the index itself becomes the symbol of what is finally and ultimately "really real." Like the icon confused with the symbol, the index when similarly mistaken narrows down urban understanding to a perpetually renewed struggle for "the survival of the fittest," only this time the fittest are the most financially shrewd and not the most physically fit. It matters little that now we speak of the bottom line instead of the strongest man. Both attitudes are indices of secondness gone wild.

If evil is the destruction of something greater than itself, then surely the misuse of indices is a leading contributor to the real presence of evil in the world. What makes indexical thinking so hard to eradicate is the fact that the index by its very nature elicits intense emotional reactions. As anyone who has tried to argue with someone mired in secondness can attest, the narrowness necessarily associated with indexical signs makes real dialogue impossible. Ideologies of whatever stripe—economic, political, or philosophical—establish a mood of intensity that balks at real tolerance of difference. In the realm of secondness, it is the collison of forces that counts. Compromise through finding a wider point of view is no part of the semiotics of secondness. A culture that confuses secondness with thirdness must in the end promote a way of resolving differences that leans toward compulsion as the ultimate arbiter of the true, the good, and the beautiful. For all its power to sway by force, secondness must finally give way to a wider vision of cultural involvement—one that moves beyond the narrow confines laid out by the intense emotional forces at work when the index comes to dominate public discourse.

Thirdness is the realm within which the order of the city, its many feelings, and its symbolic culture come to maturity. The symbol represents that mode of public discourse that fosters citizen involvement in wide axiological experience. Without symbolic interaction citizens would lack a mode of public discourse that could tie together their diverse experiential realms. As the sign of thirdness, the symbol performs a double function for city dwellers. First, it establishes continuity between the past, the present, and the future. In so doing it provides a vision wide enough to span the different temporal modalities within which city dwellers must live. If the icon necessarily focuses on the present and the index stresses the immediate future, then it is the symbol that brings all three time zones into a judicious balance.

It is this quality of temporal expansiveness that makes possible the second function of the urban symbol. When temporal width is felt with some degree of intensity, a feeling of involvement—potential as well as actual—seeps through the cityscape. Great urban symbols seize the felt intelligence of the urban populace and convert urban spacetime into an invitation to significant inclusion. By spreading wide the order within which it represents its meaning, the urban symbol plays a direct role in gathering into an affective unity the many differences that make up any city situation. By eliciting an affect of tolerance, a good urban symbol establishes a region of inclusion that beckons diverse interests to take up a place within its existential boundaries.

This is the constructive quality of urban thirdness. Within the real presence of a powerful urban symbol, authentic human involvement in urban experience can take place. All that was previously said about place echoes through these final reflections on urban thirdness.[8] It is through the sign of three that width of experience is matched with maximum participation in diversity. Just as the power to unite what usually falls apart is the signature of great places, so also the effective presence of thirdness is evidenced through the degree of inclusiveness evoked by the urban symbols in question. It is in this way that beauty once again emerges as the important dimension of city life. For urban thirdness is nothing less than the growth of real beauty emerging out of the strained relations characteristic of secondness. Where once there were two in collision, now there are three uniting past, present, and future in a continuous symbolic flow of value.

It is this constructive power that measures out wide roads of continuity that can accommodate simultaneously the presence of novelty and order. For within thirdness the shock of the new is cushioned by the massive presence of past achieved values. But this is what Alexander meant by the form of the good city and its one rule of emergence into ever-growing patterns of wholeness.[9] And it also makes clear how imperative it is for the citizenry to be schooled in normative thinking. Without a *paideia* that can sensitize city dwellers to the critical importance of intensity, integrity, depth, and wholeness, there is little hope that thirdness will find its own significant place within urban experience. What I am arguing for is the practical side of beauty. For without a widespread sensibility that values beauty for its own sake, neither continuity nor involvement nor creativity have much chance to express themselves within the urban scene. The imbalance that marks the signs of one and two will dominate city life. We will have either Las Vegas or Wall Street or some dreary combination of the two. A real city with real people who live in real neighborhoods will ever elude us.

All this makes clear why the role of the philosopher as public intellectual remains so necessary. It is the intellectual responsibility of the philosopher to raise these seemingly abstract questions about normative standards and the possibility of an urban praxis that can be measured in terms of values like beauty, novelty, balance, and integrity. This lengthy discussion of the one thought of cosmology, the many feelings derivative from thinking on this one thought of unity, and the three signs used to express those feelings makes evident an undeniable fact: The lover of wisdom is still needed within the city precincts.

The Philosopher as Master of Heartfelt Contrast

This study insists that there are always two dimensions at play in our thinking and feeling processes. There is at the forefront of our awareness a focus illuminating what is of immediate concern. But this foreground is given depth by the degree to which it connects with that which stays in the background and grants solidity and place to our present concerns. These contrasted dimensions of human experience find their most concretely interwoven expression in the subtle interactions of thought and feeling that mark city life at its best. As I argued in the previous section, these urban dimensions form "the one thought" of urban cosmological thinking and "the many feelings" of their accompanying moods. And as expressed through the three signs of urban semiotics, they make up the warp and woof of city experience.

Now, the idea of contrast has been central to this study. It is among the categories used to describe the workings of the urban environment and is also synonymous with the concept of beauty. A contrast is a harmony that brings into a balanced relation aspects of a situation that normally would not hold together. In other words, a contrast is a unique act of creativity that enlarges the cityscape by widening what is included in its boundaries. Thus, a contrast is also directly related to the dimension of thirdness that is such a vital part of good city form. Finally, because of its special character, a contrast expresses both a feeling tone and an intellectual content. In sum, a contrast is the epitome of the cosmological, semiotic, and practical parts of this study.

The contemporary philosopher can best provide an important intellectual service to urban society by developing forms of normative thinking that stress the importance of contrast as an essential ingredient in contemporary culture. As a form of unity that brings together seemingly opposed aspects of experience, a contrast offers an important form of healing for a culture bedevilled by destructive forms of dualistic thinking. Its power to heal splits in our culture is grounded in the capacity to provide a vision wider than the reigning forms of orthodoxy. When this is appropriately carried out, the narrowness excluding important parts of experience is eliminated and alternate forms of culture become real options. What is more, precisely because the philosopher deals with only vague contrasts, intense community involvement is demanded as part of the task of finding specific solutions to particular problems. The philosopher is no divine being handing down universal edicts. Rather, what the philosopher can offer the civic process is width of vision that encourages alternative ways of looking at problems. And what is more, because the philosopher is also expected (at least in the tradition of speculative philosophy) to provide intellectually coherent and applicable ideas, the community can expect testable hypotheses, not empty generalities. Thus, the philosopher is part of the experimental process of developing better ways to live together. Paying strict attention to the feedback between theory and practice ought to be a routine aspect of the philosopher's contributions to city life. The philosopher is neither an infallible guru nor a substitute social scientist. The intellectual contribution that the philosopher can make to the contemporary city lies in the direction of providing a wider understanding of what is possible within the real constraints of the urban environment. In short, the philosopher ought to become a master of contrast as a way of providing effective modes of thinking about divisive issues.

But there is more to the philosopher's responsibility than abstract intellectual effort. The contrast offered must also be "heartfelt." I employ this term (and I am aware of how sentimental the term may sound, especially to cynical ears) in order to express the connection between thought and feeling that has been so much a part of my argument. In so doing I once again consciously place myself within the tradition of American naturalism and pragmatism. Surely, when William James inveighed against vicious intellectualism, he was protesting against a form of thinking that tore the heart out of human experience. And a great part of Charles Peirce's labor to develop his semiotics of firstness, secondness, and thirdness was given over to ensuring a central place for feelings within philosophical reflection. Likewise, Dewey's insistence on the "had" quality of experience was meant to remind us that feeling is a more primary and concrete category than sensing and thinking. And there is also Whitehead's doctrine of prehensions, a bold systematic effort to refuse any ultimate distinction between thought and feeling. Heart and mind go together within the spirit of American philosophy.

My insistence on the primacy of aesthetics for understanding urban experience is rooted in a similar respect for the place of feelings in human culture. In the end we are probably far more influenced by our feelings than our thoughts. The problem is not to eliminate feelings so that so-called dispassionate thought can govern our lives. Freud has shown that such an abreaction only deepens our cultural crises. The return of the repressed is a real danger ever threatening to drown those institutions that ignore the felt dimension of experience. Nor is a life lived solely within the emotional register a satisfactory answer. The real task involves bringing thoughts and feelings appropriately together. That is essentially what I am suggesting when I call the philosopher "the master of heartfelt contrast."

In assigning such a responsibilty to the philosophical community, I am fully aware of its impossibility. But this is no real news since philosophers have always been attempting the impossible. The real danger shows itself when they suffer a failure of nerve and stop assaulting the limits of the possible. I am acutely aware of the impossibilty of doing justice to the urban environment. In *Nature*, I was similarly aware of the difficulties inherent in the philosopher's task. To assist me I developed four basic ideas (borrowed from Whitehead) as a framework for a philosophically responsible analysis of the value of nature.[10] I here reintroduce these ideas to deepen the concept of heartfelt contrast by assembling certain general notions implicit in its makeup.

These four ideas are perspective, understanding, expression, and importance. Each concept has a meaning unique to itself but at the same time must be set in an appropriate relation to the other three. In fact, it is this act of "setting in an appropriate relation" that is the supreme act of good urban praxis. For it should be remembered that to fit things together in a good way is the very definition of beauty. Therefore, these four ideas constitute a final summary of the obligations facing any philosopher who seeks to understand in a systematic way the multidimensional cultural phenomena of the modern city. The following review of these concepts offers one last opportunity to appreciate the extraordinary power of systematic philosophy. It is within the strength of such a synoptic vision that both the heart and the mind can find their appropriate place.

When constructing a cosmology, the adoption of the right perspective is of primary importance. Without a wide enough vision,
cosmology's duty to offer a scheme of general ideas that reflect the
generic traits of the matter under investigation cannot be fulfilled.
Thus, the seeming abstractness of the categoreal scheme is only jus-
tifed in terms of its usefulness in capturing in an objectively vague
way what is important about the urban environment. To speak of inscape, contrast, pattern, and transmission makes sense only if they
help to specify what goes on in a general way within a city. Likewise,
to stress the importance of creativity as the central meaning of
urban experience, is to offer the hypothesis that the emergence of
novelty is the ultimate meaning of city life. A similar search for
width of vision and application underlies my identification of four
levels of order and their accompanying moods. Such a hypothesis is
meant to allow for an inclusive understanding of the many meanings
of unity. Thus, advocating a specific perspective is not an act of hegemonic logocentrism. It is much rather the necessary result of taking
seriously philosophy's obligation to speak in such a way as not to
marginalize what is of value in city life. Thus, the upholding of cosmological perpsective is an act of intellectual daring that welcomes
the challenge of understanding and expressing the value of what is
under discussion. The heartfelt dimension of perspective is encountered when the scheme of general ideas actually does put us in contact with what is important about the city.

Given the commitments underlying this study, understanding is
by definition normative. That is why the carryover of value understood as contrastive beauty is so profoundly appropriate as the
meaning of truth within an urban environment. To understand is to
intelligently feel the many ways within which the unity of the one
and the many contrasts itself so as to create the expression of novelty within city life. Or what is the same thing, to understand is to
share in the act of felt intelligence as it conducts the public mind toward an encounter with novel beauty. The practice of cosmological
thinking is an effort to feel and understand the plural domains of
value that intersect continually within the urban situation. My
analysis of urban space as that which binds up these dimensions of
value is an effort to make clear what is axiologically at stake within
the seemingly neutral spatial structures that are established within
cities. So also the discussion of city time sought to provide a felt
understanding of the temporal weight that is suffused throughout
the contemporary city. The discussion of the contrastive power of
place to fuse spacetime into bounded volumes of value is a similar

example of felt intelligence at work.[11] To understand the city is itself an act of heartfelt contrast for it demands that the thinker feel the values expressed by the various urban events and at the same time be able to think the connections between these achievements. It is only by fully developing this mode of understanding that Alexander's "one rule"can be effectively deployed in city planning. Discovering connections that can grow into ever-increasing situations of wholeness is an art form not reserved for those proficient in city planning. It is an act of understanding that must be grounded in the felt intelligence of the community. Thus, the real test of understanding is whether or not it can be shared with others.

But what is shared within a city is the outcome for better or worse of the semiotic system at work within its boundaries. Expression is the act whereby signs are developed to represent the meanings shared by the city dwellers in question. These meanings are the values expressed by the events making up urban experience. It was because of the variety, richness, and complexity of these modes of urban expression that I introduced the semiotics of Charles Peirce. Firstness felt as the experience of fresh and spontaneous value is understood through the interpretive power of the icon. Its power to represent our initial contact with the extramental world was as critical as it was ephemeral. Our second encounter with reality is marked by a collision of values. The force of this conflict is well expressed by the unbending directness of the index. But the full development of felt intelligence awaits its unfolding in the moment of thirdness. For it is here in the symbol as the expression of a continuity of shared meaning that felt intelligence encounters the authentic presence of contrast. What was previously held apart in mutual isolation is now brought together into a unity. The resulting intensity of feelings grounds intelligence in a matrix of communally shared meanings. The consequent involvement is the very height of mentality as expressed within city experience.

But none of this would matter very much if the perspective adopted, the understanding achieved, and the expression experienced did not put the city dweller into the presence of what is important. As the final member of this quaternity of general notions, importance binds together the meanings of the other three. To be important is to make a difference. Without situations laden with importance a city and the lives of its citizens sink into a swamp of triviality. Because importance is lacking, no serious debate about values is possible, for everything is exactly like everything else. No difference emerges and therefore no alternative perspective ever offers itself for consideration. As a consequence, new forms of understanding can never arise and the need for forceful expression dissolves. The apathy afflicting various segments of the city population is in direct proportion to the disappearance of importance as a real factor in their lives.

The interwoven quality of Part Three's discussion of intelligence-in-action, community, and city justice directly reflects the way in which importance binds together the other three notions. For unless intelligence-in-action concerns itself with what makes a difference, the community will have nothing of importance to express. And in the resulting indifference, the energy needed to bring about genuine reform will never appear. The community itself is dependent upon a sense of importance for its continued existence. Without some measure of the significance of its action, any group will sooner or later dissolve. This is even more true of a genuine community dedicated to improving the lot of its members. It is no accident that the most effective way to defeat attempts at community reform is to deny the existence of such needs. When importance collapses, the triad of perspective, understanding, and expression loses its reason to be.

Importance provides the fuel necessary to carry out the arduous tasks involved in creating contrasts capable of uniting what was once divided. It is very hard work to think up ideas big enough and true enough to do the job of eliminating dualisms. Add in the abstractness afflicting much philosophic work and one can readily understand why the wait for good ideas so often disappoints a culture. But it really does no good to dismiss philosophy as no longer culturally relevant. As I hope this study has amply demonstrated, the need for masters of heartfelt contrast continues. Without a unification of heart and mind, the possibility of moving beyond the dualisms that at present sap our public will is decidedly diminished. Something like a rediscovery of the Chinese sense of HeartMind as well as a renewed sense of *li* understood as the pursuit of the common good must occur if a public place for philosophy is to be maintained in the contemporary city.[12] That place should be occupied by thinkers willing to do the hard work of systematically relating the many dimensions of human experience within a sysem of thought that gives equal weight to the importance of human feelings. The contrast between the foreground and background dimensions of our thinking and feeling is of the greatest import for philosophy. Sometimes it is our thought that is out front, and our feelings recede into the dim background. Other times see our feelings racing ahead of our thinking processes. But what is most important is the undoubted unity

that exists between both regions of experience. That unity is best understood as a contrast, and it is the philosopher who should seek to
master its intricacies in a heartfelt way.

American Philosophy at Work

This work could just as easily been entitled an American cosmology rather than an urban one. For it is derived in both spirit and
form from American pragmatism and naturalism. I wish to conclude
this study by reflecting on the importance of this tradition for American culture as it enters the next millennium. Recently a number of
important studies bearing on the significance of classical American
philosophy have appeared.[13] These works proclaim the need for philosophy in America to return to its roots and once again engage the
real problems that trouble our times. Representative of this hunger
for engagement with real experience is an essay by Robert Neville
entitled "American Philosophy's Way around Modernism."[14] Reflecting on the contributions of the distinguished American philosopher
John Smith, Neville comments on the importance of Smith's reconstruction of the theory of experience: "Smith has pointed out that
experience . . . is (1) a matter of interactive engagement, (2) interpretive, (3) corrective, in process, of antecedent expectations and (4)
aesthetic."[15]

Each of these qualities has informed my attempt to understand
the modern city from a philosophic perspective that engages in a systematic way the most important traits of the urban environment. I
have argued from the outset that the city is the special place that the
human race has created in order to first survive and then thrive in
the face of environmental pressures. It is therefore the preeminent
scene within which the human being engages the forces that it must
encounter and turn to its advantage. In the course of this encounter
experience takes on the broadest possible meaning. In fact, it really
signifies the interaction of an organism with its world. Thus, each of
the categories I developed are specific ways of seeing the texture,
shape, and action that result from the experience of human beings in
urban settings. That these categories were also used to describe the
ways in which the processes of nature could be understood is important evidence that the experience of human beings is continuous
with the natural world. A comprehensive doctrine of experience as
engaged interaction with the environment must therefore deny any
ultimacy to distinctions between the natural and the artificial, the

built and the organic. Such dualisms are only useful insofar as they enable special investigations to concentrate on particular subject matters. All this is to say that within the American tradition primacy is always accorded the continuous dimension of experience. Any attempt to freeze experience or divide it into competing dimensions is tantamount to cheating human beings of their birthright— the capacity to participate as whole beings in whatever environment they happen to occupy at the moment.

This study has insisted on the semiotic character of city life. Part Two is really an exhaustive attempt to provide a systematic framework within which the interpretive dimension of city life can be seen in all its riches. In applying the categories of firstness, secondness, and thirdness to city experience, I am doing what American philosophy in its best moments has always done: Engage the arena of its concern in such a way as to illuminate what is really going in the whirlwind of human experience. Now, to understand all experience as essentially interpretation is to admit at the very outset that fallibilism is built into philosophy. I have also tried to be faithful to this dimension of the American tradition. For example, I have applied the Peircean semiotic triad of icon, index, and symbol to the major dimensions of urban life. It is not just firstness that was examined. Rather, I took Peirce to the streets and sought to show the necessity of iconic representation as well as its potential danger in a culture driven by media hyperbole. Secondness and the index of the urban skyscraper were brought together to show the potential of advanced late capitalism for both good and evil. Finally, the neighborhood was offered as the very symbol of thirdness and its ability to establish connections between human beings by reason of intense involvement in shared meanings. And I tried to show the relevance of these philosophic tools for the citizens of the South Bronx. I offer these applications of American philosophy not as pronouncements from on high but as potentially useful ways of understanding the interpretive character of urban experience. At the same time, I welcome dissent, correction, and criticism. This attempt to shed some light on urban experience is rooted in the spirit of fallibilism that is so central a part of any attempt to deal experimentally with the critical issues facing city dwellers. To interpret is by definition to admit one's own fallibility. My hope is that the systematic character of my interpretation makes it easier for my readers to see both its good aspects and its flaws.

The third part of this study was devoted to establishing the main outlines of an urban praxis, and is therefore corrective in the sense discussed above. The last part of this book seeks to draw out the normative implications of the theory of experience developed in the first two parts. Among those implications is the real need to recast our understanding of knowing along the lines of a form of intelligence-in-action. An equally important corrective is the need for a wholesale renewal of community as the ground of city life. Finally, in correcting the rampant individualism of our own time we see the emergence of a revised concept of what city justice is really all about. Thus, this study supports the tradition in American philosophy that seeks the normative dimension of experience that is appropriate to the cultural situation being discussed.

The only socially responsible way to suggest corrections for aspects of human social arrangements is to make evident one's presuppositions and commitments. That is the reason behind the establishment and frequent recurrence of the normative ideals of intensity, integrity, wholeness, and depth. It also explains the painfully detailed presentation of the categoreal scheme and the semiotic matrix. If one is to suggest alternative ways of evaluating human experience, one is under an obligation to provide as full as possible an accounting of the intellectual grounds for such recommendations and criticism. Now, the most thorough way to fulfill such an obligation is through a systematic presentation of the theory of reality underpinning one's commitments. This readily opens one's thought to criticism, and that is the way philosophy should proceed. Such transparency has always been a forthright characteristic of American philosophy. In contrast to much postmodern philosophic discourse, American naturalism and pragmatism has never hesitated to proclaim its grounding principles. In a similar fashion, American pragmatism has always called for the testing of its presuppositions in the realm of real experience. A major reason for my own commitment to Whitehead's way of doing philosophy has always been the intellectual honesty with which he puts forward the reasons for his particular approach to human experience.

It is precisely this demand for consistency, honesty, and rigor that inspired what otherwise might seem a most peculiar way of talking about city life. I would be the first to admit that the application of a systematic metaphysics and semiotics to urban experience appears quite strange. But I know of no more effective way to express the philosophic candor demanded of those who would presume to correct aspects of cultural experience. Also, the normative thinking entailed in such corrective efforts requires an approach driven by the impossible ideal of completeness. Once again, the seemingly overwhelming contradictions of the philosophic vocation reveal themselves. On the one hand, the philosopher is obliged to take up a normative stance in the effort to provide a corrective analysis of human experience. On the other hand, the philosopher is required to publicize the fallible nature of such an effort. And to complicate the matter even more thoroughly, the philosophic spirit demands comprehensiveness and applicability. The normative versus the fallible, the general versus the particular: These are the dualisms that cry out for the creation of healing contrasts. American philosophy at work comes down in the end to the continual search for more and better contrastive thinking. I would argue that philosophy's continuing power to make important contributions to American civilization depends for the most part on its willingness to develop such ways of thinking. The fostering of cultural healing and the encouragement of human growth and development are tied to American philosophy's success in producing philosophers who are such masters of heartfelt contrast.

The mention of contrast bears directly on the last quality of American philosophy at work—its historic insistence on viewing the aesthetic dimension as the key to a unified theory of experience. A contrast, it will be recalled, is the act of putting into a unity aspects of experience usually considered foreign to each other. Every contrast produces by reason of its creative power an increase in intensity of feeling. An increase in the intensity of these feelings is tantamount to an insistence on recognition. It is these feelings that give rise to a sense of the possible emergence of meaning. Thus, value has its origin in feeling. From James to Peirce and from Dewey to Whitehead, American philosophy has always concentrated on this dimly felt axiological ground of value. Of course, they went about illuminating this ground in different ways and each cast his particular light on this matrix of the important. But such differences should not obscure their fundamental agreement on the importance of this primordial fusion of feeling, value, and meaning.[16]

In my own way I have tried to push this distinctive curve of American philosophy farther along the tangent of cultural criticism. The analysis of the aesthetic importance of place within the spatiotemporal cityscape was meant to secure the significance of the embodied feelings that ground our being in the city. So also the urban semiotics laid out in Part Two should caution us against taking too cerebral a view of the cognitive processes at play within the urban environment. Sociological analysis often goes sadly awry through a neglect of the underlying felt dimensions that support all manifestations of public mind. And finally, Part Three labored to unite feeling and intelligence in a continuous arc of action that depended as much on sensing the aesthetic tone of a situation as it did on analyzing its rational structure. It should therefore be obvious that the orientation of this effort to think philosophically about the contemporary city is an aesthetic one.

In concluding these observations on the continuity between these efforts and the tradition of American philosophy, I point toward a singular but little discussed advantage to this emphasis on the aesthetic that runs through the pragmatic tradition. It is in its own way a perfect example of how the act of contrast can contribute to dissolving the seemingly most intractable dualisms lacerating our cultural experience. Throughout this cosmology of the city I have been at pains to point out the bad effects of an overwrought sense of individuality. In addition, I made that possibility and its negative consequences the cornerstone of my critique of advanced late capitalism. Now, of course, an equally troublesome danger lurks in my insistence on the primacy of community—that of the submersion of all uniqueness in a vast undifferentiated mass. It is precisely here at this junction of the communal and the individual that the fabric of city life (or for that matter human culture in general) is most likely to tear apart. But a valid understanding of aesthetic experience precludes such a rending of urban life. True aesthetic experience always demands that we be most truly ourselves, but in the light of what we are experiencing. There is no threat of engulfment within an authentic aesthetic experience. It is only in the act of becoming the unique individuals we truly are that the fullness of feelings aroused in the presence of beauty can be experienced and expressed. Any attempt to tear apart the fundamental dimensions that make up urban experience violates wisdom's law of contrast. The community and the individual, the public and the private, the self and the social order—all these ultimates of city existence belong together. The normative measures of integrity, intensity, wholeness, and depth are to be seen as necessary tools in the cultural process of defining, sharpening, and measuring the limits of these contrasts that lie at the very heart of good city living.

Taken together, they represent a sustained effort to remain true to the tradition of American philosophy. My allies in this journey— past, present, and to come—share a common belief in the importance of philosophy for human growth and development. I would hope that this adventure in speculative philosophy contributes to this effort to bring thought to bear upon the significant issues of the day. Like all great philosophical traditions, American philosophy bears witness to the eloquence of the human soul when it meditates on the mysteries of existence. At the end of this reflection on the intricacies of city existence, I remain more than ever convinced of the fruitfulness of philosophic effort. A constant return to the beginnings of philosophy's quest for the good life is the best way to ensure its continuing relevance in the present. For what else is the contrast between city and nature but this contemporary moment's most concrete expression of the problem of the one and the many.

Notes

Introduction: Cosmology and Urban Culture

1. My mentor in learning this way of doing philosophy is Robert Neville. See especially his *Reconstruction of Thinking* (Albany: State University of New York Press, 1981) and *The Recovery of the Measure* (Albany: State University of New York Press, 1989) *passim* for a detailed presentation and thorough defense of this way of doing philosophy.

2. See Neville, *Reconstruction of Thinking, op.cit.*, pp. 79–91.

3. See George Allan, "The Primacy of the Mesocosm," in *New Essay in Metaphysics*, ed. Robert Neville (Albany: State University of New York Press, 1987, pp. 25–44.

4. See *Nature: An Environmental Cosmology* (Albany: State University of New York Press, 1997), Part One: Cosmological Method.

5. The term *haeccitas* is derived from the medieval philosopher John Duns Scotus who saw in the act of divine creation an indefinite plurality of novel instances of goodness. In turn, it is the Anglo-Irish poet Gerard Manley Hopkins who picks up Scotus's insistence on the uniqueness of each thing-event and makes it the formative principle of his poetry. Thus, "in-scape" translates *haeccitas*.

6. See Part Two of the present volume.

7. See *Nature: An Environmental Cosmology, op. cit.*, Chapter 8.

8. See Part Three of the present volume.

9. See Hall and Ames, *Thinking Through Confucius* (Albany: State University of New York Press, 1987) for a thoroughly systematic use of this

237

distinction in terms of the project of comparative cultural analysis. The original distinction was made by Alfred North Whitehead in *Modes of Thought*
(New York: Free Press, 1966).

10. See *Nature*, pp. 32 ff.

11. The standard reference to Peirce's writings is as follows: *The Collected Papers of Charles Sanders Peirce*, eds. Charles Hartshorne and Paul
Weiss (Cambridge: Harvard University Press, 1931–35) and Vols. VII–VIII,
ed. Arthur W. Burks (same publisher, 1958). Hereafter cited as *CP* followed
by volume and paragraph number. The secondary literature on Peirce has
grown along with his reputation as America's most creative philosopher. See
especially Robert Corrington, *An Introduction to C. S. Peirce* (Lanham,
Maryland: Rowman and Littlefield, 1993); and Carl Hausman, *The Evolutionary Philosophy of Charles Sanders Peirce* (College Park: The Pennsylvania State University Press, 1993) for valuable introductions. Also valuable
for situating Peirce's work within the American philosophical tradition as
well as pointing out its worth for contemporary thought is the preface and
introduction to *The Essential Peirce*, edited by Houser and Kloesel (Bloomington: Indiana University Press, 1992), pp. xi–xli. Sandra Rosenthal argues for a postmodern reading of Peirce in *Charles Peirce's Pragmatic
Pluralism* (Albany: State University of New York Press, 1994). Robert
Neville, *Behind the Masks of Gods* (Albany: State University of New York
Press, 1991), has shown the importance of Peirce's semiotic theory for theology and the comparative study of religions. Vincent Colapietro has shown
the relevance of Peirce's semiotics for a contemporary understanding of various doctrines of the human self: *The Semiotic Self of C. S. Peirce* (Albany:
State University of New York Press, 1989). Another important study con-
trasting continental and Peircean semiotics is Norbert Wiley, *The Semiotic
Self* (Chicago: The University of Chicago Press, 1994). Finally, Steve Odin
has brilliantly shown the relevance of Peirce for a comparative analysis of
The Social Self in Zen and American Pragmatism (Albany: State University
of New York Press, 1996).

12. *MT*, p. 173.

13. Ibid.

14. Alfred North Whitehead, *Religion in the Making*, p. 111.

Chapter One: Urban Space

1. See the discussion of natural space in *Nature: An Environmental
Cosmology, op. cit.*, Chapter 5.

2. See *Nature: An Environmental Cosmology, op. cit.*, Chapter 3.

3. See *Nature: An Environmental Cosmology, op. cit.*, Chapter 4.
Philosophers have begun to turn their attention to the body as a central

theme of inquiry. Merleau-Ponty's *The Phenomenology of Perception*, translated by Colin Smith (New York: Humanities Press, 1962) is the classic text in the phenomenological tradition. More recent studies in this tradition include Drew Lederer, *The Absent Body* (Chicago: The University of Chicago Press, 1990); Susan Capaldi, *Emotion, Depth, and Flesh* (Albany: State University of New York Press, 1993); John A. Schumacher, *Human Posture: The Nature of Inquiry* (Albany: State University of New York Press, 1990). The Anglo-American tradition is represented by Irvin Thalberg, *Perception, Action, and Emotion* (New Haven: Yale University Press, 1977). Eastern philosophy has richly contributed to this development. See Kasulis, Ames, and Dissanyake, *Self as Body in Asian Theory and Practice* (Albany: State University of New York Press, 1992); Shigenori Nagatomo, *Attunement Through the Body* (Albany: State University of New York Press, 1992); Yuasa Yuaso, *The Body: Toward An Eastern Mind-Body Theory* (Albany: State University of New York Press, 1987); David Edward Shaner, *The BodyMind Experience in Japanese Buddhism* (Albany: State University of New York Press, 1985); and Ted J. Kaptchuk, *The Web That has No Weaver* (New York: Congdon and Weed, 1983). Within the Asian tradition the most compelling and exhaustive examination of space is to be found in (No Author) *Concepts of Space: Ancient and Modern* (New Delhi: Abhivan Publishers 1991). The process tradition is represented by George Wolf, "The Place of the Brain in an Ocean of Feeling," in *Existence and Actuality*, ed. Cobb and Gamwell (Chicago: The University of Chicago Press, 1984), pp. 167–189. See also his "Psychological Physiology from the Standpoint of a Physiological Psychologist," *Process Studies*, 11 (1981): pp. 274–291. More popular studies include E. T. Hall, *The Hidden Dimension* (New York: Anchor Books, 1969); Ritchie Ward, *The Living Clocks* (New York: Mentor 1971); and Maxine Sheets-Johnstone, *Giving the Body Its Due* (Albany: State University of New York Press, 1992).

    4. See *Nature: An Environmental Cosmology, op. cit.*, Chapter 4.

    5. See Mircea Elaide, *The Sacred and the Profane* (New York: Harper, 1959) *passim.*

    6. See Gaston Bachelard, *The Poetics of Space* (Boston: Beacon Press, 1964).

    7. See the Introduction to this volume for a more detailed explanation of this metaphysical doctrine.

    8. See Anthony Steinbock, "Whitehead's Theory of Propositions," *Process Studies* 18, No. 1 (Spring 1989): pp. 19–29.

    9. This is also true of such topics as economic place, celebratory place, and so forth. Chapter Three deals explicitly with the felt meanings that arise in various types of urban place.

    10. The sense of ambient richness is rooted in the experience of the womb and finds its living expression in such seemingly mundane experiences as "one's favorite chair" or "a cozy nook." Circles, gardens, tombs, and other such habitats also share in the richness of ambient space.

Chapter Two: Urban Time

1. I have already provided a detailed examination and defense of the doctrine of epochal time in *Nature: An Environmental Cosmology, op. cit.*, Chapter 6. Here I confine the discussion to those dimensions most relevant to the urban experience of time.

2. *RM*, p. 111.

3. See *SMW*, p. 94.

4. See *Nature: An Environmental Cosmology*, Chapter 1.

5. See ibid., Chapter 3.

6. See ibid., Chapter 6.

7. No one has done more to make the American city a theme for philosophical reflection than John McDermott. My work has been inspired and greatly aided by his pioneering work. See his *The Culture of Experience* (New York: New York University Press, 1976).

Chapter Three: Urban Place

1. *Philebus*, pp. 59–65.

2. See the *Sophist* and its account of the *gigantomachia*. We need both being and becoming, both permanence and change, if we are to understand and appreciate the value of the temporal world.

3. See *Nature: An Environmental Cosmology, op. cit.*, Chapter 2.

4. *PR*, p. 21.

5. See Robert Neville, *The Cosmology of Freedom, op. cit.*, pp. 66–86.

6. J. J. Gibson, *The Ecological Approach to Visual Perception* (Ithaca, N.Y.: Cornell University Press, 1976). I disagree with Edward Casey's assessment of Gibson's work in *Getting Back into Place* (Indianapolis: Indiana University Press, 1993), pp. 207–208. The ground of our difference is Casey's overreliance on Merleau-Ponty's phenomenology of perception and consequent neglect of Whitehead's doctrine of symbolic reference.

7. I have provided an analysis of the feel of place in "Place, Body, Situation," in *Dwelling*, ed. David Seamon (Albany: State University of New York Press, 1989).

8. See Gibson, *op. cit.*, p. 15 and p. 24.

9. I agree with Casey's reservations about Gibson's interpretation of the optic sense. He loses a sense of depth even as he provides an understanding of the concrete textures of surfaces within the lived perception of space. See Casey, *op. cit.*, p. 373. Footnotes 60–63.

10. See, for example, Ashley Montagu's still classic study, *Touching: The Mind of the Skin* (New York: Harper and Row, 1971).

11. See Steve Odin's monumental study, *The Social Self in Zen and American Pragmatism, op. cit.*, pp. 79–122. J. Nicholas Entrikin has provided an important analysis of the connections between place, identity, and

modernity in *The Betweenness of Place* (Baltimore: The Johns Hopkins University Press, 1991). While I admire his thesis, my own project moves more emphatically in the direction of semiotics as the key to the urban experience of place.

12. See *AI* Part IV for Whitehead's comprehensive argument concerning the importance of beauty for the advance of civilization. See also *Nature*, Chapter 8, for a detailed defense of this point of view.

13. See Whitehead's development of this all-important theme in *AI* Part IV, Civilization.

14. See Neville, *The Recovery of the Measure, op. cit.*, Chapter 3.

15. *RM*, pp. 110–111.

16. John Sherrif, *A Guess at the Riddle* (Bloomington: Indiana University Press, 1994), p. 75.

17. John Dewey, *Art as Experience*, ed. JoAnn Boydston, in *John Dewey, The Later Works, 1925–1934* (Carbondale: The Southern Illinois University Press, 1987), v. 10, p. 43.

18. Robert Neville's *Eternity and Time's Flow* (Albany: State University of New York Press, 1995) provides a brilliant speculative study of the intersection of time and eternity within human culture.

Chapter Four: Urban Goodness

1. Kevin Lynch, *A Theory of Good City Form* (Cambridge: The MIT Press, 1981).

2. Ibid., pp. 99–108.

3. Ibid., p. 108.

4. See ibid., pp. 112–113, where nine criteria for performance are detailed. I have made a similar critique of the work of Paolo Soleri in "The Arcology of Paolo Soleri: Technology as Cosmology," in *The Arts and Their Interrelationships* (Lewisburg: The Bucknell University Press, 1979).

5. These terms are derived from Whitehead and explained in *Nature: An Environmental Cosmology, op. cit.*, Chapter 2.

6. See Lynch, *op. cit.*, pp. 111–220.

7. This is not meant as a condemnation. In my judgment, no one has stood up to the barons of scientific materialism more often and more courageously than Kevin Lynch. Not being a philosopher, he stops short of what could have been a radical and revolutionary revisioning of the act of city planning. Now, I am not a city planner. But I believe that just as I learned from Kevin Lynch, so can he learn from those like myself who practice systematic speculative philosophy and create for the sake of application vague categoreal schemes based on the actual values of city life.

8. See Stephen Pepper, *World Hypotheses*, for the classic study of the interrelations between system, metaphor, and speculation.

9. See Lynch, *op. cit.*, pp. 73–98.

10. Remnants of this form of thinking can be found in the utopian architecture and projects of thinkers like Soleri and Doxiades. Whenever and wherever the protection of perfection is sought, this kind of cosmic city planning forces itself into human consciousness.

11. Richard Sennett, *Flesh and Stone* (New York: W. W. Norton, 1994) traces the way in which the human body has been used as a measure for ordering divine and human spaces as well as districts of goodness and evil throughout the developmental planning of the Western city from Athens to New York. See also my essays, "on Soleri," *etc.*

12. Lynch, *op. cit.*, p. 81.

13. Lynch, ibid., pp. 86–88.

14. Lynch, ibid., p. 88.

15. Phenomena like edge cities are decrepit attempts to wring the last bit of mileage out of this obsolete city form.

16. This is the sadness of such places as Kuala Lumpur and Singapore. They turn their back on their own rich culture as they seek after the dubious gains of consumer cities.

17. Lynch, *op. cit.*, pp. 95–98.

18. Christopher Alexander, *A New Theory of Urban Design* (New York: Oxford University Press, 1987).

19. Ibid., p. 14.

20. Ibid., p. 22. Author's italics.

21. Ibid. *passim.* Author's italics.

22. But see his extraordinary treatise, *A Pattern Language* (New York: Oxford University Press, 1977).

23. In my earlier work, *Nature*, I analyzed this quality of space under the quality of a "shy openness to form." Thus my main argument concerning the continuity between city and nature receives further support by this mapping of city forms onto nature's normative dimensions. See *Nature, op. cit.*, Chapters 5, 6, and 8.

24. Ibid., Chapter 2.

25. Again, this connection between city and nature underscores my thesis that there is a direct continuity spanning city and nature. See *Nature, op. cit.*, Chapter 1. There is in other words a direct connection between contrast, beauty, and continuity. In Part One what is stressed is "ever-growing wholeness." Part Two is dominated by the discussion of continuity and thirdness. Part Three concentrates on beauty and contrast as the means and ends that bind urban goodness into effective modes of praxis.

26. It has been argued that to be complete Peirce's triadic doctrine needs a "Fourthness." See Robert Neville, *The Truth of Broken Symbols* (Albany: State University of New York Press, 1966), pp. xix–xxi (N. 2), 31–47, 66–75, 97, 116–121, 172, 241–244. I say that signs expressing this dimension have the quality of "symbolic breadth." They fuse wholeness and depth so that urban goodness can continually express itself in symbolically powerful ways. To explore this further would move my study too far away from

its proper goal, the city and its many cosmological, semiotic, and practical aspects.

Chapter Five: Mood, Order, and Sign

1. The recent resurgence of interest in Peirce's philosophy has led to a number of important studies. Among the more important from the standpoint of this study are Vincent Colapietro, *Peirce's Approach to the Self* (Albany: State University of New York Press, 1989); John Muller, *Beyond the Psychoanalytic Dyad* (New York: Routledge, 1994); Norbert Wiley, *The Semiotic Self* (Chicago: The University of Chicago Press, 1994); J. K. Sheriff, *Peirce's Guess at the Riddle* (Bloomington: Indiana University Press, 1994); and Sandra Rosenthal, *Charles S. Peirce's Pragmatic Pluralism* (Albany: State University of New York Press, 1994).

2. See Wiley, *op. cit.*, for a comprehensive defense of this position, especially in reference to the distinctions between language, semiosis, and parole.

3. In using the term *world* I mean it in the sense articulated by Justus Buchler in his article "On the Concept of World," *Review of Metaphysics*, 3/4 (June 1978): pp. 555–579. Also instructive in this regard is Whitehead's *Modes of Thought, op. cit.*, especially the section entitled "Forms of Civilized Process."

4. The best explanation of the many-sided relations between Peirce's phenomenology, cosmology, and metaphysics remains Eugene Freeman, *The Categories of C. S. Peirce* (Chicago: Open Court, 1934).

5. Robert Neville has provided a definitive articulation of the relations between cosmology, metaphysics, and ontology, which ought to be found in any serious process metaphysics. See his *Reconstruction of Thinking, op. cit.*

6. *CP* 5:311.

7. See Michael Sandel, *Liberalism and the Limits of Justice* (New York: Cambridge University Press, 1982) and his *Democracy's Discontent* (Cambridge: Harvard University Press, 1996). Richard Rorty has gone to considerable lengths to adapt the American tradition to a strong view of liberalism in *Contingency, Irony, and Solidarity*. I have argued against such an interpretation in "Confucius, Dewey, and Rorty: The Disappearance of the Public Good," in *Justice and Democracy*, ed. Bontekoe and Stepaniants (Honolulu: University of Hawaii Press, 1997). To my mind the most effective critique of advanced capitalism and its impact on urban justice remains Roberto Mangabeira Unger's *Knowledge and Politics* (New York: Free Press, 1975).

8. *CP*, 5.197.

9. See Robert Corrington, *op. cit.*, pp. 152–157 for a systematic development of this theme.

10. *CP* 3:362.

11. *CP* 3:361.
12. *CP* 3:360.

Chapter Six: The Sign of One/Qualitative Value

1. Charles S. Peirce, "A Guess at the Riddle," in *The Essential Peirce*, ed. Houser and Kloesel (Bloomington: Indiana University Press, 1992), p. 248.
2. See Chapter 2 for a discussion of the all-at-once quality of epochal time.
3. It is Jane Jacobs who has brought to the public's attention the absolute importance of a healthy street life for city goodness. See *The Life and Death of Great American Cities* (New York: Vintage, 1961).
4. See Chapter 3 for a structural analysis of the emergence of place in urban regions.
5. See Christopher Alexander, *A Timeless Way of Building* (New York: Oxford University Press, 1979).
6. See *Nature*, Chapter 7.
7. See *SMW*, chapter xiii.
8. Robert Caro has written the definitive study of what happens when all city planning falls into the hands of one expert. See his account of how Robert Moses sought to thwart the publication of his book. Robert Caro, "The City-Shaper," *The New Yorker*, Jan. 5, 1998, pp. 38–55.
9. See Steve Odin, *The Social Self in Zen and American Pragmatism*, *op. cit.*

Chapter Seven: The Sign of Two/Collision

1. *CP* 1.356.
2. *CP* 8.368. The issue of the exact nature of the indexical sign is complex. See Douglas Greenlee, *Peirce's Concept of Sign*, *op. cit.*, pp. 84 ff.
3. For empirical confirmation of the systematic speculation contained in this section, consult S. B. Landau and C. W. Condit, *Rise of The New York Skyscraper* (New Haven: Yale University Press, 1996). Also important is R. Stern, T. Mellins, and D. Fishman, *New York: 1960* (New York: Penguin, 1995). An interesting study of the interaction of architecture, nature, and market economics is to be found in William Cronon, *Nature's Metropolis: Chicago and the Great West* (New York: Norton, 1991).
4. See Chapter 3.
5. See Chapter 2.
6. See *Nature: An Environmental Cosmology*, *op. cit.*, Chapter 8.

7. See Robert Heilbroner's still relevant introduction in *The Worldly Philosophers* (New York: Simon and Schuster, 1986).

Chapter Eight: The Sign of Three/Continuity

1. I provide a detailed explanation of essential and conditional environmental features in *Nature: An Environmental Cosmology, op. cit.*, Chapter 3. Briefly, an essential feature is what gives an event its own special identity or *haeccitas*; conditional features are those environmental dimensions used by the event in question to construct its own special uniqueness of being.

2. *CP* 2.249.

3. Ibid., 2.297.

4. Ibid., 4.431.

5. Ibid., 5.475.

6. Royce saw this immediately when he sought in *The Philosophy of Loyalty* to adapt Peirce's pragmatic semiotics to the building of "the beloved community."

7. *CP* 5.475–476. Robert Corrington has provided a clear guide to the intricacies of Peirce's doctrine of the interpretant. See Corrington, *op. cit.*, pp. 159–164.

8. These are two of the three aspects of the interpretant singled out by Peirce. In addition to these emotional and dynamic dimensions, there is also the logical interpretant. At this level of urban semiotics I am only interested in the first two. The third takes on importance later in my discussion of an urban praxis.

9. The most extensive discussion of thirdness and the ultimate logical interpretant are to be found in Eugene Freeman, *op. cit.*, and Douglas Greenlee, *op. cit.*, Colapietro, Corrington, and Rosenthal also provide important guidance in this matter.

10. Sandra Rosenthal, *op. cit.*, p. 31.

11. Ibid., p. 30.

12. *CP* 5.491, Peirce's italics.

13. *CP*, 5.181; 5.197.

14. Jürgen Habermas, "Peirce and Communication," in *Peirce and Contemporary Thought* (Bronx: Fordham University Press, 1995), p. 261.

Chapter Nine: Intelligence-in-Action

1. John Dewey, *Experience and Nature* (New York: Dover Press, 1958).

2. It is to the still underappreciated work of Susanne Langer that one must turn in order to fathom the depth and reach of symbolism as a factor

in cultural life. See her *Philosophy in a New Key* (Cambridge: Harvard University Press, 1957), Chapter 1.

3. Rosenthal, *op. cit.*, p. 31.

4. The *locus classicus* for Mead's philosophy of the self is "The Social Self," in *Selected Writings of George Herbert Mead* (Indianapolis: Bobbs-Merrill, 1964). Mead's writings are scattered. A good collection is *The Works of George Herbert Mead* (Chicago: University of Chicago Press, 1967), 2 vols. There is also *The Philosophy of The Present* (Chicago: The University of Chicago Press, 1980). His writings on social psychology are contained in Anselm Strauss, ed., *Mead On Social Psychology* (Chicago: University of Chicago Press, 1977). The relation between Mead and Habermas as well as Mead's place in the development of social theory is the subject matter of Mitchell Aboulafia, ed., *Philosophy, Social Theory, and the Thought of George Herbert Mead* (Albany: State University of New York Press, 1991). Steve Odin, *op. cit.*, makes important use of Mead in discussing the cross-cultural patterns of Japanese and American Culture.

5. See Chapter 8.

6. There is an evident and significant similarity between Mead's social "body" and Merleau-Ponty's "body-subject." See Rosenthal and Bourgeois, *Mead and Merleau-Ponty* (Albany: State University of New York Press, 1991).

7. See *Nature: An Environmental Cosmology, op. cit.*, Chapter 2.

8. Langer, *op. cit.*, p. 55. Author's italics.

9. Langer, *op. cit.*, p. 100.

10. Ibid., p. 96.

11. Ibid., p. 97.

12. I defend Platonic Naturalism as an important way around the dualisms afflicting our culture in *Nature: An Environmental Cosmology, op. cit.*, pp. 190–193.

13. John Dewey, "Social Inquiry," in *The Philosophy of John Dewey*, ed. John McDermott (Chicago: University of Chicago Press, 1981), vol. II, pp. 397–420.

14. Hans Joas, *Pragmatism and Social Theory* (Chicago: University of Chicago Press, 1993), p. 248. But I also mean something much more than successful social experimentation when I use the term *praxis*. My thought is deeply influenced by George Allan's analysis of praxis especially as detailed in chapter one, "The Nature of Praxis," in *The Realizations of the Future* (Albany: State University of New York Press, 1990), pp. 1–34. It is his insistence on the ethical dimension of praxis that I find most important for my own understanding of action in a process universe.

15. This is the argument of his classic *The Public and Its Problems*.

16. Joas, *op. cit.* p. 249.

17. See Joas, *op. cit.*, pp. 256–258.

18. It would be a worthwhile project in social inquiry to work out the various ways in which Mead's "I/Me" configuration of the human self is helped or hindered by the shifting aesthetic orders in which it finds itself. I

think immediately of family systems research as an important locus for this type of analysis.

Chapter Ten: Community

1. See the work of Michael Sandel and William Sullivan. Both are forced back to the very beginnings of our political history as an independent state in order to find actual historical models for community in action. Michael Sandel, *Democracy's Discontent* (Cambridge: Harvard University Press, 1996) and William Sullivan, *Reconstructing Public Philosophy* (Berkeley: University of California Press, 1986).

2. *Symposium*, translated by Nehamas and Woodruff (Indianapolis: Hackett, 1989), 2204B. I remind the reader of Plato's earlier praise of the child as the model for the philosopher.

3. Ibid., 202D–203B.

4. George Herbert Mead, *Mind, Self, and Society*, ed. Charles Morris (Chicago: University of Chicago Press, 1967), p. 167.

5. G. W. F. Hegel, *The Phenomenology of Spirit*, trans. A. V. Miller (Oxford: Oxford University Press 1977), §§ 178–196.

6. See Sandra Rosenthal, *op. cit.*, p. 31.

7. Ibid.

8. See Robert Neville, *The Truth of Broken Symbols, op. cit.*, pp. 43–46 and *passim*. It is important to note how Neville places his thought within the great tradition of American speculative philosophy by deploying the insights of Justus Buchler as well as his own to enlarge the understanding of Peirce's semiotics. This is using the history of philosophy in the most fruitful sense because it sees philosophy's history as that which is organic to its development. The arrogance behind the ignorant rejection of philosophy's history by varieties of postmodern thinking stands in stark contrast to this kind of intellectual responsibility and generosity. Neville's highly original article arguing for our capacity to intuitively recognize harmonic unities and judge their normative excellence is a fine example of this respectful use and at the same time departure from the American philosophical tradition. See Robert Neville, "Intuition," *The International Philosophical Quarterly* VII, No. 4 (December 1963): pp. 556–599.

9. The South Bronx Churches have adopted the well-known "Iron Rule" of Saul Alinsky's Industrial Areas Foundation: "Never do for another what they can do for themselves." Hegel would approve since it is only by this kind of work that authentic self-recognition through authentic community life comes into existence. Again, it is a matter of the deft recognition and use of the "respects of interpretation" that lay at the base of every community's system of symbols.

10. See *Adventures of Ideas*, Chapter XVIII.

11. See Ralph Sleeper, "Pragmatism, Religion, and Experienceable Difference," in *American Philosophy and The Future*, ed. Michael Novak (New York: Scribner's, 1968), pp. 270–323.

12. See Neville, *Recovery of The Measure, op. cit.*, for a discussion of network and content meanings.

13. I develop these three levels of environmental participation in *Nature: An Environmental Cosmology, op. cit.*, Chapter 2. They are also the ground of my contention throughout this work of a continuity as well as significant differences between the city and other forms of social dwelling.

14. John K. Sherrif, *op. cit.*, p. 74.

15. T. S. Eliot, *The Waste Land* (New York: Harcourt, Brace and World, 1958), "The Burial of the Dead" ll. 60–70.

16. See the brilliant analysis of the problem of action in Hans Joas, *Pragmatism and Social Theory* (Chicago: The University of Chicago Press, 1993), pp. 245–259.

17. See *Nature: An Environmental Cosmology, op. cit.*, pp. 230–234.

18. See *Ethics*, Part IV, props. 35–45 and *A Political Treatise*, trans. R. H. M. Elwes (New York: Dover Books, 1951), Vol. I., c.3, pp. 301–308.

19. See *The Treatise on the Improvement of the Understanding*, which I argue is much better translated as "The Healing of The Mind."

20. John Dewey, "Philosophy and Democracy," in *The Political Writings*, ed. Morris and Shapiro (Indianapolis: Hackett Publishing Company, 1993), p. 43.

21. John Dewey, *Democracy and Education* (New York: Free Press, 1966), p. 83.

22. John Dewey, *The Public and Its Problems* (Chicago: Swallow Press, 1954), pp. 148–149.

23. Peter Manicas, "John Dewey: Anarchism and the Political State," *Transactions of the Charles S. Peirce Society* XVIII, No. 2 (Spring 1982): p. 144.

24. John Dewey, *The Public and Its Problems, op. cit.*, pp. 211, 216.

Chapter Eleven: City Justice

1. See the introduction to this volume as well as the first chapter of *Nature: An Environmental Cosmology, op. cit.*

2. See Part One, Chapter Three, "Place."

3. The phrase, of course, derives from Jacques Lacan's understanding of what makes a human being fully human.

4. See Robert Neville, *The Cosmology of Freedom, op. cit.*, pp. 61–63 for the cosmological definition of elegance as something to be prized and striven after.

5. Adam Smith, *The Wealth of Nations* (Oxford: The Clarendon Press, 1976) Book IV, chapter 2.

NOTES TO CHAPTER ELEVEN

6. When pressed on the question of utility theory, neoclassical economists like Samuelson stress its scientific character by insisting on its status as a *law* that functions continually in the face of all efforts to deter it. My colleague George Caffentzis has shared in the development of a devastating critique of this attempt to endow economic theory with the epistemological prestige of scientific materialism. See Julius Sensat and G. C. Caffentzis, "A Critique of The Foundations of Utility Theory," *Science and Society* 36, n. 2. (Summer 1975): pp. 157–179. The fact that the theory still "reigns supreme" testifies to capitalism's political power, not its theoretical rigor.

7. Donald Frey, "The Good Samaritan as Bad Economist: Self-Interest in Economics and Theology," *Cross Currents* 46, No. 3 (Fall 1996): pp. 294–295.

8. George Simmel, *The Philosophy of Money* (London: Routledge and Kegan Paul, 1978), p. 431.

9. Karl Polanyi, *The Great Transformation* (Boston: Beacon Press, 1957), p. 57.

10. F. A. Hayak, *The Mirage of Social Justice* (Chicago: University of Chicago Press, 1976), p. 115, as quoted in Douglas Sturm, *Community and Alienation* (Notre Dame: University of Notre Dame Press, 1988), p. 173.

11. See Herman Daly and John Cobb, *For The Common Good* (Boston: Beacon Press, 1989), Part Two, pp. 121–206.

12. See John Mihevic, *The Market Tells Them So* (London: Zed Books, 1995) for a chilling account of the human suffering caused in Africa by the economic fundamentalism of The World Bank. In *Generation X Goes to College* (Chicago: Open Court, 1996), Peter Sacks details the ways in which university administrations have prostituted higher education for the sake of satisfying market demand. Finally, Roberto Alejandro in *Hermeneutics, Citizenship, and The Public Sphere* (Albany: State University of New York Press, 1993) makes a compelling case for the need to move beyond "market theology" if anything like intelligent public discourse is to occur.

13. See F. A. Hayak, *op. cit.*, pp. 111, 110.

14. See John Sherrif, *op. cit.*, p. 75 for a rich analysis of the relation between feeling and meaning Peirce's semiotics.

15. The literature on the liberal-communitarian debate is vast and growing. The classic liberal text is John Rawls, *A Theory of Justice* (Cambridge: Harvard University Press, 1971). He updates his position in *Political Liberalism* (New York: Columbia University Press, 1993). The communitarian side is well represented by Michael Sandel, *Liberalism and the Limits of Justice* (Cambridge: Cambridge University Press, 1982); William Sullivan, *Reconstructing Public Philosophy* (Berkeley: University of California Press, 1986); Douglas Sturm, *Community and Alienation, op. cit.*; and Sandel's new volume *Democracy's Discontent* (Cambridge: Harvard University Press, 1996).

16. See Sandel, *Democracy's Discontent, op. cit., passim.*

17. Sullivan, *op. cit.*, p. 163.

18. This theme is brilliantly developed by Elisabeth Kraus in her distinguished commentary on Whitehead's metaphysics, *The Metaphysics of Experience* (New York: Fordham University Press, 1979). It is also at the heart of Robert Neville's "Axiology of Thinking" wherein the act of thinking is seen as first of all an act of valuation and not merely an act of reason. See *Reconstruction of Thinking, op. cit.*

19. For an interesting Buddhist perspective on the question of capitalism and normative thinking, see David Loy, "Trying To Become Real: A Buddhist Critique of Some Secular Heresies," *The International Philosophical Quarterly* XXXII, No. 4 (December 1992): pp. 403–425.

20. See Douglas Sturm's helpful discussions of "Identifying Problems of Public Order" and "Meanings of the Public Good" in *op. cit.*, pp. 52–93.

21. See Daly and Cobb, *op. cit.*, Chapter, "From Individualism to Person-in-Community."

22. Sandel in *Democracy's Discontent* presents a detailed analysis of the tradition of labor as an act of self-development in which the community had an important and vested interest.

23. See Alexander, *A New Theory of Urban Design, op. cit.*, pp. 21–22.

Chapter Twelve: The Philosopher and the City

1. Given my dependence on Duns Scotus's doctrine of *haeccitas*, it is altogether fitting that the same philosopher should supply the most convincing argument for the appropriateness of applying these "transcendentals" to reality (or being). See Duns Scotus, "Concerning Metaphysics," in *Philosophical Writings*, trans. A. Wolter (Indianapolis: Hackett Publishing Co., 1987), pp. 1–13. Frederick Ferre offers a historically detailed analysis of the move away from a value-based ontology to the fact-based objective descriptions of scientific materialism. See *Being and Value* (Albany: State University of New York Press, 1996).

2. I have argued for this understanding of goodness in *Nature*, Chapter 8.

3. I owe this insight to Ellen Chen's marvelous translation of and commentary on *The Tao Te Ching* (New York: Paragon, 1989), a contribution to the comparative study of Chinese and other cultures not yet sufficiently appreciated.

4. It thereby serves as one more proof that the underlying thesis of this study remains solid: There is a continuity between the natural and the urban and the organic and the artificial such that forms of dualism playing off these supposed differences lack ultimate decisiveness.

5. This is Whitehead's famous epigram defining the meaning of creativity as the category of the ultimate. See *PR*, p. 21.

6. See the all-important essay by John Dewey, "Having an Experience," in McDermott, *op. cit.*, pp. 554–573. It is altogether doubtful that the

present urban reality allows for, let alone promotes the type of full participation in city life that is required for felt intelligence to grow and develop
within citizens. There is just too much greed, injustice, and triviality masquerading as serious values (I mean celebrity, fame, media hyperbole, the
importance of wealth) for sustained acts of judgment to become a regular
part of the everyday existence of citizens.

7. See Part Two, Chapter 5.

8. See Part One, Chapter 3.

9. See Part One, Chapter 4.

10. See *Nature: An Environmental Cosmology, op. cit.*, Chapter 1.

11. The themes of space, time, and place are fully analyzed in Part One
of this work.

12. See my "The Disappearance of the Public Good: Confucius, Dewey,
Rorty," in *Justice and Democracy*, ed. Bontekoe and Stepaniants (Honolulu:
University of Hawaii Press, 1997), pp. 293–307 for a fuller discussion of
these themes.

13. See *The Recovery of Philosophy in America*, ed. Neville and Kasulis
(Albany: State University of New York Press, 1997) and *Philosophy and The
Reconstruction of Culture*, ed. John J. Stuhr (Albany: State University of
New York Press, 1993).

14. See *The Recovery of Philosophy in America, op. cit.*, pp. 251–268.

15. Ibid., p. 255.

16. Recognition of the central place of aesthetics in American philosophy is now a commonplace in the literature. I would draw attention to two
very significant texts. As mentioned first in my discussion of place, John
Sherrif has provided a most insightful study of the major thrust of Peirce's
thought. See *A Guess at the Riddle, op. cit.*, especially his discussion of the
relation between feeling and meaning on p. 75. Then there is Dewey's dense
but compelling evocation of the way in which value haunts all aspects of experience. See the discussion of "Qualitative Immediacy" in Richard J. Bernstein, *John Dewey* (New York: Washington Square Press, 1967), pp. 89–99.
Of course, his *Art as Experience* (Carbondale: Southern Illinois Press, 1987),
The Later Works, Vol. 10, remains America's single most important philosophic text on art.

Bibliography

Aboulafia, M. *Philosophy, Social Theory, and the Thought of G. H. Mead*. Albany: State University of New York Press, 1991.

Alejandro, Robert. *Citizenship, Hermeneutics, and the Public Sphere*. Albany: State University of New York Press, 1993.

Alexander, Christopher. *A New Theory of Urban Design*. New York: Oxford University Press, 1987.

———. *A Pattern Language*. New York: Oxford University University Press, 1977.

Allan, George. *The Realizations of the Future*. Albany: State University of New York Press, 1990.

Antoniades, Anthony. *Epic Space*. New York: Van Nostrand, 1992.

Apel, Karl Otto. *Charles S. Peirce: From Pragmatism to Pragmaticism*. New Jersey: Humanities Press, 1995.

Appleyard, Donald. *Livable Streets*. Berkeley: University of California Press, 1981.

Bachelard, Gaston. *The Poetics of Space*. Boston: Beacon Press, 1964.

Bell, Daniel. *The Cultural Contradictions of Capitalism*. New York: Doubleday, 1976.

Bernstein, Richard. *John Dewey*. New York: Washington Square Press, 1967.

Boyte, Harry. *Commonwealth: A Return to Citizen Politics*. New York: Basic Books, 1989.

253

Buck-Morss, Susan. *The Dialectics of Seeing: Walter Benjamin and the Arcades Project.* Cambridge: MIT Press, 1989.

Caffentzis, C. G., and J. Sensat. "A Critique of the Foundations of Utility Theory." *Science and Society* 36, No. 2.

Capaldi, Susan. *Emotion, Depth, and Flesh.* Albany: State University of New York Press, 1993.

Casey, Edward. *Getting Back into Place.* Bloomington: Indiana University Press, 1991.

Chen, Ellen. *The Tao Te Ching.* New York: Paragon, 1989.

Colapietro, Vincent. *Peirce's Approach to the Self.* Albany: State University of New York Press, 1989.

Corrington, Robert. *An Introduction to C. S. Peirce.* Lanham, Maryland: Rowman & Littlefield, 1993.

Cronon, William. *Nature's Metropolis: Chicago and the Great West.* New York: Norton, 1991.

Daly, Herman, and John Cobb. *For the Common Good.* Boston: Beacon Press, 1987.

Dewey, John. *Art as Experience, The Later Works.* Edited by JoAnn Boydston. Carbondale: The Southern Illinois University Press, 1987. Vol. 10.

———. *Democracy and Education.* New York: Free Press, 1966.

———. *The Public and Its Problems.* Chicago: Swallow Press, 1954.

———. *The Philosophy of John Dewey.* Edited by John McDermott. Chicago: University of Chicago Press, 1973.

Driver, Tom. *The Magic of Ritual.* San Francisco: Harper, 1991.

Duns Scotus. *Philosophical Writings.* Translated by A. Wolter. Indianapolis: Hackett Publishing Company, 1987.

Entrikin, J. N. *The Betweeness of Place.* Baltimore: The Johns Hopkins University Press, 1991.

Ferre, Frederick. *Being and Value.* Albany: State University of New York Press. 1996.

Freeman, Eugene. *The Categories of C. S. Peirce.* Chicago: Open Court, 1934.

Gallagher, W. *The Power of Place.* New York: Poseidon, 1993.

Gibson, J. J. *The Ecological Approach to Visual Perception.* Ithaca: Cornell University Press, 1976.

Grange, Joseph. *Nature: An Environmental Cosmology.* Albany: State University of New York Press, 1997.

———. "Metaphysics, Community, Environment." *Journal of Speculative Philosophy* II, No. 3.

———. "The Disappearance of the Public Good." In *Democracy and Justice: Cross-Cultural Perspectives.* Honolulu: University of Hawaii Press, 1997.

———. "As Technology Advances, Language Decays." *International Philosophical Quarterly* (June 1989).

———. "Place, Body and Situation." In *Dwelling, Place and Environment*, edited by Seamon and Mugerauer. New York: Columbia University Press, 1989.

———. "Being, Feeling, and Environment (The Metaphysical Ground of Environmental Studies)." *Environmental Ethics* (Winter 1986).

———. "Radiant Lessons from the Failed Landscape of Desire." *Places* 2, No. (1986).

———. "The Arcology of Paolo Soleri: Technology as Cosmology." In *The Arts and Their Interrelationships*. Lewisburg, Pa.: The Bucknell University Press, 1979.

Greenlee, Douglas. *Peirce's Concept of Sign*. Paris: Mouton, 1973.

Greider, William. *Who Will Tell the People?* New York: Simon and Schuster, 1992.

Hall, David, and Roger Ames. *Thinking through Confucius*. Albany: State University of New York Press, 1987.

Hall, E. T. *The Hidden Dimension*. New York: Anchor Books, 1969.

Hausman, Carl. *The Evolutionary Philosophy of Charles Sanders Peirce*. College Park: The Pennsylvania University Press, 1993.

Hayak, F. A. *The Mirage of Social Justice*. Chicago: University of Chicago Press, 1976.

Hayden, Dolores. *The Power of Place: Urban Landscape as Public History*. Cambridge: MIT Press, 1995.

Hegel, G. W. F. *The Phenomenology of Spirit*. Translated by A. V. Miller. New York: Oxford University Press, 1977.

Heilbroner, Robert. *The Worldly Philosophers*. New York: Simon and Schuster, 1986.

Hickman, Larry. *John Dewey's Pragmatic Technology*. Indianapolis: Indiana University Press, 1992.

Hookway, Christopher. *Peirce*. New York: Routledge, 1992.

Hoopes, James, ed. *Peirce on Signs*. Chapel Hill: University of North Carolina Press, 1991.

Jacobs, Jane. *The Life and Death of Great American Cities*. New York: Vintage, 1961.

Joas, Hans. *G. H. Mead: A Contemporary Re-examination of His Thought*. Cambridge: MIT Press, 1985.

———. *Pragmatism as Social Theory*. Chicago: University of Chicago Press, 1993.

Kaptchuk, Ted. *The Web That Has No Weaver*. New York: Congdon and Weed, 1983.

Kasulis, Ames, and Dissanayake. *The Self as Body in Asian Theory and Practice*. Albany: State University of New York Press, 1992.

Ketner, Kenneth, ed. *Peirce and Contemporary Thought*. Bronx: Fordham University Press, 1995.

Kojeve, Alexander. *An Introduction to the Reading of Hegel*. Translated by James Nichols. New York: Basic Books, 1969.

Kraus, Elizabeth. *The Metaphysics of Experience*. New York: Fordham University Press, 1979.

Kuttner, Robert. *Everything For Sale: The Virtues and Limits of Markets*. New York: Penguin, 1997.

———. *The Economic Illusion: False Choices between Prosperity and Social Justice*. Boston: Houghton Mifflin, 1984.

Lauer, Quentin. *A Reading of Hegel's Phenomenology*. Bronx: Fordham University Press, 1976.

Landau, S. B., and C. W. Condit. *The Rise of the New York Skyscraper 1865–1913*. New Haven: Yale University Press, 1996.

Langer, Susanne. *Philosophy in a New Key*. Cambridge: Harvard University Press, 1951.

Loy, David. "Trying To Become Real: A Buddhist Critique of Some Secular Heresies." *The International Philosophical Quarterly* XXXII, No. 4.

Lynch, Kevin. *A Theory of Good City Form*. Cambridge: MIT Press, 1981.

Manicas, Peter. "John Dewey: Anarchism and The Political State." *Transactions of The Charles S. Peirce Society* XVIII, No. 2.

McDermott, John J. *The Culture of Experience*. New York: New York University Press, 1976.

Mead, G. H. *Philosophy of the Present*. Chicago: University of Chicago Press, 1980.

———. *Social Psychology*. Edited by A. Strauss. Chicago: University of Chicago Press, 1977.

———. *The Works of G. H. Mead*. 2 vols. Chicago: University of Chicago Press, 1967.

———. *Selected Writings*. Edited by A. Reck. Indianapolis: Bobbs-Merrill, 1964.

Meltzer, Bernard. *The Social Psychology of George Herbert Mead*. Kalamazoo: Western Michigan University Press, 1972.

Merleau-Ponty, Maurice. *The Phenomenology of Perception*. New York: Humanities Press, 1962.

———. *The Market Tells Them So*. London: Zed Books, 1995.

Miller, David. *George Herbert Mead: Self, Language, and World*. Austin: University of Texas Press, 1973.

———. ed. *The Individual and the Social Self: The Unpublished*

Work of George Herbert Mead. Chicago: University of Chicago Press, 1982.

Mugerauer, Robert. *Interpretations on Behalf of Place*. Albany: State University of New York Press, 1994.

Mulcahey, Richard. *The Economics of Heinrich Pesch*. New York: Holt, 1952.

Murphey, Murray. *The Development of Peirce's Philosophy*. Indianapolis: Hackett, 1993.

Muller, John. *Beyond the Psychoanalytic Dyad*. New York: Routledge, 1996.

Nagatomo, Shigenori. *Attunement through the Body*. Albany: State University of New York Press, 1992.

Neville, Robert. *The Truth of Broken Symbols*. Albany: State University of New York Press, 1996.

———. *Normative Cultures*. Albany: State University of New York Press, 1995.

———. *Recovery of The Measure*. Albany: State University of New York Press, 1989.

———, ed. *New Essays in Metaphysics*. Albany: State University of New York Press, 1987.

———. *Reconstruction of Thinking*. Albany: State University of New York Press, 1981.

———. *The Cosmology of Freedom*. New Haven: Yale University Press, 1974.

———. "Intuition." *The International Philosophical Quarterly* VII. No. 4.

———, and Kasulis. *The Recovery of Philosophy in America*. Albany: State University of New York Press, 1997.

Novak, Michael. *American Philosophy and The Future*. New York: Scribners, 1968.

Odin, Steve. *The Social Self in Zen and American Philosophy*. Albany: State University of New York Press, 1996.

Ostrow, James. *Social Sensitivity: A Study in Habit and Experience*. Albany: State University of New York Press, 1990.

———. *Human Posture: The Nature of Inquiry*. Albany: State University of New York Press, 1989.

Peirce, Charles S. *Collected Papers*. Vol. I–VI. Cambridge: Harvard University Press, 1931–1935.

———. *The Essential Peirce*, Vol. I. Edited by Nathan Houser. Indianapolis: Indiana University Press, 1992.

Pepper, Stephen. *World Hypotheses: A Study in Evidence*. Berkeley: University of California Press, 1942.

Polanyi, Karl. *The Great Transformation*. Boston: Beacon, 1957.

258

BIBLIOGRAPHY

Rooney, John. *Organizing the South Bronx*. Albany: State University of New York Press, 1995.

Rorty, Richard. *Consequences of Pragmatism*. Minneapolis: University of Minnesota Press, 1982.

Rosenthal, Sandra. *Charles S. Peirce's Pragmatic Pluralism*. Albany: State University of New York Press, 1994.

Rosenthal, S. and P. Bourgeois. *Mead and Merleau-Ponty*. Albany: State University of New York Press, 1991.

Sacks, Peter. *Generation X Goes To College*. Chicago: Open Court, 1996.

Sandel, Michael. *Democracy's Discontent*. Cambridge: Harvard University Press, 1996.

Schumacher, John. *Human Posture: The Nature of Inquiry*. Albany: State University of New York Press, 1990.

Seamon, David, ed. *Dwelling, Seeing, and Designing: Toward a Phenomenological Ecology*. Albany: State University of New York Press, 1993.

Sennett, Richard. *Flesh and Stone*. New York: Norton, 1994.

Shaner, David. *The BodyMind Experience in Japanese Buddhism*. Albany: State University of New York Press, 1985.

Sheets-Johnstone, Maxine. *Giving the Body Its Due*. Albany: State University of New York Press, 1992.

Sherrif, John. *Charles S. Peirce's Guess at the Riddle*. Indianapolis: Indiana University Press, 1994.

Simmel, George. *The Philosophy of Money*. London: Routledge, Kegan Paul, 1978.

Smith, Adam. *The Wealth of Nations*. Oxford: Clarendon Press, 1976.

Spinoza, Baruch. *The Collected Works of Spinoza*. Translated and edited by E. Curley. Princeton: Princeton University Press, 1985.

Steinbock, Anthony. "Whitehead's Theory of Propositions." *Process Studies* 18, No. 1. (Spring 1989).

Stern, Mellins, and Fishman. *New York 1960*. New York: Penguin, 1995.

Stuhr, John. *Philosophy and the Reconstruction of Culture*. Albany: State University of New York Press, 1997.

Sturm, Douglas. *Community and Alienation*. Indiana: University of Notre Dame Press, 1988.

Sullivan, William. *Reconstructing Public Philosophy*. Berkeley: University of California Press, 1986.

Tejera, Vincent. "The Primacy of Aesthetics in Peirce and Classical American Philosophy." In *Peirce and Value Theory*, edited by H. Parret. Amsterdam: John Benjamins, 1964.

Thalberg, Irvin, *Perception, Action, and Emotion*. New Haven: Yale University Press, 1977.

Thiis-Evensen, Thomas. *Archetypes in Architecture*. New York: Oxford University Press, 1989.

Ungar, Roberto Mangabeira. *Knowledge and Politics*. New York: Free Press, 1975.

Walzer, Michael. *Spheres of Justice*. New York: Basic Books, 1983.

Warde, Ritchie. *The Living Clocks*. New York: Mentor. 1971.

White, Morton, and Lucia. *The Intellectual vs. The City*. Cleveland: Mentor, 1962.

Whitehead, Alfred North. *Symbolism, Its Meaning and Effect*. Bronx: Fordham University Press, 1986.

———. *Process and Reality*. Corrected edition by Griffin and Sherburne. New York: Free Press, 1978.

———. *Modes of Thought*. New York: Free Press, 1968.

———. *Adventures of Ideas*. New York: Free Press, 1967.

———. *Science and the Modern World*. New York: Free Press, 1967.

Whyte, William. *City*. New York: Doubleday, 1988.

Wiley, Norbert. *The Semiotic Self*. Chicago: Univerity of Chicago Press, 1994.

Wilson, William Julius. *When Work Disappears*. New York: Knopf, 1996.

Wolf, George. "The Place of the Brain in an Ocean of Feeling." In *Existence and Actuality*. Chicago: University of Chicago Press. 1984.

Wolfe, Alan. *Whose Keeper? Social Science and Moral Obligation*. Berkeley: University of California Press, 1989.

(No Author). *Concepts of Space: Ancient and Modern*. New Delhi: Abhivan Publishers, 1991.

Index

Abduction, 92–94, 151; defined, 65
Access, 4
Actuality, 42; and possibility, xx–xxi, xxxii
Aesthetic: in American philosphy, 251n. 16; defined, 55; vs. logical pattern, xxii–xxiii
Alexander, Christopher, 1, 64, 68–70, 72, 107, 159, 166; on wholeness, 206, 223
Allan, George, xii, xvii, 246n. 14
Ambient: patterns, 5–6; patterns, and symbolic reference, 11–12; space, and order, 16, 18
American philosophy, 207, 230–235; place of aesthetics in, 251n. 16; *See also* pragmatism
Appreciation, xviii
Aquinas, St. Thomas, 212, 216
Aristotle, 157, 212, 216; metaphysics of, 168

Bashō, 51
Beauty, 53–54; beautiful place, 53–55; and contrast, xxii, 214; and harmony, 213–215; and thirdness, 214; truthful, 54
Biological, participation, 186–187
Blake, William, 129
Borges, Jorge Luis, 104
Buchler, Justus, 243n. 3

Caffentzis, George, 249n. 6
Canyon effect, 128–129
Capitalism, 193–200; and urban value, 2
Carlyle, Thomas, 133
Caro, Robert, 244n. 8
Casey, Edward, 240nn. 6, 9
Christianity, 24
Civilization and Its Discontents, 133
Colapietro, Vincent, 238n. 11
Collision, and secondness, 121–136

205–206; and meaning, 166;
and symbols, 160; and truth,
212
Truth, as the carryover of value,
211–212
Two, *See* secondness

Understanding, as obligation of
philospher, 226–228
Unger, Roberto Mangabeira,
243n. 7
Unity: and city value, 210–211;
and order, 215–216; and
wholeness, 46
Utilitarianism, 212
Utility, and market economics,
196

Vagueness, xvii–xviii, 217; and
generality, xxiii; and growth,
90–91; and icons, 105–106;
and present time, 29
Value, xvii; and American philosophy, 233; of city time, 32–39;
and icons, 106; and limitation,
25
Vertical: patterns, 5–6; patterns,
and symbolic reference,
10–11; space, and order,
16–17

Warhol, Andy, xxxi
Whitehead, Alfred North, xii,
xxxiv, 42, 45; on aesthetics,

92; on beauty, 53; category of
the ultimate, xvii; on concrescence, 22; on contrast, 24–25;
on eternal objects, xvi; fallacy
of misplaced concreteness,
172; fallacy of perfect dictionary, xxx; intellectual honesty
of, 232; on minds in grooves,
116; and Peirce, 85–86; on
perception, xxv–xxviii; on
propositions, xxiv–xxv; on
school of safety vs. adventure,
xxx–xxxi; on symbolic perception, 7–9; thought and feeling
for, 226; on time and spontaneity, 23; on value, 94; on
witness of the body, xxvi, 8
Whitman, Walt, 39
Wholeness: Alexander on, 69–70,
206, 223; and growth, 91–92;
and iconic representation,
107; as normative measure,
46–47; and still places, 59–62
Width, 139, 217; and growth, 91;
and icons, 105–106; and involvement, 137–138; and
present time, 29–30
Wiley, Norbert, 238n. 11
Work, *See* labor

Zen, 24, 51; and freshness,
116–117
Zeno, 23